The woods are lovely, dark and deep
But I have promises to keep,
and miles to go before I sleep,
and miles to go before I sleep.

—Robert Frost

What am I to tell Mr. Godot, sir?

Tell him ... tell him you saw us. (pause)
You did see us, didn't you?

—Samuel Beckett.

TWILIGHT OR DAWN?

a Traveler's Guide to Free-Market Liberal Democracy

Bill Stonebarger

Gilman Street Press

Copyright 2012 by Hawkhill Associates, Inc.

ISBN # 978-1-55979-195-3

To Jane

Table of Contents

Preface

THE BOOK YOU ARE READING is an edited version of the book formerly titled *The Road to a Tea Party*. After publishing with that title in May of 2011, I realized I had made a serious mistake. The title is misleading. I emphasized in the preface that I meant *A* Tea Party, not *THE* Tea Party. But the implication remained that I am a supporter of the Tea Party and that my book is about the Tea Party. Neither is so.

Ergo. I needed a new title, one that is honest—represents more accurately what the book is about—and one that will tweak people's curiosity enough to buy a copy. I chose the former title more for the tweak than the honesty. The choice backfired as many potential readers confessed they would never read a book about the Tea Party.

So I recalculated and am republishing under the new title.

TWILIGHT OR DAWN? *a Traveler's Guide to Free-Market Liberal Democracy*

THERE WAS A LOVELY cartoon of Sydney Harris in *The American Scientist* a few years ago. A cave man's family is bedding down, and the concerned father says to his mate and children, "We have to get a good night's sleep. Tomorrow is the dawn of history."

We, too, are living in a changeover time—from the Agricultural Age to the Industrial-Scientific-Democratic Age. The Agricultural Age lasted over ten thousand years. The Industrial-Scientific-Democratic Age had its precursors in Western Europe but began to take off about the time of our American Revolution. It is still in its early childhood, if not its infancy. Just as a cave man proclaiming the dawn of history is funny, so people who think our Western Civilization is getting senile after a few hundred years are fair game for ridicule.

Ridiculous or not, that seems to be the view among many pundits today. Western Civilization, they claim, is on a deathwatch. Unless we promptly make some sharp turns—the most common suggestion today is "sustainable" living—we are goners. Vladimir Lenin, Osama bin Laden and Al Gore have all tried to teach us that our way of life in the West is decadent, unjust, and doomed to failure.

In my youth the popular choice for the next act was socialism. With the collapse of the Soviet Union the winds of socialism have calmed a bit to be replaced by the windmills and solar panels of the sustainable age. The late Osama bin Laden wanted us to return to religion—his brand of course.

This book explores these claims and concludes that collectives are not the answer. Sustainable communities won't happen. Some leaders in the West, like *Christian* bin Ladens, are urging us to return to religion. All bad ideas. What we need instead is vigorous efforts to continue the progress that began in the Renaissance, Reformation and Enlightenment of the Western World, the progress that has resulted today in the near worldwide triumph of Free-Market Liberal Democracy.

In practice this means continuing to promote science and technology, building on the proven win-win principles of capitalist economic systems, and paying closer attention to the freedom and humanistic bent of our founding father's tolerant versions of Judeo-Christianity. Pursue these directions in synergy and we will surely find that Free-Market Liberal Democracy leads to the best roads to the future as it has done in the past and is doing in the present.

BETWEEN 1940 AND 1943 the Austrian economist Friedrich Hayek wrote a seminal book *The Road to Serfdom.* He won the Nobel Prize for economics in 1974 (shared with Gunnar Myrdal). In this book and in his life work Hayek warned that government control of economic decision-making through central planning leads to tyranny. In the last sentence of *The Road to Serfdom* he summarized his message: "If in the first attempt to create a world of free men we have failed, we must try again. The guiding principle that a policy of freedom for the individual is the only truly progressive policy remains as true today as it was in the nineteenth century."[1]

I agree. Much happened in the 20th century to help us learn what works and what does not work for modern economies and governance. When we take a close look at the Cold War, at 9/11, at the rise and present state of capitalism, religion and science, and finally at the emergence of "green" environmental movements in the late 20th century, we can find clues to preserve, promote and expand free-market liberal democracy in the future.

A WORKING LIBERAL GOVERNMENT as promised and planned by our founding fathers protects freedom and supports wealth-creating private businesses, but doesn't itself create much new wealth. What the government gives to some, it must take from others. This is most often (not always) a zero-sum exchange, not a win-win one. The difference between zero-sum and win-win transactions plays a large role in the analyses and arguments in this book.

If the zero-sum trend goes too far, as I think it is doing today, it will force the government to regulate more and more of our life choices. Hayek's warning may come true. Our grand-children and our great-grandchildren will end up like indentured servants, well taken care of and even happy perhaps (that's what plantation owners in the deep south used to say about their slaves), but still servants and subjects, not citizens. Not free men and women. We may never get concentration camps or gulags, but our economic prospects will suffer grievously. We will all, rich and poor alike, end up poorer because the wealth pie will shrink dramatically. Our great-grandchildren will find themselves like workers in the now defunct Soviet Union or in present-day Cuba, North Korea or Venezuela. Poor in wealth, poor in skills, and poor in spirit.

Like the workers in the former Soviet Union they may quip, "They pretend to pay us and we pretend to work."

---

[1] Quotes from Hayek's book *The Road to Serfdom* are from the Univ. of Chicago paperbound edition copyright 1944, renewed 1972.

NOBODY SAW THE EMPEROR had no clothes until a child pointed it out. In my view the lessons of recent history are not that subtle. In this case perhaps it takes an old man to see what others have overlooked. The big picture, that is. The obvious.

Some readers, politically left or right, may be tempted to skip some of the historical narratives on the grounds that everyone knows that. Perhaps. But bear with me. The well-known can sometimes turn out to have surprising relevance to 21st-century issues.

Not that many people have lived through the Great Depression, World War II, the booming 50s, the inflationary and chaotic 60s and 70s, the prosperous 80s and 90s and now the gloom and doom first decade of the 21st century.

I have.

Not that many people today are optimistic about the future of this amazing country.

I am.

Let's start with the Great Depression ...

Rose-colored glasses and the Great Terror

In 1936 I was 10 years old starting the 4th grade at Corpus Christi School in Dayton, Ohio. I sang in the choir and was an altar boy. I looked at the world through rose-colored glasses even though we were in the middle of the Great Depression that had cost my father his business and our family its home. The depression left my father depressed, angry, and scrambling to support the family in a succession of short-lived dead-end jobs. We moved every year in my childhood because we rented houses that the bank had foreclosed on. The bank was trying to eke out a few dollars while they had the houses up for sale. When a potential buyer would come to see our latest home, my sister and I tried our best to highlight the house's fatal faults. The strategy usually failed. Despite the depression, we never went hungry, though others did. At least my mother told me that was so. "Eat your dinner," she would say, "the starving children in China would love to have those beans."

My favorite subject in the 4th grade was geography.

In 1936 I could find Russia on our classroom maps (our school maps were out-of-date so the Soviet Union was still unknown), but I had no notion what it was like there. Much later I found out that it was in 1936 that Josef Stalin launched the Great Terror. From 1936 to 1938 (while I

was moving up to the 6th grade) Stalin personally
signed death warrants for thirty-nine thousand
people, many of them prominent Bolsheviks who
had helped Lenin, Trotsky and Stalin gain power
in the 1917 Revolution. Scholars say that at least
one and a half million more Soviet citizens were
shot in those two years, all on orders from Stalin.

The *Black Book of Communism*, first published in
France in 1997, estimated that the final toll of
victims, in the many experiments in more than
thirty-five countries searching for a socialist
utopia in the 20th century, was between eighty-
five and one hundred million. This is more than
twice the total civilian and military losses in the
two World Wars of that century combined.

Our family was reliably Catholic in religion and
reliably Democratic in politics. Worry about
money and speculation about sports were topics
of conversation in our house, but almost never
politics or religion. I remember that once when
we were especially short of money, I asked my
father why President Roosevelt did not print
more dollars and give them away to people like
us. I don't think he had an answer.

Today I am old. I still speculate about sports but
for many years now I have also been interested
in politics, history, money and religion. This book
leaves out sports for the most part, but summa-
rizes my present thinking about politics, history,
money and religion.

I make a case that (1) the Cold War of the 20th century was not only the most important story of that century, it has a lot to do with the challenges of the 21st century. And (2) among the challenges of the 21st century, none is more important than the future of free-market liberal democracy.

Introduction

AT THE BEGINNING OF the 20th century, in 1902, Vladimir Lenin wrote a short book, *What Is To Be Done?* He borrowed the title from a popular socialist-utopian novel in 19th-century Russia. In his answer to the title's question, he gave his recipe for creating the world's first communist country. The key, he wrote, was small, tightly disciplined, intellectual leadership that would use any and all means, including whatever violence was needed, to gain power.[2] Fifteen years later his organization, the Bolsheviks, did gain power in Russia and proceeded to give birth to the world's first communist country, the Union of Soviet Socialist Republics (USSR).

Within a few decades, communism expanded rapidly until it controlled almost one-half of the world's people. By the end of the century communism had collapsed on the world stage, the cold war was over and only one-half of one percent of the world's peoples were still controlled by Marxist-Leninist ideology. They were concentrated in just two small countries, Cuba and North Korea.

TOWARD THE END of the 18th century, a small group of patriots led by George Washington, Benjamin Franklin, John Adams, Alexander Hamilton, James Madison and Thomas Jefferson gained power by free election in the new world of North America and established the world's first democratic (they called it republican) government, the United States of America.

Within the next two centuries, democracies became the world's richest, most admired, and most imitated countries. By 1950, democracies ruled about one third of the world's peoples, mostly in Europe, North America

---

[2] Some Marxist analysts dispute this interpretation. See Hal Draper, <http://www.marxists.org/archive/draper/1990/myth/myth.htm>

and Australia. By 2000, democracies were the governing system for more than sixty percent of the world's peoples on all continents.

THIS RISE AND FALL of communism, along with the explosive growth of democracy led by the United States, was without question the most important story of the 20th century. The western democracies, led by the United States, won the Cold War that brought down totalitarian Marxist-Leninist Communism. In the 21st century, Western free-market liberal democracies are being challenged again on two major fronts.

One: by a Radical Islamic ideology that strives to destroy the "Great Satan" America, as well as all free-market liberal democracies in Europe and elsewhere in the world, with weapons of propaganda and suicidal violence.

Two: by a blend of left-over-Marxist and new quasi-religious ideologies that strive to undermine and eventually destroy free-markets, and in the end—liberal democracies—in the name of economic justice, environmental purity, and alleged scientific facts.

So ... what is to be done?

This book is one man's analysis and one man's answer. First some science ...

Memes and genes

The lessons you learn early at home and in school leave lasting imprints on the mind. This is not big news. One important lesson I learned after school days came from the biologist Richard Dawkins in his book, *The Selfish Gene*. He hypothesizes that some lessons, he calls them "memes," are every bit as important as genes in guiding the individual's fortunes, and in the long run nudging the course of human history.

Memes, said Dawkins, are units of cultural information. Songs, catch-phrases, symbols, words, ideas, attitudes, concepts, all these and more qualify as memes.

"Just as genes propagate themselves in a gene pool by leaping from body to body via sperms or eggs," Dawkins wrote, "so memes propagate themselves in the same pool by leaping from brain to brain."[3]

Like genes, memes also mutate. They leap from brain to brain by means of music, books, talk, television, schools, churches, Internet, etc. They can even "have sex" with one another. And often the offspring of these quasi-sexual unions are new and improved versions. Unfortunately they can also be disastrous versions.

---

[3] *The Selfish Gene*, page 92

Just as there is a geosphere (inanimate matter) and a biosphere (living matter), so there is a "noosphere"[4] (world of thought) that complements, interacts with, and sometimes dominates the geosphere and the biosphere. In the 21st century, the Internet "cloud" version of this noosphere is supplementing, expanding, and in-as-yet-unknown ways revolutionizing all of our lives.

If this noosphere is real (and I think it is), the Cold War of the 20th century was the grandchild of many memes. Memes that were invented and passed along in some cases for thousands of years, and in others for only hundreds, or even decades. It was also the parent of many 21st-century memes that are now mutating and leaping from brain to brain with far more ease and speed than ever before in human history.

There are small memes and large ones. Small memes like "eat your beans, the starving children in China would love to have them," or "why doesn't Mr. Roosevelt print more money so we could have our allowance." Medium-size memes like Mr. Roosevelt, the New Deal, money, corporations, the Pope, the Third World, computers, Karl Marx, energy, Osama bin Laden,

---

[4] "Noosphere" was popularized by the French Jesuit theologian Pierre Teilhard de Chardin. It is discussed in a 1999 book, *The Biosphere and Noosphere Reader; Global Environment, Society and Change*. See also the discussion by Robert Wright in *Non-Zero: The Logic of Human Destiny*, pp. 4, 297, 309, 316, 329.

the Tea Party, welfare and terrorism. And then there are some very large memes (perhaps better thought of as whole chromosomes of the mind) like socialism, capitalism, communism, Christianity, Islam, environmentalism, natural resources, populations, science, democracy. Most of these large memes had their origins centuries past, but today are leaping, crossing, splitting, multiplying, and mutating like crazy.

If you don't believe in Richard Dawkins' memes it doesn't matter that much, so long as you agree that what people are thinking, individually and in groups, in their conscious moments, and for that matter even more in their unconscious ones, matters to human history.

Let's first take a fresh look at the Cold War, its history, its critics, and its lessons for today.

PART ONE

THE COLD WAR

Chapter 1

The Rise of Communism

THE COLD WAR IN THE second half of the 20th century pitted the western free-market liberal democracies against the command-economy totalitarian communist dictatorships. The United States led the democracies. The Soviet Union led the dictatorships. The democracies won.

The war against terror of the 21st century pits the western free-market liberal democracies against radical Islamic theocracies. The United States is leading the democracies. A small terrorist group called al-Qaeda is leading the theocracies. So far neither side has prevailed.

Some, including this writer, think that another cold war in the 21st century is pitting free-market capitalists and liberal democrats against a disparate but powerful amalgam of environmental radicals, globalization deniers, corporation bashers, multicultural educators and command-economy enthusiasts. So far this war is indecisive.

The Cold War of the 20th century was the longest lasting, most expensive, and most deadly war in all of human history.

How long the war against Radical Islamic terror will last is unknown. It has already proved expensive and deadly.

How long the second cold war against leftover-Marxist, and new quasi-religious ideologies like radical environmentalism, will last is unknown. So far it, too, has proved expensive. It has also proved deadly and may become more so as the century progresses.

I CLAIMED IN THE PREFACE to this book that the big picture, the "obvious," would emerge from an understanding of what happened in the Cold War, 9/11, and the challenges of radical leftists and environmentalists today. Let's look first at what happened in the Cold War. It will give clues about the other wars, cold and hot, we face today.

Unlike most wars, most of the casualties of the 20th-century Cold War were not on bloody battlefields of Korea or Vietnam (or even of the

Second World War itself, the immediate precursor to the Cold War). Horrific as all of the battlefield and civilian casualties were in wars of the 20th century, most of the violent deaths in that century came from totalitarian regimes murdering their own citizens. The atrocities of Hitler's National Socialist (Nazi) regime in Germany are well known. The atrocities committed by totalitarian Communist regimes against their own people before and after the Second World War are not as widely known, or at least not as widely acknowledged.

Movies, books and TV specials about the Nazi Holocaust far outnumber movies, books and TV specials about communist massacres, famines and gulags. Celebrities in the political or entertainment world routinely use the Nazi Holocaust in Germany as their example of atrocity far more often than they use the atrocities in communist countries of the 20th and 21st centuries. Evil geniuses like Lenin, Mao, Castro and Che Guevara[5] are often romanticized rather than excoriated.

When I was in college some sixty years ago, the 20th-century Cold War was just beginning—or so the standard version of the story goes. Some list the beginning as two years after the end of World War II in 1948 when the wartime Prime Minister of Great Britain, Winston Churchill, accompanied by the new U.S. President Harry Truman, gave a speech at Fulton, Missouri. Here are excerpts from his long speech.

> The United States stands at this time at the pinnacle of world power. It is a solemn moment for the American Democracy. For with this primacy in power is also joined an awe-inspiring accountability to the future. ... Opportunity is here now, clear and shining, for both our countries. To reject it or ignore it or fritter it away will bring upon us all the long reproaches of the aftertime.
>
> I have a strong admiration and regard for the valiant Russian people and for my wartime comrade, Marshal Stalin. There is deep sympathy and goodwill in Britain—and I doubt not here also—

---

[5] See article in *Slate Magazine* for details on this "episode in the moral callousness of our time." <http://www.slate.com/id/2107100/>

toward the peoples of all the Russias and a resolve to persevere through many differences and rebuffs in establishing lasting friendships.

It is my duty, however, to place before you certain facts about the present position in Europe.

From Stettin in the Baltic to Trieste in the Adriatic an *iron curtain* has descended across the Continent. Behind that line lie all the capitals of the ancient states of Central and Eastern Europe. Warsaw, Berlin, Prague, Vienna, Budapest, Belgrade, Bucharest and Sofia; all these famous cities and the populations around them lie in what I must call the Soviet sphere, and all are subject, in one form or another, not only to Soviet influence but to a very high, and in some cases, increasing measure of control from Moscow.[6]

Forty-one years later, a key link in that iron curtain chain was broken when the Berlin Wall came down. Two years after that, a Russian flag replaced the Soviet flag over the Kremlin and the Soviet Union was history. The Cold War was over. The democracies had won. What happened during those forty-three years? What was it about the Cold War that made it so long lasting, so expensive and so deadly? What lessons, if any, does the cold war have for us in the 21st century?

TO ANSWER THESE QUESTIONS we need to go back not forty-three years, but at least one hundred and sixty years. In the middle of the 19th century the Industrial Revolution and capitalism were rapidly making countries of Western Europe and North America the richest and most powerful nations on earth.

Workers, farmers and families of 19th-century Western Europe and North America were richer, healthier and had longer lives than peasants, slaves and servants of all previous centuries everywhere in the world. Many workers, farmers and families, however, were also more alienated

---

[6] Readers can access the complete speech at: <http://www.hpol.org/churchill/>

from their work and their world. They could see more clearly now the gulf between their lives and those of the wealthy industrialists who owned and managed the new factories, mines and sweatshops, as well as the wealthy landowners who profited mightily from their backbreaking agricultural work. A combination of new wealth and new freedom coexisted with a breakdown of traditional religions and cultural values, newly perceived poverty and rampant exploitation. All of this paved the way for revolutionary change.

The most important catalyst for this change was the brilliant German scholar, Karl Marx. He wrote the influential book, *Das Capital,* in which he claimed to have discovered the scientific meaning of human history. Capitalism, he wrote, was the most powerful economic force ever invented. And capitalism, along with the industrial revolution, was responsible for the greatest leap forward in human wealth in all history.

But all history, Marx claimed, is a story of class warfare. In capitalism the new wealth is concentrated in a few hands, the owners of industry, the bourgeoisie. The workers, the proletariat he called them, are wage slaves. They would, his analysis showed, sink deeper and deeper into poverty until they rebelled and took power for themselves. They would then, with the leadership of the communist party, establish true socialist utopias where there were no longer any classes, and where the means of production were owned by the workers. Resources and wealth would then be fairly and equably distributed. Production would not be for profit, but for the welfare of all.

Marx, along with his rich English industrialist partner, Friedrich Engels, produced one of the most influential pamphlets ever written, the *Communist Manifesto.* The last paragraph of this pamphlet promised …

> The communists disdain to conceal their views and aims. They openly declare that their ends can be attained only by the forcible overthrow of all existing social conditions. Let the ruling classes tremble at a Communist revolution. The proletarians have

nothing to lose but their chains. They have a world to win. Proletarians of all countries, Unite!

Thus did Marx and Engels set the tone and write the bible for what some would call a new secular religion—communism. To Marx communism was science, not religion. He called all religions "the opiate of the masses." But to others communism, for its true believers, was very like many religions of the past.

"I had the feeling," wrote Leon Trotsky, "I was joining a great chain as a tiny link." Stalin said that his communist faith "was not only a theory of socialism: it's an entire world view, a philosophic system." The British Marxist historian, Raphael Samuel, put it directly, "The ambitions of the Communist Party were unmistakably theocratic ... Reports were handed down with all the majesty of encyclicals and studied as closely as if they were Bible texts."[7]

Just as many Christian Churches used "excommunication" as a strong weapon against dissenters, so in the Communist "church" one of the more severe penalties for deviationists was expulsion from the party. Not the most severe. Like the medieval Church which did not flinch at burning heretics, the modern communist "church" was always ready to murder heretics—people like Leon Trotsky, Nikolai Bukharin, Karl Radek and tens of thousands of other old and new Bolsheviks—who did not or would not see eye-to-eye with Lenin's or Stalin's utopian visions.

This new scientific religion of socialism would solve once and for all the age-old problems of wealth and poverty, of health and disease, of crime and exploitation, of peace and war. It would replace the vicious world of greedy capitalists, exploited workers, hypocritical priests, and phony democracies with true "people's democracies." Instead of sin and penance and "pie in the sky when you die," it would produce a new man and a new woman who would live happily ever after in an earthly socialist paradise.

---

[7] See *The Rise and Fall of Communism* by Archie Brown, page 126.

This socialist dream was (and is) deeply inspirational for many people. The writer Maxim Gorky, for instance, a friend of Lenin and a dedicated socialist himself, gave the vision color and life in *Mother: The Great Revolutionary Novel* ...

> There will come a time, I know, when people will take delight in one another, when each will be like a star to the other, and when each will listen to his fellow as to music. The free men will walk upon the earth, men great in their freedom. They will walk with open hearts, and the heart of each will be pure of envy and greed, and therefore all mankind will be without malice, and there will be nothing to divorce the heart from reason. Then life will be one great service to man! His figure will be raised to lofty heights—for to free men all heights are attainable. Then we shall live in truth and freedom and in beauty, and those will be accounted the best who will the more widely embrace the world with their hearts, and whose love of it will be the profoundest; those will be the best who will be the freest; for in them is the greatest beauty. Then will life be great, and the people will be great who live that life.[8]

That was the vision.

The only catch was that to get to this paradise it would be necessary, as the Manifesto said, to "overthrow all existing social conditions." This overthrow would require violence. As it turned out, the quest for a new earthly paradise, and for a new man and a new woman, led to more violence than Marx or Engels ever imagined.

The composer Dmitri Shostakovich in his book of memoirs, *Testimony,* tells a story that was typical of the kind of violence used to "overthrow all social conditions."

---

[8] *Mother: The Great Revolutionary Novel,* page 185.

Since time immemorial, folk singers have wandered along the roads of the Ukraine. They're called *lirniki* ... They were almost always blind men—why that is so is another question that I won't go into, but briefly, it's traditional. The point is, they were always blind and defenseless people, but no one ever touched or hurt them. Hurting a blind man—what could be lower? And then in the mid-thirties the First All-Ukrainian Congress of Lirniki was announced, and all the folk singers have to gather and discuss what to do in the future. "Life is better, life is merrier," Stalin had said. The blind men believed it. They came to the congress from all over the Ukraine, from tiny, forgotten villages. There were several hundred of them at the congress. It was a living museum, the country's living history. All its songs, all its music and poetry. And they were almost all shot; almost all of those pathetic blind men were killed. [9]

In the late 19th century the communist vision was a powerful and exciting one that made many converts. The new Marxist religion soon split into many variations. Like the split in Christianity a few centuries before, there was more than one Marxist faith before the 19th century ended. Some branches became known as social democrats. They believed socialism could arrive through peaceful democratic means. Some of these social democrats, and there were many varieties, were among the founding fathers of modern welfare states in Western Europe and North America.

Another offshoot, actually a small minority of Marxists led by a stern Russian named Vladimir Lenin, preached a harder line. "To belittle the socialist ideology in any way," wrote Lenin, "to turn aside from it in the slightest degree *means to* strengthen bourgeois ideology." In his influential small book published in 1902, *What Is to Be Done?*, Lenin claimed that the socialist vision demanded leadership by a rigidly organized communist party that would not hesitate to use extreme violence in order to destroy

---

[9] Dmitri Shostakovich, *Testimony*, p. 214-215.

bourgeois capitalism and its phony democratic veneer. The leadership was to consist of radical intellectual leaders, not real workers, above all no trade unionists. And in fact the actual Bolshevik council that Lenin formed to bring down the Russian government in 1917 had only one proletarian worker, and he turned out to be a police spy.

In the 20th century it was this variant of the Marxist faith, Marxism-Leninism, that did gain real power, total power.

In the wake of the First World War in 1917, dedicated followers in Russia led by Lenin, Josef Stalin and Leon Trotsky, used guile and violence to overthrow a newly formed democratic government and proclaim the world's first communist state in Russia. They called it the Union of Soviet Socialist Republics (USSR). In one of his first speeches to the newly assembled parliament (which lasted just one day, to be replaced by a dictatorship the next day), Lenin kept it simple: "We will now proceed to construct the Socialist order."

From the beginning Lenin was clear about the methods to be used. "The scientific term dictatorship," Lenin wrote, "means nothing more or less than authority untrammeled by any laws, absolutely unstructured by any rules whatsoever, based directly on violence."[10]

Lenin said what he meant and did what he promised. Contrary to what many believe, he was every bit as brutal as his successor, Josef Stalin. Here, for instance, is Lenin's definition of democracy: "Democracy is a form of the state: one that welds together the proletariat, and enables it to crush, smash to atoms, wipe off the face of the earth the bourgeois."

When he wanted to punish Estonia and Latvia for attempting to become independent in 1918, Lenin ordered the army to "cross the frontier somewhere, even if only to a depth of half a mile, and hang 100-1,000 of their civil servants and rich people."

Lenin characteristically told an acquaintance, "We're engaged in annihilation . . . Break, beat up everything, beat and destroy! Everything

---

[10] See *The State and Revolution*, Vladimir Lenin.

that's being broken is rubbish and has no right to life! What survives is good."

Here are his words in a directive to Communist officials soon after he had attained dictatorial power and won the ensuing civil war.

> The kulaks [better-off peasants, whose wealth sometimes consisted of owning one cow] are the most beastly, the coarsest, the most savage exploiters. These bloodsuckers have waxed rich during the war on the people's want. These spiders have grown fat at the expense of peasants, impoverished by the war. Comrades! The uprising of the five kulak districts should be mercilessly suppressed. The interests of the entire revolution require this because now 'the last decisive battle' with the kulaks is under way everywhere. One must give an example. (1) Hang (hang without fail, so the people see) no fewer than one hundred known kulaks, rich men, bloodsuckers. (2) Publish their names. (3) Take from them all the grain. (4) Designate hostages – as per yesterday's telegram. Do it in such a way that for hundreds of kilometers around the people will see, tremble, know, shout: *they are strangling* and will strangle to death the bloodsucker kulaks. Yours, Lenin.[11]

From the beginning Lenin also made it plain that the communist vision and struggle was an international one. In a speech in 1920 he said: "We knew that our victory will be a lasting victory only when our undertaking will conquer the whole world, because we had launched it exclusively counting on the world revolution."

Of special note today in our search for a better health care system are Lenin's instructions to Stalin in regard to Soviet health care. He told Stalin to spend as much "gold" as he could to establish a health-care facility for high-ranking Bolshevik officials. Make sure, he told him, to have "strictly scrupulous doctors and administration—not the usual Soviet bunglers and slobs," that is, the ones who provided care for ordinary citizens.

---

[11] See Richard Pipes, *Communism: A History.*

For seventy-five years the Soviet Union set records for radical social engineering, for totalitarian power, and for merciless violence. In addition to violently assaulting "social conditions" in the Soviet Union itself, leaders like Lenin and Stalin created an international unit called the Comintern to support communist revolutions in all countries of the world. Article 17 of the twenty-one rules for joining the Comintern made the aim explicit: "The Communist International has declared a resolute war on the bourgeois world and all yellow Social-Democratic parties."[12]

In many countries the war succeeded. Dedicated communists in China, in Korea, in Cuba, in Vietnam, in Poland, in Hungary, in Czechoslovakia and in other countries of Eastern Europe and Southeast Asia were able to take power in the 20th century with the aid of Soviet Union money, arms and propaganda—sometimes with the aid of the Soviet army as well. These new communist dictatorships, like their Soviet model, proceeded to act with violence and terror to overthrow existing social conditions. Just past the middle of the 20th century, communist governments controlled almost one-half of the world population. To many observers, communism seemed well on its way to conquering the entire world as Marx and Engels had confidently predicted.

Reliable estimates are difficult because communist regimes were always particularly skilled and efficient at lying, at controlling the press, and at concealing crimes against their own people from their own people, as well as from the outside world. Since the opening of many Soviet archives in the early 21st century, the consensus among scholarly researchers is that the pursuit of a socialist utopia in the Soviet Union cost at least sixty million Soviet citizens their lives. These deaths came from political assassinations, government-sponsored massacres, government-induced famines, and forced labor in slave-labor camps (gulags) under such inhuman conditions that premature and painful death was the inevitable result.

---

[12] See "Works of Lenin":
<http://www.marxists.org/archive/lenin/works/1920/jul/x01.htm>

Stalin, for instance, the most hideously wholesale of the communist dictators, ordered the death of seventy percent of his own 17th Congress in 1934. He explained, "The death of one man is a tragedy, the death of a million is a statistic."

In addition to these Soviet crimes, communist regimes in China led by Mao Zedong murdered at least forty million Chinese citizens. Scholars today say that number jumps to over 100 million if you count unintended, but very real, deaths caused by two ill-fated utopian programs launched by Mao, *The Great Leap Forward* and *The Cultural Revolution*.

Cuba, North Korea, Vietnam and many countries of Eastern Europe also proved to be deadly to their own citizens—and, faithful to the prediction in the Manifesto, to existing social conditions like private property, private businesses, religions, personal privacy, scientific, social and philanthropic associations, sports, hobby and arts groups. The small country of Cambodia must take the prize as, per capita, the most murderous of all. Under the Paris-educated communist Pol Pot, his Khmer Rouge followers literally emptied all the cities of people and slaughtered two million Cambodians. That is two million out of a total population of seven million.

These horrendous totals are larger than the total battlefield and civilian casualties, including Nagasaki and Hiroshima, of all countries in the First and Second World Wars combined. That gruesome total was "only" around thirty-three million. [13]

Note, too, that these almost unbelievably large casualties due directly to government-caused crimes to their own citizens in the 20th-century communist world—well over 100 million human beings—are twenty times as large as the well-known genocide of six million Jews, gypsies, homosexuals and handicapped people in the Holocaust carried out in the final years of Hitler's Fascist regime in Germany.

---

[13] For data on deaths from non-war democide, mostly communist, see article by R. J. Rummel, reproduced at:
<http://www.hawaii.edu/powerkills/WSJ.ART.HTM.>

Despite this gruesome record, many intelligent and well-meaning people in western democratic countries were taken in by this new *scientific* religion of Communism. France and Italy after the Second World War, for instance, had large communist parties with prestigious intellectual leaders like the philosophers Jean Paul Sartre and Simone de Beauvoir and world-famous artists like Pablo Picasso. The communist parties in both France and Italy came close to winning post-war elections and taking power.

In the United States and Canada communist parties were always small. Only a tiny minority of intellectuals, politicians and workers were dedicated communist party members. However, a much larger group of intellectuals, writers, artists, scientists, academics, business and union leaders, moviemakers, and ordinary citizens were fellow travelers. That is, without belonging to the party, they were sympathetic to its goals, forgiving as to its means, and dependable supporters of its actions. The memes, in other words, of socialism were widely distributed and very popular, especially among elite segments of western society like the press, academia, Hollywood, and other art and communication disciplines.

With this background in mind, what actually happened in the second half of the 20th century during what is called the Cold War? And what relevance, if any, does this Cold War have for our 21st-century challenges?

Antioch, religion and Korea

In 1949 I was a student at Antioch College in Yellow Springs, Ohio. Having served two years in the U.S. Navy after high school, the GI Bill supported me in my college education. Antioch was a small liberal arts college with a strong liberal bent and a broad but comprehensive curriculum. Some of my friends and classmates who later became famous include Coretta Scott (later Coretta Scott King), Rod Serling (TV writer/producer of the popular *Twilight Zone* series in the 50s and 60s), Leon Higginbotham (civil rights lawyer and one of the first African-American U.S. District Court judges), Ed Fisher (award-winning *New Yorker* cartoonist), and Cliff Geertz (a philosophy major at Antioch who later became a famous anthropologist).

Antioch was a marvel to me in those days. It was the first time that I found ideas could be interesting. For the first time I began to read serious books, think, and discuss ideas. We had books, radio and good bull sessions but no television, cell phones, calculators, computers, video games, or Internet.

Like most liberal college students in those post-war days, I was a firm believer in democracy, but I was not so sure of capitalism. I knew there was a communist challenge from the Soviet Union, but it seemed remote. They were our allies in

World War II and whatever their shortcomings, any challenge they presented seemed tame compared to our recent wars with Hitler and Hirohito. Like most of my classmates at Antioch, I knew that U.S. democracy needed fixing, especially in its treatment of people we called "negroes." I also knew that women were still being treated too often as second-class citizens, and that we should do something about this.

I was not much of a political activist, however. At that time I was more interested in poetry, philosophy, and girls than in money, protests, or power.

I was interested in religion, more to the point, the Catholic religion that I was brought up to follow. Sometimes I was obsessed with it. My reading both in the Navy and now in college had brought me to question the dogmas I had learned from my catechism in grade school, and the teaching of the priests and Brothers of Mary that I had absorbed in high school. I was elected to give the valedictory speech at our high school graduation. The subject I chose myself was "Return to Religion." My parents, especially my mother, could not have happier or more proud of their only son.

I remember one fall day at Antioch I was particularly depressed and went for a long walk in a nearby nature preserves. At least part of my depression was due to pangs of guilt for a recent decision to reject my Catholic faith, get married outside the Church, and thus be what I called an apostate. I confessed my doubts to a local priest who advised me to pray. I talked it over with a history teacher at Antioch, and his contribution was to say that "apostate" was an awfully ugly word. He was right about the word, but it didn't help. I still felt sad and depressed.

On that lonely autumn walk I became more and more emotional. I wasn't sure whether I had abandoned God or He had abandoned me. At one point I collapsed onto the falling leaves and sobbed. In my tears I constructed a crude cross from a few broken twigs, prayed to it, and cried some more. I never got a response. I left the woods as confused and depressed as ever. Despite some, many, backsliding days weeks and months thereafter, eventually I said goodbye to the Catholic faith, and do not regret that decision today.

All of these opinions, prejudices and inclinations, these weakly and strongly formed memes, were real but some, like recessive genes, needed time to assert themselves and major shocks to mutate.

The year after graduation, 1951, the Cold War became a hot war in Korea. My wife and I, just married the year before and with no children yet, moved to Colorado Springs where she went to a graduate school in painting and I taught science and math at a local high school, my first real teaching job. Since I had already served two years in the Navy and was married now, I was not worried about being drafted to serve in Korea but we were opposed to the new war. (Actually we were opposed to all wars and considered ourselves pacifists on the example of Mahatma Gandhi.) Looking back now I think our anti-military views may have been close to those of the Vietnam War protesters a quarter of a century later. Just as some young Vietnam critics moved to Canada, we briefly considered moving to Costa Rica, where we understood there was no army or military budget. In the end we stayed in Colorado, moving the next year to New York City.

That year in Colorado was a year of indecision and painful growing up. College was new, exciting, and fun. Keeping a steady job was a bit of a jolt, not very exciting, and not nearly as much fun. "Working" for me, at that point in my life, had been mostly school "work." Even in the Navy, most of my two-year duty was spent learning about physics, math and electronics in Navy classrooms.

Like some philosophy graduates today, wouldn't you know, I ended up driving a cab in Colorado Springs the summer of 1951. I drove the night shift and actually liked that job better than some I had later in New York City (while waiting for lightning to strike and tell me what I should do with my life). I kept a book of poetry in the cab and when business got slow around 3 AM I would buy a cup of coffee and sit in my cab reading and memorizing poems. I also began writing poems of my own, and made that a big part of my life for the next few years in New York City.

By 1951 the Berlin air-lift crisis was past history, Stalin was still alive and it was many years later before I realized my wife and I were wrong about the Korean War. That mistake, I realize now, has everything to do with my later political changes. I believe now, on a much bigger scale, it had everything to do with our country's challenges in the 21st century. Let's take a close look now at what actually happened in the Korean War, before and after.

Chapter 2

Truman, Stalin, Berlin and Korea

IN WORLD WAR TWO from 1939 to 1945 the United States, Canada, the United Kingdom, France, Australia and democratic countries of Western Europe were allied with the totalitarian Soviet Union in a desperate war of survival against aggressive fascist totalitarian empires of Germany, Italy and Japan. The allies were uncomfortable bedfellows—democracies allied with a totalitarian power—and almost immediately after the war ended, another war began between the former allies. It was called a Cold War, but it was not always so cold.

In World War II, the Soviet Union, due at least partly to its scorched-earth and human-wave battle policies, suffered far more homeland destruction and far more civilian and military casualties than any other belligerent. The Soviets lost nine million soldiers and more than eighteen million civilians in the World War II. This was five times the German losses. Whatever the cost, the Soviets deserve a major portion of the credit for destroying Hitler's armies.

Josef Stalin, the Soviet dictator, had been in power since a few years after the premature death of Lenin in 1923. He was a small man, only 5'6" tall. Many people, including Franklin Roosevelt and Harry Truman, as well as British Prime Minister, Winston Churchill, thought "Uncle Joe" had considerable personal charm. He wrote poetry, loved music and literature (*some* music and literature). When it came to raw power and cold-blooded cruelty, however, he had few matches in all of world history.

Stalin met with Roosevelt and Churchill in conferences before the war in Europe ended, and later with President Truman and Churchill after the war ended. At both the Yalta and the Potsdam conferences, he demanded a free hand in territories occupied by the Red Army in Eastern Europe, the Balkans and the Korean peninsula. And he got it. Poland, Hungary, Czechoslovakia, Yugoslavia, Romania, Bulgaria and North Korea ended up with communist governments. Governments that were either put in place by the occupying Soviet army, or by local communist parties allied to the Soviet Union.

Germany was in almost total ruin; its major cities and most of its industrial infrastructure were destroyed. Germany's former capital city, Berlin, was divided into a free sector occupied by the western democracies and an eastern sector occupied by the Soviet army.

The United States, except for Pearl Harbor, had not had any war destruction at home and at the end of the war was by default the wealthiest and most powerful nation in the world.

The first major cold war action came just two years after the war ended in March 1947. Greece and Turkey were on the fringes of the free democratic world of Western Europe and Eastern Asia. Local communist insurgents, helped by the Soviet Union, threatened both with communist takeovers. President Truman asked Congress for four hundred million dollars (four billion in today's currency) in aid for the two countries. "It must be the policy of the United States," he argued in what became known as the Truman Doctrine, "to support free peoples who are resisting attempted subjugation by armed minorities or by outside pressures." In this case the U.S. aid was effective. It helped stop communists from taking control in Greece and Turkey. Both of these countries remain free-market democracies today in the 21st-century.

Remembering the bitterness and disastrous mistakes the victorious allies made following the World War I, under the leadership of President Harry Truman and his visionary Secretary of State, General George Marshall, a "Marshall Plan" was proposed and enacted by Congress in 1948. It went into effect with amazing speed to help Western Europe rebuild war-devastated cities and economies, and in the case of Germany and Italy, to rapidly form new democratic governments. Instead of robbing Germany, the Marshall Plan spent thirteen billion dollars ($1.3 trillion in today's dollars) to help it recover from the war. Admittedly the motives for the aid were not totally altruistic. We wanted Germany as an ally in possible conflicts with our former ally, the Soviet Union. We also wanted Germany to recover so that it could be an effective and contributing partner in post-war global trading. Seldom had a conquering power been so magnanimous, so effective and so wise.

This was also one of the first times a sovereign nation had rejected agricultural-age zero-sum economics in a major way. For many centuries war had been a way for countries to obtain resources and wealth by stealing them from their neighbors. The theory was that resources, living space and wealth were a fixed limited quantity. Wealth was like a big pie, so the only way to get more resources, living space and wealth, a bigger piece of the pie, was to expand into nearby or far-off places and grab as much as you could. This was called imperialism. In any war the idea had always been to the winners go the spoils. That was what happened in the Trojan War of ancient Greece and that was what happened after World War I when France, Great Britain and the United States demanded heavy reparations from the defeated Germany.

This time the United States and her allies were wiser. Free-market capitalism operated on a different base idea than the zero-sum feudal agricultural-age one. Where it used to be in a nation's self-interest to bleed a conquered nation white, it was a different game now. Rather than grabbing the spoils, it made more sense to help your enemies become prosperous again so that they could contribute to a worldwide wealth-pie expansion. That way both victor and vanquished could end up gaining still more wealth in a win-win economic game.

Win-win globalization accelerated. And it worked. Instead of festering in its defeat and setting the stage for another Nazi-like take-over as happened in the years after the First World War, this time Germany recovered and rebuilt with remarkable speed. Very soon Germany became a contributing partner to worldwide prosperity and a reliable ally of the victorious free-market liberal democratic countries.

THE THEORY ALSO WORKED in Japan. Japan was occupied by U.S. troops after the atom bomb ended the Pacific War. The Japanese were allowed to keep the Emperor as a figurehead but General Douglas MacArthur and the American military were given power to run the country, to rebuild its cities and factories, to nurture a free-market private business climate, and to write and install a democratic constitution that included a provision for permanent disarmament. In a dramatic and convincing way, this contradicted the oft-repeated claim that you cannot impose democracy at the point of a gun. That is exactly what we did in Japan. And Japan, sixty years later, is still operating as a successful free-market liberal democracy, a strong economic competitor, and a reliable ally under that post-war imposed democratic constitution.

The U.S. offered to extend the Marshall Plan to Eastern Europe and to the Soviet Union itself. Stalin, however, rejected this aid and instead stuck to the traditional winner-takes-the-spoils position. Stalin stripped much of eastern Germany and other allies of Germany of their factories, gold and stored wealth. He also made sure that communist dictatorships governed the defeated populations. It took another forty years to realize the magnitude of this mistake.

THE COLD WAR HEATED UP in divided Berlin in the summer of 1948. Berlin was an island in the Soviet occupation zone of East Germany so that the western free part of the city was completely surrounded and at the mercy of communist military forces. The Soviets considered this free zone of Berlin a thorn in their side and decided to apply pressure to force the westerners out. They blocked off all roads, canals and rail links to the free zones of Berlin, gambling that the French, British and American occupying forces would be forced to leave when West Berlin citizens could not get food, coal and other vital supplies to survive coming winter months.

President Truman was faced with a hard choice. Should he challenge the blockade at the risk of war or should he order his troops out? Very soon he found a way to avoid direct military action and to keep freedom alive in Berlin. He ordered the U.S. Air Force to conduct 24-hour a day air lifts to supply needed food, supplies and coal to West Berlin citizens. After many tense weeks (would the Soviets attack the planes?) and difficult technical problems (at the beginning we did not have enough cargo planes to carry enough to supply a major city), the strategy worked. The Soviets lifted the blockade in the late spring of 1949 and West Berlin survived as an island of freedom in a sea of coercion.

Some analysts today point out that Stalin probably did not attempt to shoot down any of the U.S. planes even though he had the capability to do so because at that time the U.S. still had a monopoly on nuclear weapons, and the Soviet Union was still recovering from the catastrophic destruction and huge loss of life the World War II had caused.

Truman's response to the Berlin blockade as well as most other U.S. actions in the cold war were based on a strategy called *containment*. In 1946 George Kennan, a top advisor to our ambassador in Moscow, sent a famous long cable that outlined this strategy.

Kennan cabled that the Soviets perceived themselves to be in a state of perpetual war with capitalism. The war with Hitler had severely weakened their military and economic power, however. As a result, in the immediate post-war period they were not likely to be as militarily aggressive as Hitler and Hirohito had been. The Soviets, however, would use "controllable Marxists" in the capitalist world as allies wherever and whenever they could. To survive this perpetual war, Kennan advised, the U.S. should be prepared to confront the Soviets with threatened force that would "contain" Soviet ambitions but would avoid all-out war or aggressive rollback of Communist gains.

To implement this strategy in Europe the western democracies in 1948 formed North Atlantic Treaty Organization (NATO). The first head of NATO admitted that the purpose was "to keep the Russians out, the Americans in, and the Germans down." The success of the Marshall Plan soon made the third goal unnecessary. By 1955 West Germany had recovered enough to establish its own stable democratic government and was admitted into NATO. The communist countries countered NATO in 1955 with a Warsaw Pact.

EARLY ALONG THE COLD WAR became a hot war on the eastern frontier, though not one directly involving the Soviet army. Japan had occupied and made Korea a part of the Japanese Empire in 1910. After Japan surrendered to end World War II in 1945, Soviet armies in the north and U.S. armies in the south occupied the Korean peninsula. The occupying armies set the 38th Parallel as an arbitrary dividing line between Soviet-dominated North Korea and U.S.-dominated South Korea.

Both newly established Korean states wanted to unify Korea and both states asked the superpowers for help in invading the other. The U.S. under newly re-elected President Truman refused South Korea's request for help. Instead the U.S. withdrew its troops. Sensing an opening, Stalin, the Soviet dictator (along with Mao Zedong, dictator of Communist China) gave the green light to the North Korean communist dictator, Kim Il-sung, to launch a military invasion in 1950, with the goal of uniting North and South Korea under one rule, a communist one.

Caught by surprise, Truman petitioned the new United Nations Security Council to condemn the invasion and to authorize military force to repel it. (The Soviet Union had a veto power on the Security Council but did not vote due to a self-imposed embargo of the Council at that time). Truman's petition was adopted, and soon United Nations troops (mostly American) under the leadership of General Douglas MacArthur came back to South Korea to help the South Korean army defend their country.

"Communism was acting in Korea," said Truman, "just as Hitler, Mussolini and the Japanese had ten, fifteen, and twenty years earlier. ... If the Communists were permitted to force their way into the Republic of Korea without opposition from the free world, no small nation would have the courage to resist threat and aggression by stronger Communist neighbors."

Initially North Korea, with a much larger and more heavily equipped army, was dominant and would have easily defeated South Korea's smaller ill-equipped army. Once MacArthur's troops got to Korea they slowed the communist advance and then surprised the enemy with a daring behind-the-lines landing at Incheon. After a series of bloody battles, the United Nation troops advanced almost to the Yalu River border with China.

Alarmed by the U.S. advance, Mao Zedong ordered a tsunami wave of Chinese Communist troops (the number of troops is still in dispute. Some authorities claim it was as many as 3 million men) to intervene and drive the UN forces back. The UN forces controlled the air but the Chinese troops, with their overwhelming manpower advantage, drove the UN forces back, at one point capturing Seoul, the South Korean capitol city. China suffered huge casualties in this offensive. Some experts put the figure as high as a million men killed-in-action. Among those killed was Mao Zedong's eldest son.

MacArthur requested permission to recruit soldiers from Chiang-Kai-shek's army in Taiwan and to bomb targets over the border in China, even at one point threatening an atomic bomb attack. Truman, worried about a possible global war with China or the Soviet Union, refused. When MacArthur made public statements disagreeing with the president, Truman in a courageous but unpopular decision relieved the general of his command.

The war ended in a stalemate with an armistice that divided Korea again at the 38th parallel, just where it was before the war began, and where it still is today. This sometimes "forgotten" war (Truman called it a "police action," not a war) cost the U.S. over 50,000 lives and set a pattern that was repeated twenty years later in Southeast Asia when a communist North Vietnam attacked U.S. supported South Vietnam.

Although it was thought for a long time that there was never a shooting war between the United States and the Soviet Union recent evidence has confirmed that is not so. During the Korean conflict it turned out that the Soviets did have fighter planes manned by Soviet pilots in the air over Korea. And these planes did shoot at American fighter planes. Both the United States and the Soviet Union kept this information secret at the time and for many years thereafter.

Even though the Korean "police action" ended in a military stalemate, the stalemate represented a significant victory for South Korea and a disaster for North Korea over the next fifty years.

VERY SELDOM IN HISTORY do you get a chance to have controlled experiments as you routinely have in the physical and life sciences. Korean history after the war is about as close as you could come to such a controlled experiment. In one case you had South Korea supported by a free-market liberal democracy, the United States. In the other case you had North Korea supported by command-economy communist dictatorships, China and Soviet Union.

Before the war each side had roughly comparable populations (South Korea was a bit larger), roughly equal resources (North Korea had more industry and mineral resources), roughly equal wealth, roughly equal land areas, roughly equal poverty levels, and ethnic cultures that were very similar. After the armistice each side had suffered roughly equal destruction and human causalities (though the Chinese lost far more military personnel than did the armies on the United Nations side). The only major variable was the difference between a command economy and a free market economy after the armistice. So what happened?

Both sides left the war with authoritarian governments. In South Korea, however, the authoritarian military government of Syngman Rhee eventually evolved into a full free-market liberal democracy and is so today. In North Korea, the communist dictatorship became, if anything, more totalitarian as time passed and remains so today.

What was the result of this "experiment?"

The gross national product per capita in U.S. dollars today is about $900 in North Korea, over $13,000 in South Korea.

In North Korea, one of only two Marxist-Leninist communist countries in the 21st century (the other is Cuba), up to two million people died of starvation in the 1990s. That was out of a total population of twenty-two million. The life of the survivors was, in the words of one survivor, "worse than a pig's life in China." South Korea has, like the United States, a surplus of dieters.

South Korea is a full member of the United Nations, has the fourth largest economy in Asia, the fifteenth largest in the world, is a major producer and exporter of automobiles, ships, electronics, robotics and petrochemicals, and ranks high on a list of the countries with the most economic freedom in the world. North Korea ranks at or near the bottom on freedom, near the top on poverty level, with next to no significant production for export (except military weapons and some minerals), and only too little for internal use.

On the *Index of Economic Freedom* for 2011[14] North Korea came out dead last, 179th out of 179 measured countries. (Cuba was 176 out of 179.) South Korea came out a respectable number 35, better than Israel, number 43, but worse than Belgium, number 32.

North Korea has a much larger military establishment than South Korea and is said to be developing first-strike capabilities for nuclear bomb attacks using long-range missiles. South Korea is exporting Hyundai automobiles known for superior safety and good gas mileage.

Conclusion: Free-market win-win capitalism works. Command economy zero-sum socialism does not work.

Second conclusion: Our police action was not in vain and the 50,000 men who lost their lives in Korea did not die in vain. There does remain some question whether we made a mistake in not pursuing the war to a victory instead of being content with a stalemated armistice. In that failure North Korean citizens today are the big losers. To make matters worse, South Korea and western liberal democracies are being challenged today by the threat of nuclear strikes from the totalitarian regime still in power in North Korea.

RELEVANT CONCLUSIONS about our wars in Iraq and Afghanistan are not easily drawn. At a minimum, though, we should note that if critics like my wife and I (and most of our fellow students and professors at liberal-left colleges like Antioch) had had our way, East Germany, Berlin, Greece, Turkey and South Korea might be communist countries today.

---

[14] For details on this useful tool from the *Wall St. Journal* and the *Heritage Foundation,* see <http://www.heritage.org/index/>.

Faulty Predictions

If my wife and I had had our way in 1950, South Korea would be a communist country today. With all that that implies. Of course my wife and I had no responsibility in the matter in 1950, so it is easy to say our views did not hurt anybody. That is the excuse fellow travelers use today when confronted by the facts of communist horror in the 20th-century. Is it that easy though? Memes can be as powerful as genes and when they infect masses of people, as the socialist zero-sum memes did (and still do), there are consequences.

In my day Antioch College, from which I graduated in 1950, was, like most liberal arts colleges then and now, on the left-center of the political spectrum. In the decades since that time Antioch moved steadily to the far-left end of that spectrum. In fact, it moved so far left and became such a poster college of radical progressive movements (a popular t-shirt of the day claimed that Antioch was the "boot-camp for the revolution") that it lost most of its student body as well as most of its financial support by the end of the century. As a result the College went defunct in 2008. (I understand it hopes to be reborn in 2011.) The experience of the college, in a reverse way, mirrors my own intellectual and political experience in the decades since 1950.

Values, attitudes and ideological leanings (memes all) were not necessarily taught as such in the classroom but somehow came through in the college noosphere then, as they still do today. Communism was not OK, but profit was a bit of a dirty word and capitalism was often looked on as synonymous with greed. Socialism was cooler. Social democracy was considered the norm. Fairness and equality were often considered more important than freedom. The poverty of what we called "third world" countries in Africa, Asia and South America was almost always blamed on the imperialism of western democracies and the greed of western business interests. In progressive circles it still is today.

The Soviet Union, if we thought about it at all, was probably not all that bad. Even though we won the war against fascist totalitarianism, considering the way we treated Negroes and women, and the depth of poverty still prevalent in our country, we in the United States did not have all that much to be proud of. As I remember it, some of our professors at Antioch in those days were talking about the evils of corporate capitalism and the "fascist" tilt of both democratic and republican political parties in much the same way many leftists do today. A few professors went so far as to suggest we consider seceding from the U.S. and forming social-democratic utopian cells that somehow would protect us from the ravages of corporate tyranny, just as some radical environmentalists do today.

In the first presidential election in my coming-of-age I voted for Harry Truman, but I was tempted to vote for the far-left candidate and fellow traveler, Henry Wallace. He was the favorite of many professors and fellow Antiochians. I emphatically did not trust "anti-communists" like the congressmen on the House Un-American Activities Committee (HUAC) who voted to investigate Antioch the year after I graduated. And, of course, I was appalled at the soon-to-be-infamous Wisconsin senator, Joe McCarthy. In short, I was in those days a weak fellow traveler, uncomfortably close to what George Kennan called a "controllable Marxist."

The history of controllable Marxists in the mid-20th century has uncanny, and uncomfortable, parallels with the history of environmental and far-left liberals in the early 21st century. Let's look now at the Cold War Controllable Marxists.

Chapter 3

Controllable Marxists

TH U.S. RESPONSES to the Berlin blockade and the Korean invasion were clear-cut and for the most part successful. The U.S. responses to the Soviet use of "controllable Marxists" inside the western world were muddied, controversial and not always successful. At enormous cost in human lives during the Second World War the Soviets were successful in repelling and destroying Hitler's armies. They were successful, also, at very little cost, in planting spies in the U.S. and British governments and defense industries, notably the Manhattan Project (the multi-billion dollar effort to create and deliver an atomic bomb for use in the war).

At the end of the war the U.S. had a monopoly on atomic bomb technology. However, it turned out later that Soviet spies stole important secrets of the atomic bomb that made it easier for the Soviets to build their first nuclear weapons in 1949.

Two cases, in particular, became national scandals in the early 1950s.

Klaus Fuchs, a high-level British scientist working on the Manhattan Project in New Mexico, confessed to stealing secrets about the detonation details of the atomic bomb and passing them along to Soviet agents in the U.S., including Julius and Ethel Rosenberg. The FBI intercepted some of the communications, and prosecutors brought Fuchs and the Rosenbergs to trial in 1952. Fuchs pleaded guilty; and in consideration of his aiding the prosecution, received a sentence of ten years in prison.

In a much-publicized (and much criticized) trial both Ethel and Julius Rosenberg were convicted of espionage and sentenced to death. Both were executed, though many legal experts think the evidence was stronger against Julius than it was against his wife, Ethel. The presiding judge in Boston, Irving Kaufman, wrote, "I consider your crime worse than murder. ... I believe your conduct in putting into the hands of the Russians the A-bomb years before our best scientists predicted Russia would perfect the bomb has already caused, in my opinion, the

Communist aggression in Korea, with the resultant casualties exceeding 50,000 and who knows but that millions more of innocent people may pay the price of your treason."

In another widely publicized and controversial trial, Alger Hiss, a senior U.S. State Department official and an important advisor to President Franklin Roosevelt during the war, was accused in 1948 of being a secret agent of the Soviet Union. He denied the accusation but was subsequently convicted of perjury in 1950 and sentenced to five years in prison. Hiss had many supporters in high places, including Dean Acheson, Secretary of State under Harry Truman. His trial and conviction were divisive and controversial. As were a series of highly emotional hearings and investigations of communist activities in both the U.S. Senate and House of Representatives.

In the late 40s and early 50s the House Un-American Activities Commission (HUAC) conducted widely publicized hearings on communism in the government, in academia and in Hollywood. These HUAC hearings ruined some careers in Hollywood when executives in the movie industry started a "blacklist" of writers, actors, directors and movie technicians who were suspected of being communists, or of being sympathetic to communist activities. Some on the blacklist were active party members. Most people on the list, however, were fellow travelers, "controllable Marxists."

LOOKING BEYOND HOLLYWOOD, in the depression, in the war years, and after the war, the list of famous fellow travelers in the 20th-century is long, surprising and sobering. It includes well-known playwrights like Lillian Hellman, Arthur Miller, George Bernard Shaw and Clifford Odets; writers like Dalton Trumbo, Howard Fast, Ernest Hemingway, Howard Zinn, Sidney and Beatrice Webb; actors like Charlie Chaplin, Paul Robeson and Edward G. Robinson; folk singers like Pete Seeger and Woody Guthrie; journalists like I.F. Stone, Lincoln Steffens, Edgar Snow, Walter Duranty and William Shirer; philosophers like Bertrand Russell, Jean Paul Sartre and Simone de Beauvoir; scientists like

Albert Einstein, J. Robert Oppenheimer, George Wald and Linus Pauling; musicians like Leonard Bernstein, Kurt Weill and Aaron Copland; capitalists like Cyrus Eaton and Frederick Vanderbilt Field; union leaders like Sidney Hillman, Saul Alinsky and Harry Bridges; diplomats like Joseph Davies and Alger Hiss; even a former vice president, Henry Wallace—as well as hundreds of thousands of other intellectuals, college professors, union leaders, businessmen and socially prominent leaders. These leaders did not all directly support the Soviet Union, but they did support memes that were "communist-friendly." And they were, in Kennan's words, "controllable Marxists."

Some examples:

In 1919 the American muckraking journalist Lincoln Steffens wrote of the Soviet Union: "I have seen the future, and it works!" Actually he apparently wrote these often-quoted words when he was on a train in Sweden before he even entered Russia. Later he modified his praise when he wrote from a luxurious spa in Czechoslovakia: "I am a patriot for Russia, the future is there; Russia will win out and it will save the world. That is my belief. But I don't want to live there."[15]

Joseph Davies, the American ambassador to Moscow during the height of Stalin's reign of terror in the late 1930s, said of the sadistic dictator, "if Stalin had been born in America, my guess is that Stalin would have gone into public life because of his sympathy for the underprivileged and his desire to bring about a better life for the masses."

The famous *Life* magazine photographer Margaret Bourke-White went into rhapsodies of praise for the greater freedom for artists under Stalin. "This freedom to experiment—and the opportunity to experiment without worrying about the rent and the grocery bill," she wrote, "points up, more sharply than anything else I can think of, the tremendous

---

[15] *Communism: A History*, by Richard Pipes. Page 98-99

difference between the opportunities of the artist under a system like that in the Soviet Union and the situation here in America."[16]

The most read and most respected newspaper in America, the *New York Times,* was complicit at times in this naïve support of communism under Stalin. Their bureau chief in Moscow, Walter Duranty, won a Pulitzer Prize for his pro-Stalin reports. Duranty reported approvingly that Stalin was, " a guardian of the sacred flame" whose five-year plans would bring a new life to the people of Russia. Duranty flatly denied that Stalin had anything to do with the famine in the Ukraine that deliberately starved so many millions. He supported Stalin in the infamous "show trials" of the 1930s that condemned so many Bolsheviks to death on evidence obtained by torture and forced confessions.

The liberal magazine, *The Nation,* was also often complicit in support of Stalin and the Soviet Union. In a review article they described Duranty's work as "the most enlightened, dispassionate dispatches from a great nation in the making which appeared in any newspaper in the world."[17]

Another example of how widely the noosphere power of fellow traveler memes extended (especially in the elite provinces of New York and Washington) is the story of a New York dinner in November 1933. It was given for Soviet Foreign Minister Maxim Litvinov in New York's Waldorf Astoria Hotel. Each of the attendees' names was read in turn, politely applauded by the guests, until Duranty's. Whereupon, T*he New Yorker* critic, Alexander Wollcott wrote, "the one really prolonged pandemonium was evoked ... Indeed, one quite got the impression that America, in a spasm of discernment, was recognizing both Russia and Walter Duranty."

The New York Times continued to defend Duranty, and to this day they have not acknowledged the injustice of the Pulitzer Prize award, even after it became apparent how false and harmful his reporting was.

---

[16] *NY Times,* April 29, 1986. Reprinted:
http://www.nytimes.com/1986/04/27/books/the-big-red-paintpot.html?pagewanted=2

[17] For more on Duranty and the controversy about his reporting see:
<http://en.wikipedia.org/wiki/Walter_Duranty>

Did all this make a difference? Arnold Beichman in *The Weekly Standard* reviews the Duranty and *New York Times* link. In the article he quotes the historian Robert Conquest in his book on the Ukraine famine, *Harvest of Sorrow*, "as one of the best known correspondents in the world for one of the best known newspapers in the world, Mr. Duranty's denial that there was a famine was accepted as gospel. Thus Mr. Duranty gulled not only the readers of the *New York Times* but because of the newspaper's prestige, he influenced the thinking of countless thousands of other readers about the character of Josef Stalin and the Soviet regime. And he certainly influenced the newly-elected President Roosevelt to recognize the Soviet Union."

The British philosopher Raphael Samuel, and "new leftist" after he broke with the communist party, wrote movingly of the appeal of communism: "The Communism of my childhood was universalist. We no longer advocated World Revolution, but we believed that socialism was a cosmic process, and though allowing for the existence of national peculiarities (we only half believed in them), we thought of the transition from capitalism to socialism as beings 'identical' in content everywhere. Communism, like medieval Christendom, was one and indivisible, an international fellowship or faith ... 'one great vision' uniting us, in the words of a communist song, internationalism was not an option but a necessary of our political being, a touchstone of honour and worth."[18]

Many of these fellow travelers in the U.S. (in only a few cases were they dedicated party members) got their start in the 1930s depression when it did seem to many citizens in the West that capitalism was on its deathbed, and that communism was the best hope for the future.

Besides the apparent failure of capitalism in the depression there are other explanations for the fellow-traveler support of communist goals and activities.

(1) THE MARXIST VISION has always had strong appeal for many people in its quasi-religious hope of utopian bliss in the future. Many

---

[18] *The Rise and Fall of Communism*, by Archie Brown. p. 126.

fellow travelers believed it was more than a hope—it was a sure thing, scientifically certified and inevitable. All this in contrast to what many saw as the exploitation, hypocrisy and misery they felt was brought on by capitalism in the depression years. (Many leftists today are still convinced the utopia will arrive in the future, perhaps not under the "communist" name, but as an endgame to social democracy. The dream has simply been delayed by the collapse of some totalitarian versions in the late 20th century.)

(2) The zero-sum economic fallacy and its emotional appeal to "fairness" has had ten thousand years (the length of the agricultural age on earth), as well as the dominating influence of strong memes from all major religions to support its claims. Intellectuals especially are susceptible to this appeal. This is partly because, unlike the poor, they usually have enough leisure and education to learn a bit about history, and to know of the exploitation of the poor by the rich in past ages. Secondly, intellectuals often think they deserve a bigger piece of the supposed zero-sum pie than they are presently getting for their efforts. And finally, since their own income is often based on government programs, any shift to socialism is of direct benefit to them. Benefits and pensions in government jobs are substantially better than comparable jobs in the private sectors.

(3) It was, and it still is, easy to confuse support for communism with support for genuine democratic social welfare progress. Not all of the ideas of Marx and other reformers and revolutionaries of the 19th and 20th centuries led to tyranny and brutality. Only the Marxist-Leninist branch led to totalitarian states like the Soviet Union and Mao's China. Other Marxist-influenced offshoots often paired forces with religious activists, to pioneer social-democratic reform movements that are still active in improving capitalist and liberal democratic states today.

Germany was a leader in social-democratic welfare ideas all the way back to the time of Bismarck in the 19th century. Before the Soviet revolution changed world politics, communists expected that the first triumph of the party would not be in Russia, but in Germany. In the wake of World War I, however, extraordinary inflation, a blizzard of street fighting between Communists, Nazis and social-democrats, a reactionary policy of the winning allies (especially France), and the failure of social-democratic governments to keep order opened the way for Hitler to take command and lead his anti-Semitic totalitarian Nazi thugs to world catastrophe in the Second World War.

Some analysts, like Friedrich Hayek, claim that social-democratic movements, in Germany especially, laid the groundwork for what turned out to be the Soviet totalitarian state. They also greased the path for Fascism and Nazism. In other words, socialism and fascism are both "roads to serfdom," because they both take away freedom and substitute collective social planning. As he wrote, "The relative ease with which a young communist could be converted into a Nazi or vice versa was generally known in Germany, best of all to the propagandists of the two parties. Many a university teacher during the 1930s has seen English and American students return from the Continent uncertain whether they were communists or Nazis and certain only that they hated Western liberal civilization."[19]

Liberals claim, with evidence, that in both the 19th and the 20th centuries socialist and social democratic parties and movements made significant and progressive changes in the industrialized democratic countries of Western Europe and North America. Union leaders like Samuel Gompers and Eugene Debs, suffragettes like Susan B. Anthony, politicians like Franklin Roosevelt, Harry Truman and Lyndon Johnson, and African-American leaders like Martin Luther King brought ideas to democratic practice, some of which were also championed by Marxist thinkers. Liberal ideas like universal suffrage, free education, civil rights laws, and the liberation of women. Progressive ideas like unemployment compensation, social security, progressive taxation and indeed much of the modern welfare state.

For myself, I'm not sure about progressive taxation and some welfare programs, but I agree that the liberation of women and African-Americans were significant, liberal and progressive.

---

[19] *The Road to Serfdom.* Page 29.

IN THE U.S. SENATE, TOO, there was a communist scare in the 1950s. A senator from Wisconsin, Joseph McCarthy, got international fame (or infamy depending on your point of view) for his charge in a West Virginia speech that "I have in my hand the names of 205 (or 76, there was no written record at the speech and the number is in dispute) State Department officials who belong to the Communist Party of America."

There were indeed some communist party members and more than a few fellow travelers in government, business, unions, academia and intellectual circles. McCarthy's reckless and unsubstantiated charges were eventually to bring his downfall when he accused the Army of being heavily infiltrated with communist saboteurs.

As a young college graduate and teacher in the McCarthy days, like pretty much all of my friends and colleagues I was solidly anti-McCarthy. I could see that many of his accusations were based on flimsy or nonexistent evidence and that they were harming innocent people. Looking back today, however, I have to admit that McCarthy, while he was an obnoxious personality who drank too much, and made too many unfounded accusations, was onto something real. We may find history is kinder to him than to some of his harshest attackers, like the left-wing journalist I. F. Stone or the fellow traveling playwright, Lillian Hellman.

Recently translated and decoded secret Soviet transcripts, for instance, have produced evidence that journalist I. F. Stone may have been a paid secret Soviet agent all the while he was leading the pack in denouncing McCarthy.[20]

And Lillian Hellman (like many other fellow travelers of the 30s and 40s) consistently and openly praised Stalin and supported his "show trials" in the 1930s that did not stop at ruining a few reputations, but used torture and forced confession to send most of Stalin's revolutionary

---

[20] *Commentary Magazine*, May 2009.
http://www.commentarymagazine.com/viewarticle.cfm/i-f--stone--soviet-agent-case-closed-15120

Bolshevik colleagues to a quick death (along with three or four million other unfortunate citizens).

Hellman claimed later in life that "whatever our mistakes, I do not believe we did our country any harm." I suppose all fellow travelers, all "controllable Marxists," could make that same defense. But is it valid?

One of Hellman's most successful plays (recently revived on Broadway in 2010) was *The Little Foxes*. The villains of the play are a family of capitalist exploiters whose greed is destroying people in the South. One of the heroes is a young daughter in the nasty family who says to her greedy mother, "There are people who raped the Earth, and those who stood around and watched them do it. Well, Mama, I'm not gonna watch you do it." When it turned out that it was communist tyrants who did most of the raping, it was Hellman who claimed that even if they were wrong in supporting these tyrants, "we did no harm to anyone." How about by watching them do it? Even worse, by applauding as they did it!

William Phillips, editor of the *Partisan Review* (one of the few intellectual journals that did not come to the defense of the Hollywood blacklisted celebrities), wrote later in defense of Hellman's attack on his magazine.

> First of all, some were Communists and what one was asked to defend was their right to lie about it ... Another considera-tion was the feeling ... that Communists did not have a divine right to a job in government or in Hollywood ... Furthermore, it was not just a case of disagreeing with the Communists. They had branded us as the enemy. They were under orders not to speak to us. Their press called us every dirty name in and out of the political lexicon. And, of course, they were apologists for the arrest and torture of countless dissident writers in the Soviet Union and in other Communist countries ... how could Lillian Hellman not know these things?" [21]

---

[21] *A Partisan View: Five Decades in the Politics of Literature* by William Phillips. P. 174-175.

It is true that McCarthy and other anticommunist crusaders made too many false accusations and these sometimes ruined the careers of some people. What about the naïveté of so many fellow travelers in the West? What harm did they do? The U.S. was never seriously threatened with a Communist take-over. Nor did we ever suffer from American communists creating an American gulag. All that is true.

What we did suffer from, however, was a failure of will, due in large part to fellow travelers in the mass media, the universities, the entertainment industry and the intelligentsia. These are the folks (and I include myself) who created and expanded a noosphere that praised socialism and belittled capitalism; that exalted equality and downgraded freedom; that condoned the crimes of communism while condemning free-market democracies of racist imperialism and of exploiting the poor and downtrodden.

Alas, this national failure of will did quite a bit of harm. It condemned many millions in Southeast Asia, Eastern Europe, and Latin America to many years of communist oppression, tyranny, poverty, and in millions of cases, violent death.

Our abandonment of the South Vietnamese, for instance, after the armistice in a war that our military forces had won, is but one cruel example. Our failure to finish the war in Korea condemned twenty-two million North Koreans to fifty years of oppression, famine and "lives worse than a Chinese pig." Our ambivalence in the Bay of Pigs invasion of Cuba; our reluctance to support East Europeans in Hungary, Czechoslovakia, and Poland; our acquiescence in détente, implicitly agreeing that democracy and tyranny were equal; all of these are other depressing examples.

Even such a small thing as *The New York Times* policy[22] in obituaries has had consequences difficult to quantify but clearly prejudicial to memes that in the end play such a large part in determining history's directions. This obituary policy seems to direct writers to call a Nazi a Nazi, but

---

[22] Eric Breindel review of *Not Without Honor: The History of American Anticommunism.* WSJ, Jan 10, 1999

considers it bad form to refer to a long-time supporter of Stalin as a "communist." Instead they are to be labeled a "progressive."

Once Ronald Reagan and his supporters reversed some of these national policies in the 1980s and committed our country to move from containment, détente and Mutually Assured Destruction (MAD) strategies to "We win, they lose," we recovered some of our leadership and courage. Ideas have consequences. Memes make a difference.

The French anti-communist intellectual Jean-Francois Revel was not exaggerating when he wrote referring to *The Black Book of Communism*: "A conclusion leaps out from the pages: Communism was something far worse than an 'illusion.' It was a crime. To have been a Communist was to have been an active participant or accomplice in a colossal crime against humanity."[23]

I emphasize this truth in this book because I think it was not only true then, it is true now. As we in the early 21st century face the twin challenges of Islamic terrorism and of far-left economic and environmental zealots, it helps to remember the history of controllable Marxists.

And I was one of those fellow travelers.

---

[23] *Last Exit to Utopia* by Jean-Francois Revel. p. 71

Progressive, liberal, conservative?

Timothy Ferris, in his book *The Science of Liberty*, has a useful update on the left-right spectrum (which as he points out, was born in the seating arrangements of the French Chamber of Deputies after the French Revolution in 1789). Instead of left to right in a straight-line spectrum, he suggests a triangular model. At the points of the triangle we would have three political directions: (1) liberal, (2) progressive, and (3) conservative.

Liberals, Ferris suggests, are people in the classical liberal tradition of John Locke, Adam Smith, Baruch Spinoza and John Milton. They are strongly in favor of freedom, especially freedom from governmental and religious restraints.

Progressives lean strongly toward equality and social welfare, especially as represented in the works of Karl Marx.

Conservatives are strongly attached to tradition and slow evolutionary change as represented by leaders like Edmund Burke and Ronald Reagan.

I fall somewhere between liberal and conservative, leaning to the liberal, and suspicious of the progressive.

The 50s, 60s and 70s were tumultuous decades for the country and for me personally. Marriage, children, a teaching career in New York city, psychoanalysis, summers directing a progressive camp in New England (where Pete Seeger was a sometime visitor), moving back to the Midwest (Wisconsin instead of Ohio), founding a summer theater, involvement with the human potential movement, encounter groups, brief flirtations with hippie counter-culture, divorce, falling madly in love again, remarriage, and finally leaving teaching and launching my own small educational media company.

During all of those years I was never much of a political activist, more an "inspector of snow-storms," as Thoreau once described his talent. Despite being in one of the helping professions for many years, I could understand and sympa-thize with Thoreau when he wrote in *Walden*: "As for Doing Good that is one of the profes-sions which are full ... If I knew for a certainty that a man was coming to my house with the conscious design of doing me good, I should run for my life."

In New York my first wife and I were not swingers, but we did go to a few liberal parties where artists and writers often came with lurid sexual reputations, that were sometimes borne out in action. In at least one case we made a kind of arms-length contact with celebrity, when my wife lent our modest apartment to Norman

Mailer, who needed a place for a rendezvous with his current mistress.

My first wife is an artist and while in New York she had a long-running affair with our best friend, another artist. It was a source of great pain to both of us, but we did not divorce. Instead I got an offer of a teaching job in the Midwest and we moved to Wisconsin.

When we moved to Wisconsin we were both still on the liberal-progressive arm of the political triangle. During the 70s and 80s, however, I was ever so slowly moving from a liberal-progressive outlook to a liberal-conservative one, where I began to see more clearly the benefits of freedom and tradition and the shortcomings of socialism and its many offshoots.

Chapter 4

Khrushchev to Nixon

STALIN DIED IN 1953 and was replaced by the ineffective Georgy Malenkov, who was in turn replaced in 1955 by a flamboyant risk-taker, Nikita Khrushchev. In 1956 Khrushchev shocked the Soviet Union (and the world) by making a speech in the Kremlin denouncing the crimes of Stalin. When contents of the speech leaked to the world press, it caused a major tremor in the communist world and shook the confidence of many western party members and fellow travelers. Khrushchev pointed out that on one day—November 12, 1938—Stalin and Molotov had approved the execution of 3,167 people. One day!

Khrushchev in his entire speech spoke only of Stalin's crimes against Bolshevik comrades and opponents. He did not mention Stalin's many other crimes—including politically instigated famines, random massacres and concentration camp gulags—against so many millions of Soviet citizens.

Khrushchev brought change in the communist world with his denunciation of Stalin. However, he did not waver from the ultimate message Marxism-Leninism was sending to the world. In his memoirs, written after his own peaceful removal from office, he echoed the earlier insistence of Lenin that there should be no compromise:

> The struggle will end only when Marxism-Leninism triumphs everywhere and when the class enemy vanishes from the face of the earth. Both history and the future are on the side of the proletariat's ultimate victory … We Communists must hasten this process by any means at our disposal, *excluding war* … There's a battle going on in the world to decide who will prevail over whom: will the working class prevail, or the bourgeoisie? … Every right-thinking person

can see clearly that the basic questions of ideology can be resolved only when one doctrine defeats the other ... To speak of ideological compromise would be to betray our Party's first principles—and to betray the heritage left to us by Marx, Engels, and Lenin. [24]

President Truman did not run for reelection and was replaced by General Dwight Eisenhower who served two terms from 1953 to 1961. During the Eisenhower years there was an epidemic of fear over a supposed "missile gap." By the mid-1950s the Soviet Union was seen as aggressively adventurous with its new nuclear arsenal, and was thought to present a deadly threat to America. The new Soviet Premier, Nikita Khrushchev, once vowed to "bury us," though he later claimed he meant this in an economic, not a military way. When Khrushchev visited America in 1964 he was royally entertained by politicians and by some capitalist industrial leaders. Trade union members snubbed him, however, due to his harsh suppression of trade unions in the Soviet bloc.

Some citizens built bomb shelters in their back yards that they hoped would protect them when Russian missiles with nuclear warheads rained down from the skies. Some schools had "A-bomb" drills. Hollywood produced a series of movies like *Dr. Strangelove: or, How I Learned to Stop Worrying and Love the Bomb* and *Fail-safe* starring Henry Fonda, that stoked the fear. The supposed missile gap was intensified by the launching of the first earth satellite, Sputnik, by the Soviet Union in 1957.

A young senator, John F. Kennedy, ran for President to succeed Eisenhower with a campaign built around this supposed missile gap between the U.S. and Russia. "The nation is losing the satellite-missile race with the Soviet Union," claimed the Senator, "because of ... complacent miscalculations, penny-pinching, budget cutbacks, incredibly confused mismanagement, and wasteful rivalries and jealousies."[25]

---

[24] *The Rise and Fall of Communism* by Archie Brown, p 253.
[25] See: http://goliath.ecnext.com/coms2/gi_0199-1230060/Who-ever-believed-in-the.html

After Kennedy was elected president in 1961, one of his first challenges was how to deal with the first communist government in the Western Hemisphere in Cuba, led by Fidel Castro. Kennedy reluctantly supported an Eisenhower-planned invasion of Cuba by Cuban dissidents trained by our CIA. This invasion, labeled the "Bay of Pigs," failed ignominiously when the CIA bungled the details, and Kennedy declined to support it with air cover.

A year later, in 1962, the missile gap came to a head when Khrushchev installed Russian nuclear-armed missiles in Cuba. By now the policy of "containment" of communism had been augmented by a policy of Mutually Assured Destruction (MAD). That policy, adopted on both sides, said that any use of nuclear weapons by one side would assure use by the other side and thus both sides would be destroyed. MAD would, the theory went, make any hot war unlikely since for both sides it would be national suicide.

When new U.S. satellite photos revealed the secret missile sites in Cuba, President Kennedy addressed the nation in a speech aimed at Khrushchev, demanding that the Russians remove the missiles immediately. Kennedy ordered the U.S. Navy to intercept any Russian ships headed to Cuba and to forcibly remove any missile parts. Many of his advisors recommended an invasion of Cuba to make sure the missiles (and Castro and his government) were removed.

It was a tense time in the Cold War and many people around the world were terrified that a devastating hot war might break out at any time. 21st-Century archives show that Castro was urging the Russians to fire nuclear-armed missiles at the U.S. should the U.S. make any move to invade his country. His Russian advisors spelled out to Castro that any nuclear strike against the U.S. would also result in disastrous fallout over Cuba.

Khrushchev (despite Castro's angry objections) backed down, ordered his supply ships to return to Russia and took the missiles out of Cuba, on the assurance from Kennedy that we would not invade Cuba, as well as a secret concession that we would remove some of our missiles from

Turkey. The world breathed a sign of relief that this time at least MAD was avoided.[26]

The Cold War became a hot war again in 1963, however, when President Kennedy ordered 16,000 American military advisors into Vietnam to support and advise the South Vietnam government under attack by a communist-led insurgency (we called them the Viet Cong), which was supported, supplied and eventually joined by regular army troops from communist North Vietnam. A few months after these first American troop advisors arrived in South Vietnam, Kennedy was assassinated in Dallas, Texas.

When the new U.S. President, Lyndon Johnson, took office, South Vietnam was on the verge of being overrun by the insurgent Viet Cong, as well as regular army communist troops from North Vietnam. Johnson had to decide whether to commit substantial forces to Vietnam as Truman did in Korea, or to withdraw. He chose the first option on the same "domino" theory that Truman had used in Korea. This time the war became a long-running major disaster for the United States and for Vietnam, as well as neighboring Laos and Cambodia.

In the early years of the Vietnam War there was strong, if not unanimous, support in the United States Congress as well as the citizenry. (In many ways the situation then was remarkably similar to the situation now with Iraq and Afghanistan. Some of the people who supported the wars at the beginning, later—when things did not go well—became the most virulent critics.)

As in Korea, the U.S. military slowed and then stopped the aggressive communist forces from inside and outside South Vietnam. As the war dragged on and a military draft brought many new inductees to Vietnam (most from poorer families, since college students could and did get deferments), protests against the war gained strength in Congress and on the streets.

---

[26] A detailed account of the Cuban Missile Crisis prepared by Maureen M. Lynch, Lieutenant Colonel in USMC is available on
<http://www.globalsecurity.org/wmd/library/report/1995/LMM.htm>

When the North Vietnamese staged their biggest offensive in 1968 (the *Tet Offensive*), the U.S. and South Vietnam armies soundly defeated them. However, the very size of the offensive, coupled with misleading reports on television news in this country, served to further inflame protesters in American cities and especially on college campuses. Chants of "Hey, Hey, LBJ/How many kids have you killed today?" and tragic incidents like the killing of student protesters by National Guard troops on a college campus in Ohio, made for a virtual "war at home."

Hoping to cool the protests and end the war Johnson declined to run for a second term. Protests continued, however, and became ever stronger and more violent after the election of Richard Nixon. Nixon curtailed the draft, tried to shift troops home and make the war a strictly Vietnamese affair. In this process he also secretly expanded the war by authorizing the bombing of Viet Cong sanctuaries in Cambodia and Laos.

After eight years of war in which more than 55,000 American troops lost their lives, President Nixon, along with his Secretary of State Henry Kissinger, finally arranged an armistice with the North Vietnamese in 1974. After the armistice all the U.S. troops came home and Congress refused to support the South Vietnam government with any further aid, military or economic. North Vietnam, on the other hand, continued to get strong support from both the Soviet Union and from Mao's China.

Without our support South Vietnam soon fell to the North Vietnamese who sent their troops into Saigon in 1976, forced an emergency evacuation of our embassy, and proceeded to establish a full fledged communist dictatorship on the Vietnam peninsula that still exists today.

It was a humiliating defeat for the United States, and the Vietnam War left a bitter legacy that has still not completely dissipated. Unlike the Korean War, which eventually laid the foundation for prosperity in South Korea, the Vietnam defeat laid foundations, instead, for bitter times in Southeast Asia. Over a million Vietnamese were sent to harsh "re-education camps" where thousands perished. Hundreds of thousands of refugees fled Vietnam in small boats. Hundreds of thousands of Hmong people were persecuted by communist governments in Laos, and in

Cambodia over two million Cambodians died at the hands of the Khmer Rouge communists. Only now in the 21st century, forty years later, are Vietnam, Cambodia and Laos beginning to recover economically. Like China, these southeastern Asian countries are slowly moving today from command zero-sum economies of communist days to a modified free-market capitalist economy, still under authoritarian controls.

Many people, including me, have speculated that traumatic as the Vietnam War was, if we had continued our support of the South Vietnam government after the hard-won armistice, South Vietnam (and Cambodia) would have been spared the post-war tragedies that occurred. Even further, South Vietnam would, like South Korea, be a vibrant free-market democracy today, fully integrated into the global economic free world. Could our failure here be due at least in large part to the overwhelming influence of the fellow-traveler noosphere nourished so strongly by celebrities like Lillian Hellman, Jane Fonda, Pete Seeger, Noam Chomsky, Allen Ginsberg, the *New York Times*, etc. etc.?

I, for one, think so.

I also see obvious parallels to our undeclared war today with Radical Islamic terrorism and our commitments in both Iraq and Afghanistan to bring the Islamic World into the modern world.

The new left and me

More personal politics. I never warmed to
Richard Nixon, though I admired his work to end
the Vietnam War and to open relations with
China. On the progressive-left side I did support
John F. Kennedy. I was a wholehearted supporter
of Lyndon Johnson's "Great Society," and of his
effective leadership in civil rights legislation.

It was about that time, in the late 60s, that I gave
up writing poetry and became enamored of the
theatre. It started with community theatre where
I found new satisfaction acting and then writing
plays, and eventually founding, and producing
plays for a new summer theatre in our suburban
town in Wisconsin.

Some years later I worked a bit for Jimmy Carter.
I got a press pass when he was running for
president, and flew on his campaign plane along
with high-profile newsmen like Sam Donaldson
and Ed Bradley. I had a personal interview with
Carter and made an educational program called
How to Get Elected President.

I strongly supported the civil rights laws of 1964
that liberated African-Americans from a sea of
injustice, as well as the earlier Supreme Court
decision in Brown vs. the Board of Education
(1954) that declared segregated schools
unconstitutional. And I support today laws and
executive decrees that will give equal rights to

homosexuals in the services and in any and all civilian pursuits, including the right to marry and raise children.

I tell all of this now because it was about that time that I began to be disillusioned with many left-progressive views, and by the time Ronald Reagan came onto the political stage, I was converted to a more free-market, libertarian, unapologetic pro-Western, pro-capitalist point of view. Reagan, too, began his political career as a liberal social democrat. He was also a strong union supporter and was president of the *Screen Actors Guild.*

Part of my change in political views was due to the reading I was doing then in history, science-society issues and politics as well as the interviews we were having with prominent scientists for our educational video productions. Much of this reading and interviewing was at odds with the views I had held since college. Some of my change was no doubt a reaction against the "New-Left" that grew powerful in the Vietnam years.

Maybe it was my growing up experience in the Great Depression and in World War II, but I could never stomach the anti-American fulminations of New Left heroes like Abbie Hoffman, Tom Hayden, Noam Chomsky, Jane Fonda, William Kunstler, Allen Ginsberg, et al. Ginsberg's famous poem "Howl" was not a favorite of mine.

When I read that first line, "I saw the best minds of my generation destroyed by madness," I could have forgiven him if he meant folks like Vladimir Lenin, Josef Stalin, Pol Pot, Mao Zedong, Fidel Castro and Che Guevara. I don't think he did.

This "New Left," it seemed to me then, and seems to me today in its 21st-century reincarnation, is not progressive, and it is certainly not liberal. Today some of these same Vietnam-educated new-left activists, along with their students, are very powerful players in the media, in the government and in education at all levels.

In all of these powerful pulpits, new left activists cultivate a barely disguised suspicion of science and technology (not disguised when it comes to nuclear power, genetic engineering, intelligence testing and animal research); they encourage a vague but real disgust with modernity; they condemn out of hand "corporate America"; they mock middle-class values and life-styles; they often glorify primitive ways of life (see the hit movie *Avatar*) even if they don't want to live that way; they are zealous in promoting organic foods, "natural" cures, alternative medicine and "green" lifestyles; and while they are negative about traditional religions, they make environmentalism, sustainability and multiculturalism into new quasi-religions that denounce free-market capitalism and globalization, preaching instead a return to a modern variation of zero-sum economics.

All of these trends are destructive of free-market liberal democracy, which has as its base, science, capitalism and humanistic religion.

Is it just a coincidence how many of these new left directions resemble Radical Islamic complaints about the "Great Satan America?" More of this later. For the moment let's consider a new wrinkle in the Cold War—détente.

Chapter 5

Détente

GERALD FORD, VICE PRESIDENT under Nixon, served two years as president after Nixon resigned due to the Watergate scandal. A Democrat, a relatively unknown peanut farmer, nuclear engineer and former governor of Georgia, Jimmy Carter, succeeded him. Carter was elected on a pledge to "cool" the Cold War and he tried to do just that. He claimed that "anti-Communists" were exaggerating the threats and were harmful to the long-term interests of the U.S. and the western world. "We are now free of that inordinate fear of communism," he said in an address at Notre Dame University in 1977, "which once led us to embrace any dictator who joined us in that fear. I'm glad that that's being changed. ... Now I believe in détente with the Soviet Union."[27]

After Khrushchev denounced Stalin's crimes in 1956, the Soviet Union did seem to be mellowing. Some called it a "thaw" in the cold war. The Soviets were apparently no longer sending massive numbers of prisoners to slave labor camps. If anything, the communists under Mao Zedong in China, however, were accelerating their campaigns of terror and bloodshed. Mao's utopian "Great Leap Forward" from 1958 to 1961 cost at least forty-five million Chinese citizens their lives, most of them in famines that the rest of the world never knew about. And then, from 1966 to 1976, Mao's "Cultural Revolution" brought still more chaos, misery and death. Some scholars claim the total death toll in China surpassed sixty million from these disastrous utopian campaigns. Sixty million! And yet all the while in America I knew personally quite a few controllable Marxists who were still defending Mao as a great improvement over Chiang Kai-shek.

Tony Judt, Professor of European History at New York University, reported, "I well remember sitting in the graduate lounge of Cambridge

---

[27] Carter's speech at Notre Dame can be found on:
<http://teachingamericanhistory.org/library/index.asp?document=727>

University in 1969 while a tenured member of the economics faculty assured us that the Chinese Cultural Revolution, then at its paroxysmal height, was the last best hope for humankind."[28]

New gulags were also being established in Cuba, Vietnam and North Korea.[29] In Cuba, for instance, we can give credit to Castro for some advances in literacy and health care, but even today almost one quarter of adult men are in the active military, and the prisons and mental hospitals are full of political prisoners, including men and women whose only "crime" is being homosexual.

A theory of détente had been championed first by President Nixon and his secretary of state, Henry Kissinger. It was later adopted and expanded by President Carter. Détente was also a favorite of many intellectuals in the U.S. and Western Europe. In the Soviet Union it was called "peaceful coexistence." This was of course a whopper. Just as Stalin had preached a "common front" when it suited his purposes, "peaceful coexistence" for the Soviets was a way to pacify the imperialists, while working to destroy them. As Lenin once predicted: "The capitalists will sell us the rope with which we will hang them!"

The basic idea of détente was that we should try to understand and live with two systems in the modern world, communist dictatorships and free-market democracies. Each was felt to be legitimate and each could and would live side by side for the foreseeable future. Détente would in effect freeze the cold war, not attempt to end it.

The theory of "détente" was severely strained by Soviet actions in the late 20th century in East Germany, in Hungary, in Czechoslovakia, in Poland, and in Afghanistan. In East Germany in 1961, the communists built an ugly wall to separate East Berlin from West Berlin and prevent citizens of the communist side from fleeing to the freedom side. In 1964 a freedom threat in Hungary sent Soviet tanks into Budapest to suppress any deviations. In 1968, Czech reformers were threatening to replace the

---

[28] *Capitalism, Democracy, and Ralph's Pretty Good Grocery*, by John E. Mueller. p. 119.
[29] See *The Vietnamese Gulag* by Doan Van Toai and David Chanoff. Also *Against All Hope: A Memoir of Life in Castro's Gulag* by Armando Valladares.

communist government with a democratic one. The Soviets felt threatened again and sent Soviet tanks into the Czech capital to put down the "Prague Spring."

In 1979, Soviet troops invaded Afghanistan in a futile effort to support their communist allies, then in power. (In the case of Afghanistan, the U.S. supported Muslim insurgents with critical arms and supplies that later helped to bring the Taliban to power. This support came back to haunt us in the 21st century when some of the same Muslim fighters we aided, like Osama bin Laden, attacked the U.S. on 9/11/2001.)

And finally, in Poland in 1980, an increasingly powerful trade union movement, Solidarity, was seen as a mortal threat. The Soviets ordered the subservient Communist government to squash it with any means necessary.

Throughout all of these late 20th-century events many experts in the U.S. were still supporting détente. The French writer, Jean-Francois Revel, was a powerful European voice opposing communism and rejecting détente. When he came to the U.S. to help sales of his new book, *The Totalitarian Temptation,* he was well received by unions but was given a chilly reception in university circles. He wrote later, "They were then imbued with a spirit of détente vis-à-vis the Soviet Union and a lively admiration for Communist China."[30] Stephen Cohen, a leading Russian scholar at Princeton University, confirmed the view of many university experts in the late 1970s, "there was no alternative to détente."

As it turned out, there was an alternative, that of our next president, the former actor and union leader, Ronald Reagan.

---

[30] *Last Exit to Utopia*, by Jean-Francois Revel, footnote on p. 24.

Mendel in Brno, McDonald's in Moscow

By the time Ronald Reagan was elected president, I was learning more about history. I was also travelling more to learn about science and politics in other countries and cultures. I traveled to the Soviet Union, East Germany, and to Czechoslovakia in the cold war days of Leonid Brezhnev. Twice later, I visited the Soviet Union with my wife Jane and son Andrew (a specialist in Russian language and culture).

I remember crossing the border into communist Czechoslovakia in 1985. There were only two people on the bus, a Russian officer, and me. We were met by barbed wire and two soldiers with machine guns who made us get off the bus and empty our pockets, billfolds and suitcases. I had nothing incriminating in my suitcase or billfold, but I was carrying two 35 mm cameras and a lot of film. The soldier with the machine gun looked quizzically at me and asked in English, "Why you want to come to this country?" I lied a bit and said I was just a curious tourist. (Actually, I wanted to go to Brno to see and photograph the monastery where Gregor Mendel made his historic discoveries in genetics.) I don't think he believed me. His smile seemed to imply "You must really be cuckoo to want visit this country!"

Once inside Czechoslovakia, I found a bus to take me to Brno where the government tourist agency, Čedok, found me a room in a Holiday Inn-knock-off hotel. My room was on the 8th floor, and the first inkling I got that this was a command-economy hotel, was discovering I needed to take the stairs to my room because none of the elevators was working.

When I went to a Čedok agency again in Brno to ask about the address of Mendel's monastery, they claimed they had never heard of it, or of Mendel. This was in the days of Trofim Lysenko, the bogus Soviet agronomist, who claimed that environmental influences were always dominant over genetic ones. From various maps I had brought with me, I eventually did find the monastery. It was in a sad state of disrepair. (When my wife and I came back in the late 1990s, after the Czech Republic had become a free-market democracy, we found the monastery had been restored and was now a fine museum!)

Before leaving Czechoslovakia I found more examples of command-economy efficiency. I had three hours to kill before my train left Prague for Berlin. I was tired and hungry so I decided to splurge and have a slow dinner at a fancy expensive hotel near the train station.

It turned out that I was the only customer in the plush dining room, with three or four waiters at my service. One brought me a large elaborate menu printed in embossed letters and with impressive tassels. I couldn't read Czech so I just guessed and pointed randomly at some presumably fine dish. The waiter shook his head, no, that was not available today. I tried another. Same response. After pointing at five or six, I gave up and in sign language asked, "Well, what is available?" He pointed to one dish and I agreed that that would be fine. It wasn't.

In the Soviet Union, on my first trip in the Brezhnev era, I went with a small group from Antioch College. We stayed in what were considered first class hotels in Moscow, Leningrad and Kiev. The hotels were comfortable enough, though far below the standard of Hilton or Marriot. At least the elevators worked. I noticed that there were armed guards at the front doors of all the hotels, and that all the other doors, side and back, were locked with crude-looking padlocks. It soon became clear that ordinary Soviet citizens were not welcome. These hotels were for tourists or high ranking *nomenklatura* only. The same was true for what they called *Beriozka* shops. Here foreign tourists and privileged Russian officials could buy luxury goods like chocolate bars, western gin and whiskey, supermarket food, silk stockings, etc.

I learned later that the Soviets had a complex system of distribution. At the very top, leading bureau chiefs, scientists and artists could shop at the *Beriozka* stores that were ordinarily reserved for tourists. There were then two or three more layers with successively more meager wares until you came to the bottom level, stores that could sell to the overwhelming majority of Soviet citizens and workers.

I walked alone through the streets of Moscow and did find stores that sold to the ordinary citizen. This was in 1984 and it was clear that after sixty-seven years of command-economy experiments, the payoff for the ordinary Soviet citizen was pathetic. On a small grocery store shelves I saw a few generic cans, some sacks of rice and beans, some bread, quite a few bottles of cheap vodka, and that was it. If there were any fresh produce, meat, eggs or dairy goods, they were carefully concealed. I did see one long line waiting outside a store that had a small sign in the window that a passer-by translated for me. "Cuban oranges today!" Small wonder that one story has it that when a Soviet visitor to an American supermarket entered the store and looked around, she fainted.

Jane and I signed up for a second trip to Moscow with another group from Antioch. This was in 1991. We watched the Soviet flag come down and the flag of the Russian Republic go up on New Years Eve. That same night we went to the Bolshoi Theatre for a performance of *Swan Lake*. After the show we all went for dinner at the most popular restaurant in Moscow—the brand new McDonald's. It had just opened a few blocks from the Bolshoi.

Unlike most restaurants and stores in the Soviet Union, this new Russian McDonald's was squeaky clean, had good food and the people behind the counter smiled at you when they took your order. We were told that McDonald's had to conduct intensive training programs for clerks to achieve these smiles. They also had to buy, organize and supervise their own farms in Russia in order to produce the hamburgers, milk shakes and fries at a quality up to their standards.

Jane and I did a lot of traveling outside this country in the 80s and the 90s to get information and video for new programs in science and social studies for our small educational media company. Included in our travels were visits to Tanzania, Mali, Morocco, South Africa, Brazil, Venezuela, Ecuador, Haiti, Costa Rica, Panama, Cuba, Mexico, Canada, Turkey, Greece, Scotland, Ireland, England, as well as multiple visits to many countries in Eastern and Western Europe.

At the turn of the century Jane and I took a three-month trip around the world. We stopped for three weeks in China (Shenzhen and Yunnan Province). We also stopped in Japan, Taiwan, Thailand, Cambodia, India, the Netherlands, Finland, Germany, Denmark, Russia and England.

We took away from these foreign trips a new respect for ordinary people everywhere. We did not meet any anti-American sentiment, even in Muslim countries like Mali, Morocco and Turkey.

(The only exception was a brief run-in with New Left hippies in the richest country we visited, Switzerland.) On the contrary, the ordinary people we met in all of these varied countries went out of their way to be helpful.

One of the hallmarks of many progressive liberals today is to follow Howard Zinn or Noam Chomsky in claiming that anti-Americanism is the norm around the world.

Not in our experience.

Chapter 6

"We win, they lose."

THE COLD WAR TOOK still another turn when Jimmy Carter was succeeded by a former actor, union activist, governor of California, and outspoken anti-communist politician, Ronald Reagan. Reagan had always been ambivalent about the "containment" policy and lukewarm about "détente," which he saw as a way of perpetuating the cold war rather than ending it. He hated MAD and set as a goal for his administration abolishing all nuclear weapons. When asked by a reporter what his theory of the cold war was, he said, "We win, they lose."

A few years after Reagan came to power in the U.S., the Soviet Union also had a new leader, Mikhail Gorbachev. Gorbachev came from a different mold for a Soviet premier. He was relatively young. He realized that the command economy of the Soviets was not working and they were falling further and further behind the western democracies. He also was aware that the draconian restrictions on freedom of speech, publication and openness were severely handicapping their economic and political progress.

To repair these defects, he pushed a two-part program of reform called "perestroika" and "glasnost." The first was supposed to reform the economy by introducing more incentives for production and the second was supposed to soften the repression by introducing more openness. In the end neither perestroika nor glasnost worked as planned, but instead probably contributed to the failure and then to the final collapse of the communist world movement.

Reagan and Gorbachev met three times to find breakthroughs in the cold war competition. Reagan championed what some called a "Star Wars" concept. The idea was that the U.S. would pioneer in anti-missile rockets that in theory could shoot down any nuclear-armed missiles before they arrived at their targets. This, Reagan felt, would make the

MAD strategy obsolete. He even offered to share the technology with the Soviets and hoped that this would make all nuclear arms obsolete.

Gorbachev did not agree. Nor did many experts in the U.S. and Western Europe. Nevertheless, some think the very threat of anti-missile technology along with a U.S. military build-up was one key to the final winding down of the cold war and the virtual demise of communism on the world stage.

PROBABLY THE MOST IMPORTANT new dimension that Reagan brought to the cold war was moral power. That is where Reagan's rhetoric hurt. What better place to employ that weapon than where the difference between western freedom and communist oppression was the most obvious, the Berlin Wall.

In 1987, Reagan gave a speech at the Brandenburg Gate, in front of the Berlin Wall, that contained a challenge most of his advisors thought inadvisable:

> General Secretary Gorbachev, if you seek peace, if you seek prosperity for the Soviet Union and Eastern Europe, if you seek liberalization: Come here to this gate! Mr. Gorbachev, open this gate! Mr. Gorbachev, tear down this wall!

Thousands of leftists in West Berlin marched against Reagan when he was giving this speech. Some western intellectuals and media leaders thought Reagan was being "un-Presidential" issuing this challenge. Many westerners were still in favor of détente and did not think it wise or effective to challenge the Soviet ideology. Dan Rather, the powerful CBS anchor, claimed, "despite what many Americans think, most Soviets do not yearn for capitalism or Western-style democracy."[31]

Two years later the East Germans did just what Reagan had urged. They tore down the Berlin Wall. Jubilantly. Some of it with bare hands!

---

[31] CBS Evening News. June 17, 1987.

And just two years after that, to the further astonishment of the world, the Soviet Union ceased to exist. Quietly. And for the most part peacefully.

During this same time, in the late 80s and early 90s, all of the formerly satellite communist countries overthrew their communist governments. Quietly. For the most part, peacefully. They became either free-market liberal democracies or non-communist authoritarian states with more freedom than they had under their communist leaders. Almost all were eager to join the increasingly globalized free-market world economy.

The new President of Russia, Boris Yeltsin, gave an address in 1992 to the U.S. House of Representative. In this speech he said: "The world can sigh in relief. The idol of Communism, which spread everywhere social strife, animosity and unparalleled brutality, which instilled fear in humanity, has collapsed. It has collapsed never to rise again."

Other former communist leaders and some fellow traveler sympathizers confessed their mistakes in honorable despair. Paul Noirot, for instance, a famous French fellow traveler wrote movingly: "Rationality is the last thing to ask of all those—and I was one of them—who took part in that chimerical enterprise. At the end of the day we built nothing that lasted: no political system, no economic system, no communities, no ethic, no aesthetic. We wanted to realize the highest human aspirations and we ended up birthing monsters."[32]

THE COLD WAR WAS OVER. The West had won.

Astonishment indeed. For most of the 20th century many people, east and west, believed that communism was the wave of the future. Ten years after the World War II ended, close to one-half of the world's people lived under communist rule. Most people in the western democracies, including me, thought it highly unlikely that the cold war would end in any of our lifetimes. And yet it did end. Suddenly and unexpectedly.

---

[32] Paul Noirot, *Le Trou noir du communisme après le naufrage*, Panoranmicques no. 4. (Arlea-Corlet, April 1992)

And not only in Russia! In different ways before the 20th century ended, Marxist-Leninist Communism, as well as socialist-dominated and socialist-leaning economic systems, were on the way out in China, in Vietnam, in India, and in South America (Venezuela, Bolivia and Ecuador, going the other direction, are exceptions today). Some, like China and Vietnam, still cling to the name "communist" for their government, while dramatically changing their economic base from a command-economy socialist one to a free-market capitalist one.

In China, for instance, where under Mao one hundred percent of the land and property was owned by the state, private businesses now employ over a hundred million people. And these private enterprises contribute over half of China's gross national product, and over two-thirds of its industrial output.[33]

After controlling almost one-half of the human population in the middle of the 20th century, the only true communist states left in the 21st century are two small countries with less than one-half of one percent of the world's population, Cuba and North Korea. And very recently, in 2010, Cuban President Raul Castro (who replaced his brother, Fidel, in 2008) abruptly announced that they were letting go one million state workers in hopes that they could jump-start a private economic sector!

---

[33] For devastating accounts of the Mao era in China read the books of Jung Chang's who lived through them: *Wild Swans: Three Daughters of China* and *The Unknown Story of Mao*.

entrepreneurs in St. Petersburg, prostitutes in Havana

In one of our final trips to Russia, Jane and I took a train from Helsinki, Finland to St. Petersburg, Russia. We hired a cab driver for the day to show us the sights. It turned out that our cab driver, Aleksandr, spoke good English and was a fine guide. His cab was an ancient Russian Lada. He was proud of it because now that Russia was capitalist, he was a private entrepreneur and he owned his own cab. He was a former hockey player who had a secret hope, he told us, of defecting, of leaving the Soviet Union on an elite hockey tour and not coming back. "Unfortunately," he said. "I wasn't that good."

His Lada ran okay but had its quirks. He was worried about it being stolen. He always took off the windshield wipers. "Thieves prize windshield wipers," he said. He also had a large club-like piece of sturdy metal that he not only locked onto the steering wheel, but also onto the accelerator and brake pedal.

Somewhat reluctantly (I didn't want, as a tourist, to insult his country) I told Aleksandr that a video camera had been stolen off my back when I was getting out of the St. Petersburg subway. It was so neatly and so cleverly done that I wasn't even aware the camera was gone for ten or fifteen minutes. He laughed and topped my story with a

tale of his own about the day he first voted in the
newly established Russian Republic.

This was just after he bought his own cab, and
was the same day he and his wife were moving
into their own apartment! For many years, like
many couples in the Soviet system, they had
been forced to live with her parents due to the
severe shortage of housing. He loaded up his cab
with all of their belongings to make the big move.
They left the cab just long enough to wait in the
voting line, and when they came from voting for
Boris Yeltsin, they found someone had stolen all
of their belongings from the cab!

Aleksandr laughed again when he told us his
story. Yes, he admitted, petty crime was a bigger
problem now than it had been in Soviet days,
when it was the government you had to look out
for, not small-fry criminals. Still, life was better
now and he no longer dreamt of leaving.

A friend here in Madison, now retired from
teaching social studies in a local high school,
volunteered a few years ago to critique the script
of a new series I was producing, on *The Totalitarian State*. In the script I included the story of
President Reagan giving a speech in Florida
where he famously called the Soviet Union an
"evil empire." My teacher friend wrote in the
margin, "My students would laugh this out of
class!"

He and his students were not alone. Activists like
Helen Caldicott promised to emigrate from the
U.S. should Ronald Reagan become president.
She was convinced a nuclear war would result.
Students at my friend's school, as well as the
faculty at one of the nearby University of
Wisconsin branch campuses, were unanimous
(not a single dissenting voice) in opposing some
of Reagan's cold war policies and pronounce-
ments.

By the end of the 20th-century, the only two
Marxist-Leninist countries were North Korea and
Cuba. No one is defending North Korea today,
but Cuba still commands respect and admiration
from many leftists in this country and abroad.
Michael Moore, the popular moviemaker, made a
big deal about Cuba and its supposedly superior
health care system in his recent movie, *Sicko*. And
of course Che Guevara, the handsome romantic
rebel who played a major part in Castro's
successful rebellion before getting himself killed in
a hoped-for Bolivian revolution, is still a pop star
among some young people and aging hippies.

Jane and I traveled to Cuba in 2001. The first
thing we noticed in Havana was the extreme
state of decay in ninety-five percent of the
buildings. The second thing was the prevalence of
prostitutes, male and female. Both of these seem
to be due to the poverty of the country
combined with a radical commitment to equal
outcomes.

The government owns everything and apparently cannot afford to keep any but a few government and tourist buildings maintained. Everyone is equal to everyone else, so brain surgeons and street sweepers get the same salary. When we visited, that salary was in pesos, the equivalent of about sixteen dollars a month. Food, education, medical care and shelter are heavily subsidized, so sixteen dollars suffices for survival but not much else. Grocery stores that accepted pesos had bags of very cheap rice and beans, maybe a pineapple or two, vodka and, on occasion, a chicken. That was it. There were a few farmers' markets that had expensive produce purchased mostly by tourists or government officials.

Families are so stretched for funds that the only way to get more than bare survival goods is to abandon their professions and get a job in the tourist trade—or send their daughters or sons out to sell themselves to European tourists. One time when I walked alone down a quiet residential street, a good looking young woman with a small child came up to me and offered her services. I politely declined, but she, I think, thought the child had put me off and indicated that she could get rid of him for a few hours if I wanted. A handsome young friend of mine went to Cuba a year later, alone and on his own, and said whenever he left his tourist hotel it was hard to walk anywhere without being repeatedly propositioned by women and men, pretty and ugly, young and old.

If you want to know more about the charming unpublicized life of Cuba I recommend *Dirty Havana Trilogy* by Pedro Juan Gutierrez, a writer and painter who lives the dirty life in Havana today. It is billed as a novel but it reads as personal memoir. Here is a sample:

> I went back to my room on the roof with its common bathroom, the most disgusting bathroom in the world, shared by fifty neighbors who multiply like rabbits, since most of them are from the east of the island. They come to Havana in clumps, fleeing poverty. In Guantanamo a person joins the police force and then arranges to be trans- ferred to Havana (no Havana native wants to be a policeman in the city), dragging his whole family along. And somehow they all live in a twelve-foot- square room. ... Each day no fewer than two hundred people shit, pee, and wash in that bathroom.[34]

Our taxi driver had been a lawyer, but like many professionals, he gave up his government job in order to earn more in tips driving a cab for tourists. He told us that he had many doctor,

---

[34] *Dirty Havana Trilogy* by Pedro Juan Gutierrez. p. 80.

lawyer and other professional friends who had become cab drivers, waiters in resort hotels, and barmen for the same reason.

We stayed in a private apartment that had an official license from the government to operate a kind of bare-bones bed-and-breakfast. The hostess (who rented her apartment from the government) was quite friendly. The apartment was a disaster, though. It had a bathroom shower with a Rube Goldberg arrangement for hot water. You had to turn on an electric switch while the water was running. This maneuver eventually warmed the water to lukewarm, but had the disadvantage that you might electrocute yourself instead when the bare wires from the switch contacted your wet hands. After watching the sparks fly once or twice, we decided to stay dirty.

As to the famous Cuban health care system, our second tour guide, a young handsome and friendly black man supplied by the government, had nothing but praise for the system. He had recently been in a motorcycle accident, he said, and the government had done an admirable job fixing his bones and healing his injuries free of charge.

On the other hand I read a book when we got home by a former American communist, Ronald Radosh. In his book, *Commies*, he tells of his first trip to Cuba with an American communist group.

Among other VIP sights, they were taken on a
tour of a mental hospital in Havana. He was
impressed. The patients were well dressed, the
furniture was modern and plentiful, and the
patients seemed remarkably calm, almost
spookily so. When he asked the secret of their
success, "We are proud," the doctor answered,
"that in our institution, we have a larger proportion of hospital inmates who have been loboto-
mized than any other mental hospital in the
world."[35]

"We were flabbergasted," writes Radosh,
"particularly a young man named Larry, a radical
therapist who taught at a New Jersey College.
'This stinks!' Larry screamed, as we got back on
the bus. 'It's exactly what we're working against
at home.'"

"Castro loyalist Suzanne Ross glared at Larry,
shot us all a contemptuous look, and said harshly,
'We have to understand that there are differences between capitalist lobotomies and socialist
lobotomies.'"

Radosh also discovered that some of the inmates
were homosexuals, since the Cuban health care
system considered homosexuality a disease
justifying commitment to either a mental
institution or a prison.

---

[35] *Commies: A Journey Through the Old Left, the New Left and the
Leftover Left* by Ronald Radosh. pp. 126-127.

Chapter 7

How and Why We Won

HOW CAN YOU EXPLAIN this turn of events, the most surprising political and economic events of my lifetime?

Some think President Reagan's policies had much to do with the final Soviet collapse. He did say in one of his speeches that communism was "another sad, bizarre chapter in human history whose last pages even now are being written." He turned out to be right, but whether his policies put the nails in communism's coffin is in dispute. One theory goes that the Soviets (like all communist countries) had always spent a far larger portion of their budget on military expenses and now they could no longer compete with the U.S. after the Reagan-initiated U.S. military build-up. With the "Star Wars" threat they realized they were even further behind, especially in electronics, and they would never be able to catch up.

While Reagan's actual policies, military and political, may or may not have had a decisive role in the collapse of communism, his moral stands certainly did. Memes are powerful, more powerful than many imagine. Reagan, with his infectious optimism, his light-hearted but deeply felt confidence in free-market capitalism, his denunciation of collectivist socialism and his sense of humor, made anti-communism respectable again. In the end it helped crush the pro-socialist agenda both in the United States and abroad.

It is more likely though that the final nails in the coffin of communism were supplied and driven in by the communists themselves. Perestroika and glasnost policies championed by Soviet premier Mikhail Gorbachev were desperately needed by the Soviet economy but, in the end, proved fatal to the Soviet system.

Political scientists point out that tyrannical systems do not often collapse when the tyrants have total control, but often they do collapse when reformers try to modify and soften the system. That seemed to be true in the Soviet case. Lenin, Stalin and Khrushchev kept power because they were ruthless. Gorbachev lost power when he tried to rule without terror.

Marx claimed that contradictions within the capitalist system would inevitably lead to its collapse. Lenin said that capitalists would sell them the rope to hang them. Ironically it was the communist systems that gave birth to contradictions that led to their demise. While free-market capitalist systems around the world were bringing wealth and progress for the workers, command systems like Marxism-Leninism were bringing poverty and alcoholism for the workers.

In contrast to the increasing prosperity of the free-market liberal democratic world in the late 20th century, it became obvious to leaders (and to citizens), of communist countries in the late 20th century that their system was not working. They were falling further and further behind, especially in computers and electronics.

A satirical novel, *The Yawning Heights,* by the Soviet political essayist Aleksandr Zinoviev (published abroad) gave voice to this gap. "On top of all that," he wrote, "there's abroad. If only it didn't exist! Then we'd be home and dry. But they're eternally dreaming up something new over there. And we have to compete with them. To show our superiority. No sooner have you pinched one little machine from them than it's time to pinch the next one. By the time we've got it into production, the bastard's obsolete!"

They were having trouble growing enough food to feed their populations. Their manufactured goods were shoddy, scarce and plainly inferior to the goods coming out of western factories. Factories were inefficient, corruption was pandemic and with little incentive to produce, productivity was low. A joke in Moscow had it that "they pretend to pay us and we pretend to work." Their citizens were becoming educated (a good thing) but that very education enabled them to see how far their society was slipping behind.

They did have better housing after the Khrushchev reforms in the 60s. Instead of many families sharing small rooms communally as they had to do under Stalin, single families now could sometimes have small private apartments where they could talk to one another without fear of being denounced by informers and sent to gulags. And talk they did.

In 1985 reformers pushed through new laws to curb alcoholism in the Soviet Union. These laws cut down on the highway deaths from drunk drivers. They also resulted in a serious problem for state finances. For many years a substantial part of the Soviet budget had come from taxes and markups on state-monopoly vodka sales. The new laws led to even more alcoholism and higher death rates at home when, to escape the long lines at high-priced government liquor stores, many citizens began making their own bootleg vodka.

With perestroika and glasnost in the 80s, more of the leaders (and educated citizens) could now travel to western countries and see for themselves how far behind they were. The new leadership of Mikhail Gorbachev was also more reluctant to use the KGB or brute military force to suppress dissent in the Soviet Union itself, as well as in eastern European communist satellites.

With expanded education, more travel and especially with more access to information from abroad due to new electronic media, Soviet citizens could see that the Marxist dogmas they had been taught were leaky. Marx had predicted, and that was what their teachers had always said, that workers in the capitalist system would become ever poorer and more taken advantage of by the capitalist owners of industry. That certainty clashed with the views they were getting from travel and the news media that showed ordinary workers in Western Europe and North America with two high-powered cars, plush suburban homes, fancy appliances, vacations at the beach, big recreational vans, and supermarkets that had every kind of food you could imagine. All that in contrast to dingy cramped apartments and long lines for a rare shipment of Cuban oranges at home.

Another glaring failure of glasnost came with the worst nuclear accident in world history at the Chernobyl nuclear power station in 1986. The accident happened on April 26 but the Soviet press waited a full two days before making even minimal information available. Only after reports of nuclear fallout began coming in from western European countries did the Soviet information ministries begin to report the serious nature of the accident.

Chernobyl was devastating news for Gorbachev. It revealed, he said, "the sicknesses of our system ... the concealing or hushing up of accidents and other bad news, irresponsibility and carelessness, slipshod work, wholesale drunkenness ... scientists, specialists, and ministers have been telling us that everything was safe. ... But now we have ended up with a fiasco."

Most important of all, the rapid explosion of new electronic means of communication that were difficult to censor—cell phones, computers, satellite television and the Internet—were making contrasts all the more obvious to more and more people in all countries of the world. The memes of freedom were trouncing the memes of equality.

THAT POWER OF NEW electronic gadgets is becoming ever more important in the 21st century. China, for instance, abandoned the command-economy, government-owns-all dogma of Marxism-Leninism in the 1980s, though it has retained dictatorial control of the population in political matters. In the 21st century, that control, too, is being challenged by the massive expansion of the Internet and other electronic communication tools.

At this writing, the giant Internet corporation, Google, is itself challenging the Chinese government about its censorship policies. In 2005 over 250 million Chinese citizens had cell phones and over seventy million had direct access to the Internet. Those figures are increasing exponentially every year. As the last British governor of Hong Kong said, "there is no Marxism left in China, though there are bits of Leninism." Electronic gadgets may make Leninism a lost cause, too, in the near future.

Using a capitalist free-market economic system, China became the world's largest exporter in 2010. Between 1978 and 2010 the "restructuring of the economy and resulting efficiency gains have contributed to a more than tenfold increase in gross national product (GDP)."[36]

UNDERLYING THESE DIRECT CAUSES there is a basic flaw in communist and socialist theory about human nature. Free-market capitalism assumes that humans usually act in self-interest and that diversity of talents and rewards leads to progress for all, so long as private property, free trade and free markets are given a chance to work their magic. Liberal democracy insists that the individual human being has rights and privileges that need to be acknowledged and protected, that freedom of speech, of religion and of the press are essential to a civilized society. On the whole both democracy and capitalism say self-interest, diversity of talents and individual rights are good things. And finally, both democracy and capitalism are pragmatic, not utopian. They are open to change and to new ideas and do not have a grand fixed vision-of-the-future, nor a dogmatic set of rules on how to get there.

Socialism, on the other hand, does tend to be utopian. In its pure form it envisions a future where everyone is equal and near-perfect justice is the norm. Socialism assumes that humans are altruistic by nature and that they can and will be their natural good-seeking selves once capitalism is abolished. Socialism stresses that community needs should take priority over individual rights, that private property should be strictly limited if not abolished, and that there should be equal outcomes, as well as equal opportunities. (In communist Cuba today, for instance, a brain surgeon and a day laborer receive the same salary—as well as the same ration cards.) Socialism demands that people be unselfish, that they sacrifice their private concerns for the public good. And socialism preaches that in the future a new man and a new woman, freed of petty greed and self-interest and dedicated only to the common good, will emerge.

The change in China in recent decades provides interesting on-the-job evidence to test the results of capitalist economics and of socialist

---

[36] See <https:///www.cia.gov/library/publications/the-world-factbook/geos/ch.html>

economics in a near controlled-experimental way. Back in the time of Mao when socialist rhetoric and control were dominant in China, workers in Chinese factories were among the most unproductive in the world.

A study in the 1970s, for instance, compared the efficiency of an average autoworker in a Chinese plant with the same worker in an American plant. It showed that the American worker took a few days to do the same amount of work the Chinese worker did in a few weeks. At this same time Chinese workers overseas—in Hong Kong, Malaysia, the Philippines or America—were always among the most productive of all workers.[37]

After Mao's death in 1976, China began to change. In 1979 a new leader, Deng Xiaoping, steered the economy in a free-market capitalist direction. The same workers who used to sleep on the job, in a few years became the most productive in the world, and the Chinese economy became the envy of the world. Exports soared, wealth increased and it was China who had money to lend, not to borrow. And they have been lending large amounts of it to the United States in the 21st century to support our welfare state demands.

The difference in productivity almost certainly can be attributed to the change of incentives. When people know their own work can improve their own situation, they work hard. When they are simply rhetorically harangued to work for the benefit of all, they become lazy and find ingenious ways to shirk the job. When questioned why he abandoned the command economy for capitalism, Deng Xiaoping neatly dodged the question by saying, "It doesn't matter if the cat is white or black, so long as it catches mice."

The socialist dream may have worked for religiously motivated people and voluntary communities. Early Christians had such a dream, and in isolated locations lived the dream. St. Ambrose, the Bishop who was the mentor of St. Augustine in the 4th century wrote: "Nature has poured forth all things for all men, to be held in common. For God commanded

---

[37] Thomas Sowell. "People Respond More Readily to Incentives than Rhetoric." *The Capitol Times*, Madison, WI. Apr. 30, 1986.

all things to be produced so that goods should be common to all, and that the earth should be a common possession of all. Nature, therefore, created a common right, but use and habit created private right."

When applied to an entire society however, socialism tends to destroy incentives for economic, scientific and social progress. Where it has been tried in entire countries (for more than half a century), instead of leading to equality, prosperity and altruism, it has led most often to apathy, repression and alcoholism. It has restricted innovation and compromised art. In the end it has only been able to take and keep power by coercion. Friedrich Hayek goes further, and claims that the collective planning characteristic of socialism, and even of social-democracy, inevitably leads to either totalitarian communism or totalitarian fascism.

After seventy years of experimentation on statewide levels, and despite the over on hundred million victims who paid with their lives, the socialist utopia seems more remote than ever.

Yet despite the failure of Marxism-Leninism in the 20th-century, a few national leaders like Hugo Chavez in Venezuela, Rafael Correa in Ecuador and Juan Evo Morales Ayma in Bolivia are attempting to rehabilitate it in the 21st Century. The odds are not in their favor.

PART TWO

THE CHALLENGE OF 9/11

Where were you on 9/11?

I remember when Pearl Harbor was bombed in December of 1941. I was just starting high school that year. It was Sunday afternoon and I was out playing touch football in the street with friends from the neighborhood. I think it was my sister (two years younger) who came out to tell me that the Japanese had bombed Pearl Harbor and there was going to be a war.

To tell you the truth, I don't remember reacting very much.

Four years later I had graduated from high school, volunteered for the Navy and was stationed on a mountaintop in Hawaii when the first atom bomb dropped on Hiroshima. I was an electronic technicians mate 3rd class at a radio station responsible for keeping a transmitter running. We were broadcasting to submarines all over the Pacific. I was on an all-night watch, alone, when the small radio I was listening to interrupted the all-night music program with a news bulletin. A new kind of bomb of enormous force had hit the Japanese city of Hiroshima and brought unprecedented death and destruction.

All I remember was a feeling of great numbness at the horror and death in Hiroshima.

The other two major death events of the 20th century I remember were the death of President

Roosevelt and the President Kennedy assassination. The day Kennedy was assassinated I was teaching high school biology and had just gone outside for a short break and a cigarette, when someone interrupted with the news that the President had been shot in Dallas, Texas.

I was shocked and saddened.

I remember a more visceral reaction when the *Space Shuttle Challenger* broke apart right after launch in January of 1986. Seven astronauts including the first *Teacher in Space*, Christa McAuliffe, died. I happened to be at an educational media convention in Chicago when a messenger came into the conference room with the terrible news. I remember retreating to my hotel room, turning on the television, and sobbing.

On 9/11/2001, I was about to play a weekly round of golf with three retired buddies at a local municipal golf course. The television in the clubhouse was tuned to a morning news show and when I walked in I saw an airplane hit the World Trade Center. On first glance, like many people, I thought it was some kind of weird accident. The golf pro, who had been watching longer, said to me quietly, "It was no accident."

Chapter 8

The Rise of Radical Islam

MORRE PEOPLE WERE KILLED in the 9/11 attacks on the World Trade Center and the Pentagon than in the Japanese attack on Pearl Harbor in 1941 that began the World War II for the United States. The aggressors on 9/11 were foreign but they were not Japanese imperialists, Nazi thugs or communist radicals. They were Islamic radicals from a hitherto obscure group called al Qaeda, led by an equally obscure Islamic radical named Osama bin Laden.

Immediately after the attack there was an international outbreak of sympathy with the United States. A headline in the leading French leftist newspaper in Paris read: "We are all Americans now!" On the other hand there was jubilant dancing in the streets of some Arab and Islamic countries now that bin Laden had struck such a deadly blow to what some called the "Great Satan" America.

In their attack on the World Trade Center in New York and the Pentagon in Washington, the Islamic radicals demonstrated in dramatic fashion their contempt for free trade, for capitalism, for liberal western values and democratic ways of life.

Not too long after the attack there came another response both in Europe, and in some literary, academic and leftist circles in the U.S. It reminded me of similar anti-American, pro-Soviet and "controllable Marxist" statements of fellow travelers in the cold war era.

The prominent novelist Norman Mailer said of the twin towers: "They were like two huge buck teeth and now that they are down the ruins are more beautiful than the buildings were."

In response to the attack on the Pentagon, a professor at the University of New Mexico, Richard Berthold, was quoted as saying: "Anyone who can blow up the Pentagon gets my vote."[38]

A professor at Rutgers, Barbara Foley, piled on: "We should be aware that the ultimate cause for 9/11 is the fascism of U.S. foreign policy over the past many decades."

Isthmus, our local free weekly newspaper in Madison, Wisconsin had a lead editorial by the editor, Marc Eisen, the week after the attack. It happened that he had been in Washington on 9/11 and had been taking his children through the White House on a tour. When the White House guides got a message about the New York and the Pentagon attack and the possibility of an attack on the White House itself, they quickly ushered everyone out.

In his editorial on the attack the following week he never mentioned the attack, but vented his anger on what offended him more, being bossed around by the White House guides. "One of our basic rights as an American is not to be bossed around by people in uniform," as he put it.[39]

Maybe the German Enlightenment philosopher, Georg Hegel, was right when he wrote, "the only thing we can learn from history is that we learn nothing from history." I hope not.

It is true that American foreign policy has not been mistake-free. The chasm, however, between the American foreign policy mistakes, when compared with the hideous crimes of Hitler, Stalin, Pol Pot, Mao Zedong and other communist and fascist leaders is too vast for any rational person to take the above critics seriously. As we have seen, however, many intellectuals in the western world do take these claims seriously.

To understand this "war on terrorism," this war against Al Qaeda, this war against radical Islam, we need to go back not one hundred and sixty years but a thousand and five hundred years.

---

[38] Washington Time editorial, http://www.tampaforums.com/forums/free-4-all/anyone-who-can-blow-up-pentagon-gets-my-64697/

[39] *Isthmus*. Sept. 13 and Sept 20, 2011 for Eisen column and the *Letters to Editor* responding to his column the next week.

FOLLOWING (AND CONTRIBUTING TO) the collapse of the Roman Empire in the fifth century A.D. it was the Christian vision that triumphed in the western world. A hundred years later an Islamic vision, founded by a prophet in what is now Saudi Arabia named Mohammed, challenged this Christian world. And thus it was that fifteen centuries ago followers of Jesus and of Mohammed—Christians and Muslims—laid the religious foundations for rich civilizations that still flourish today.

Both Islamic and Christian civilizations were dominated by strong monotheistic religious ideas that had a common origin in the Jewish Biblical lands of ancient Israel. Neither Christianity nor Islam encouraged the pursuit of earthly happiness since both religions preached the ultimate importance of salvation, life after death. Both Islamic and Christian civilizations could lay claim to birthing some ideas that eventually would lead to modern democracy's belief in the "unalienable rights" of individual human beings given them by Islam's Allah, or by Christianity's God.

This was the theory. In practice both Islamic and Christian civilizations were strongly aristocratic and maintained some of the same class distinctions and tyrannical practices bequeathed by the Roman, Greek, Jewish and Arab civilizations out of which they grew.

Both Christianity and Islam honored a strong warrior class as essential to the civilization's survival and power. Both were founded in an agricultural age and saw wealth in terms of land, shepherds, peasant or slave laborers and gold. Both had their roots in a zero-sum economic system where any gain to one meant a loss to another.

Both believed in a jealous god and fought many barbaric wars through many dark centuries trying to prove their religion was the one true religion, their god the one true god.

One difference was the way they viewed government. For Christians both religion and state were important but they were not the same. Jesus said "give unto Caesar the things that are Caesar's and to God the things that are God's." In matters spiritual, the Pope in Rome was supreme. In matters secular, nobles and kings in small feudal kingdoms throughout medieval Europe and western Asia ruled by divine right, but separate from the supreme spiritual authority.

In Islam, on the other hand, religion and government were never separate. Since the laws of Allah must govern all of life, no distinction was made between religion and state. Islam did not have priests or a Pope. It did have religious leaders called caliphs and imams. They ruled supreme in both temporal and spiritual affairs in all the provinces of a vast Islamic Empire that once extended from Spain in the West to what is now Indonesia in the East.

There were other differences. Islam did not condemn slavery and Islamic countries for many centuries considered slavery natural and ordained by Allah. Islam did not believe that women should be accorded equal status, rights or privileges as men. Islam did support science and technology, so long as they did not infringe upon religious dogmas. Throughout the Middle Ages—the time roughly between 500 and 1300— Islamic countries were world leaders in medicine, in agriculture, in astronomy, mathematics and physics.

Islamic countries placed a higher status on trade than did Christian kingdoms. As a young man the Prophet Mohammed himself, founder of Islam, was a merchant. In medieval times Islamic countries also tended to be more tolerant of Jews and of Christians within their borders than the Christian countries were toward Jews or Muslims within their borders. They called Christians and Jews, "people of the book."

While they did have peasants and serfs, Christian kingdoms for the most part did not have slaves—though there were exceptions. Gypsies, for instance, were enslaved for hundreds of years in many Christian countries of Eastern Europe.[40]

In the 16th, 17th and 18th centuries hundreds of thousands of Africans were purchased or kidnapped by both Christian and Muslim traders. (Also by Hindu, Buddhist and other religious traders.) These Africans were transported to the Middle East and Asia and forced to become slaves. After the European discovery of the new western continents, they were

---

[40] See *Bury Me Standing: The Gypsies and Their Journey* by Isabel Fonseca.

sent on cruelly packed slave ships to North and South America and to all the Caribbean Islands. They were forced to work on plantations as slave-laborers in Christian-dominated communities.

Jews, while not enslaved, were often persecuted, outlawed and often murdered by Christians. The persecution of Jews became worse in times of great natural disasters like the Black Death, or in times of great religious and military zeal like the Crusades of the 11th to the 13th centuries.

Though all ancient and agriculturally based civilizations were male dominated, most historians agree that Christian kingdoms gave a higher status to women than did Muslim, Chinese or Hindu Kingdoms.

CHRISTIAN CIVILIZATION IN EUROPE was dramatically changed by three important happenings, happenings that for the most part did not happen in Islamic countries—the Renaissance, the Reformation and the Enlightenment. In the Renaissance some of the values, arts and sciences of classical pagan civilizations of Greece and Rome were reborn in Christian versions. In the Reformation the Christian world split into two parts, Catholic and Protestant. Subsequently both of these parts split into the many variations that still thrive today. And then in the Enlightenment, especially in England and Holland, new secular ideas and values of science and democracy came to the western European and North American continents.

Islamic civilizations, too, changed over the centuries, but for the most part the changes tended to be reactionary rather than progressive. Islamic countries tended to retreat back to a medieval world-view where Islam was dominant and aggressively powerful on the world stage. Today that same reactionary movement in Islam, funded by new oil wealth, has awakened with renewed ferocity and suicidal power in what some call Radical Islam.

Radical Islam is not the same as the Muslim religion. Indeed some predominantly Muslim countries like Turkey, Indonesia, Morocco, Pakistan, Iraq, Bangladesh and parts of India are changing in a positive way and seem to be moving haltingly to enter the modern world. And there are individual leaders in all Muslim countries who are moderate in their views and offer hope that Islam will change and accommodate itself to the modern world, just as Christianity did two or three hundred years ago. And, just as in the Christian world, the majority of Muslims worldwide are lukewarm if not indifferent to the dogmas of the religious leaders, whether radical or moderate.

It is dangerous, however, to delude ourselves that the radical terrorists in so many Muslim countries are simply a small "criminal" group that can be handled the same way we handle criminal groups in the West—by patient and effective police work and normal jury trial procedures. Their leaders are a relatively small group it is true. So were Lenin, Trotsky, Stalin and the other Bolsheviks when they pioneered the communist cause that led to so many heinous crimes in the Soviet Union, China and the world. And in fact so were Hitler and his Nazi followers before they rocketed to popularity in the late 1920s.

The Osama bin Ladens of the early 21st century have much in common with the Bolsheviks and the Nazis of the early 20th century in their messianic zeal, their cunning, their utopian visions, their intellectual power, their demand that state and religion be one and the same, their fierce intolerance, their hatred of free-market capitalism and liberal democracy, as well as their embrace of violence. These Islamic radicals do not have the conventional armies that the communists or the Germans could rely on once the Soviet Union or the Nazis came to power. But they do have a weapon the communists or the Nazis did not have—a plentiful supply of suicide volunteers. And in the 21st-century chaos of the Middle East and Southeast Asia, they are dangerously close to having nuclear weapons that would enormously magnify the power of this suicide weapon.

As in pre-revolutionary Russia, the ordinary citizens of many Muslim countries today—over a billion human souls—are for the most part poor, uneducated and exploited. They provide rich soil for demagogic leaders. And then there is the fast-growing population of more educated Muslims in the Middle East, in Asia, in Europe and in America that offers rich soil for leadership roles in terror. Terrorist leaders themselves, like the Communists before them, rarely come from the poor. More typically terrorist leaders and suicide bombers come from the educated middle class or the wealthy.

Just as the Soviets tried to convince westerners that communism was for "peaceful coexistence," Muslim leaders in the West like to portray Islam as a religion of peace and good will. Western fellow travelers chose to ignore Article 17 of the communist international Comintern that said in plain words: "The Communist International has declared a resolute war on the bourgeois world and all yellow Social-Democratic parties."[41] It may not be wise to ignore a quote from a Muslim Brotherhood Strategic Memorandum on North American Affairs that was obtained in a 2007 Holy Land Trial.

This memorandum is devoted to "enablement of Islam in North America ... establishing an effective and stable Islamic Movement led by the Muslim Brotherhood." Here is part of what it says:

> The process of settlement is a "Civilization-*Jihadist* Process" with all that means. The *Ikhwan* [the Muslim Brotherhood] must understand that their work in America is a kind of grand *Jihad* in eliminating and destroying the Western civilization from within and 'sabotaging' its miserable house by their hands and the hands of the believers so that it is eliminated and Allah's religion is made victorious over all other religions.[42]

---

[41] See: <http://www.marxists.org/archive/lenin/works/1920/jul/x01.htm>
[42] "It's Never Just the Economy, Stupid" by Brian T. Kennedy. Hillsdale College *Imprimis*, Jan. 2011. p. 3.

sentimentality, iPhones and X-rated films

In my later years I confess to sentimentality. I tear up when the *Star Spangled Banner* is sung at baseball and football games. I tear up at scenes in old movies like *Casablanca* when Paul Henreid, to upstage the Nazi brass, leads the night-club band in *La Marseille*, or when Claude Rains says, "I'm shocked, shocked, there's gambling here," as the casino clerk surreptitiously hands him his winnings. Or his other great line: "Round up the usual suspects," after he watched Humphrey Bogart shoot the Nazi officer in cold blood.

Songs, poems and quotations from long ago often jump into my head. An Irving Berlin song from the Great Depression days is one. It should get a revival today.

> If today your heart is weary
> And every little thing looks grey
> Just forget your troubles and learn to say
> Tomorrow is a lovely day.

If our parents and grandparents could appreciate that sentiment in the 1930s, we can sing along today. Tomorrow is even more likely to be a lovely day now that the threat from Marxism-Leninism is on the ash-heap of history. Even though the challenge from Radical Islam is real, I'm not convinced that it is in the same league.

There is an irony though. Free-market liberal democratic states won the cold war against command-economy totalitarian communist states. They have also converted formerly desperately poor command-economy-leaning countries like India, China, Vietnam and Brazil into prosperous free-market tigers. Yet today within the democratic countries many left-leaning critics are still fighting the lost battle, under different names, with different issues, and on the losing side.

Marxist-Leninists lost the 20th century war but some progressive activists today are rephrasing some of the issues in that war into wholesale condemnations of corporate greed, of western life style consumerism, of globalization, of modern science and technology, and especially of free-market capitalism. Many of these criticisms of America and of other western liberal democracies come close to the views of radical Islamic terrorists, even though the western critics leave out the suicidal methods and the other-worldly religious propaganda.

So … what's to be done about Radical Islam?

I'm only half joking when I make one small suggestion. As the poet A. E. Housman wrote, "And malt does more than Milton can/to justify God's ways to man." Muslim people are people like the rest of us people. The radical leaders make big noises about the decadence of

Western life styles. When push comes to shove, however, most people in the world like good food, good housing, good entertainment and even a bit of naughty luxury if they can get it.

That is why some of our strongest weapons may not be arms or drone airplanes, or heavy propaganda and news shows, or missionary-like USAID programs. Instead, the insidious infiltration of Hollywood films, McDonald's fries, iPhones, Facebook connections and Victoria's Secret shops may prove more effective.

Recently I saw a film from a young independent producer who went alone to the streets of Baghdad with a small video camera during the most dangerous days of the recent war. He reported that the most popular place in the city was a newly opened theatre that showed X-rated films. Sold out for five showings a day. I'm not suggesting that the government should subsidize porn films, but I am suggesting that the often derided-by-liberals private sector may be our most significant asset in our religious war against Islamic radicals.

Chapter 9

What is to be done about Radical Islam?

IN THE 20TH CENTURY, THE free-market democracies led by the United States won the cold war against command-economy Communists led by the Soviet Union. In the 21st century, the free-market democracies are being challenged by Radical Islamic theocrats who use suicidal terrorism as their preferred weapon, as well as by some western activists who oppose globalization and consumer-driven economies.[43] I will leave the response to these homespun challengers for another chapter.

How do we answer the question, "What is to be done about Radical Islam?"

A U.S. military strategist, Eliot A. Cohen, has pointed out key features that the new war against Al Qaeda shares with the cold war against the Soviet Union. "That it will involve a mixture of violent and nonviolent efforts; that it will require mobilization of skill, expertise and resources, if not vast numbers of soldiers; that it may go on for a long time; and that it has ideological roots."

Note especially his phrase, "that it may go on for a long time."

There are differences, of course. Differences in the ideological roots, and in the source and depth of our adversaries power. Those differences are important in deciding what to do in the "war" against Islamic terror.

The communist challenge during the cold war was based on a Marxist-Leninist ideology that viewed the U.S. as a greedy capitalist imperial power. Marxists, however, actually admired our western standard of living, our consumer-rich way of life, our scientific and technological prowess and to some extent even our democratic freedoms (they said we need to postpone real "people's" democracy until all the world was communist).

---

[43] A few days after 9/11, our local *Wisconsin State Journal* had a brief column where they interviewed a coordinator of the Human Issues Department at Edgewood College. Students asked, "Why do they hate us?" She answered "by talking about the environment and natural resources of the world and how much of these we use, how that makes a percent of the world extraordinarily angry at us."

For all their secrecy, their violence, their hopelessly inefficient economies and their cruelly repressive instincts, they saw themselves as more modern, more scientific and more progressive than we were.

The Radical Islamic fighters also view the U.S. as greedy and imperial. They agree with the communists that state and religion should be one and the same. They just have a different religion. Communist law and ideology were based on a secular religion as laid down in Karl Marx's *Das Capital.* Radical Islamic ideology is based on Allah's revelations as found in the *Koran* (and as interpreted today by Radical Imams.)

Unlike their communist cousins, Islamic radicals reject modern western society and values. They see Western lifestyles with their consumer-driven economies, as decadent and destructive. They claim modern Western education is sinful, not liberating. Education, say Radical Muslims, should be confined to men and then primarily, if not solely, to the study of the Koran. They deplore women's rights and women's education as sacrilegious and deeply offensive. Science (especially biology and the social sciences) is seen as threatening to their dogmatic religious beliefs. Even humor and music are often seen as sinful in Iran, Somalia, Afghanistan under the Taliban, and other fundamentalist Muslim countries in the Middle East and in Africa.

To Radical Muslims, all other religions are inferior. More than inferior, believers in any other faith in fact are guilty of blasphemy, and fit only to be conquered and/or destroyed in the name of Allah. Insults to Mohammed are to be punished by death, as are many other crimes like adultery, fornication and homosexuality. Like true communists, the Radical Muslims see their religion as international, the only true religion, the only way to achieve justice in this world and paradise in the next.

CHRISTIANITY USED TO SHARE some of these same values and opinions—five hundred years ago. In time, prodded and altered (often with blood as well as philosophy) by the Renaissance, the Protestant Reformation, and the Enlightenment, Christianity mellowed, modernized and has often participated in progressive movements. Not only participated, but led. Some branches of Christianity in the 19th, 20th and 21st centuries, for instance, have nurtured and inspired leaders in the democratic quest for equal rights, universal education and health care in modern welfare states of Western Europe, North America and the Pacific Rim.

Can the same thing happen with Islam? One can be forgiven for hoping so. Remember, once it was Islam that was the world leader not only in science, in art, in music, and in architecture, but also in tolerance!

Lenin answered his question of *What Is to Be Done?* by creating a small tightly-disciplined organization of intellectual leaders and terrorists. We, in the 21st century democracies, can counter the challenge of Radical Islam in a different way. We will need the patience and power of a vital working democracy, free people committed to a free press, free markets, free enterprise, and free politics. The same power of example and patient strength that won the cold war against communism can win the war with Islamic terror. Like Truman, we may need to sometimes "contain" the terror first, but we need not be satisfied with détente. Instead, we need to have the faith and power to believe that in the long run the winning strategy will be the same one Reagan used in the cold war against communism, "We win, they lose."

Sometimes victory may require military force, just as the Cold War did. President Obama said as much in his speech accepting the Nobel Peace Prize in 2009. "Make no mistake: evil does exist in the world. A nonviolent movement could not have halted Hitler's armies. Negotiations cannot convince al Qaeda's leaders to lay down their arms. To say that force may sometimes be necessary is not a call to cynicism—it is a recognition of history; the imperfections of man and the limits of reason."[44]

Not only could a nonviolent movement not have halted Hitler's armies, it could not have won the cold war against the communist movement throughout the 20th century. Fortunately we never had to

---

[44] For complete transcript of Obama's speech see: <http://nobelprize.org/nobel-prizes/peace/laureates/2009/obama-lecture-en.html>

directly confront the Soviet army, but we did have to use military power in major wars in Korea and in Vietnam. It was, also, without doubt the credible threat of U.S. military power that protected Western Europe, Greece, Turkey and other countries in Asia, Latin America and Africa from communist aggression. The former Prime Minister of Great Britain, Tony Blair, in his political biography *A Journey,* acknowledged as much, "As the defeat of Communism showed—and let's be clear, without America, it would not have been defeated—our alliance with the U.S. mattered."[45]

So, too, the wars in Iraq and Afghanistan may prove their worth in achieving a lasting final victory over Radical Islam—if we do not give up and pull out our troops before new democratic-leaning governments can survive and evolve. We kept a large number of troops and military bases in Germany, Japan, Italy and South Korea after our victory in WW2. It has worked well.

Vietnam was, unfortunately, a different story. We not only pulled all of our troops out, we abandoned the Western-leaning government of South Vietnam. The result was disaster for all parties. We should beware now of pulling out of Iraq and Afghanistan before these countries are ready to give liberal democracy a fair chance.

I emphasize victory over Radical Islam. This does not mean the death of Islam as a religion. Christianity still thrives despite the changes brought on by the Renaissance, Reformation and Enlightenment. It does mean promoting freedom of religion, as pioneered in the U.S., in all countries. Including Muslim ones where Islam is not only dominant but legally the only permitted religion.

In the long run, in other words, President Reagan gave us a standard and an achievable goal in the war against Radical Islamic terror just as he did in the cold war against Marxism-Leninism: "What I am describing now is a plan and a hope for the long term—the march of freedom and

---

[45] *A Journey,* p. 400. Also notable in the same book Blair wrote about the Kosovo conflict, "In truth, without the U.S., forget it; nothing would happen. That was the full extent of Europe's impotence." p. 231.

democracy which will leave Marxism-Leninism on the ash heap of history…"[46]

To achieve that final victory military power may be necessary. Nation building may also be necessary. But our strongest ally will be our own ideology of freedom. In the end, memes will rule. Cell phones, television, satellites, and computers helped the western democracies expose the weakness and sterility of Marxist-Leninist ideology. Those same meme-creating and meme-expanding tools can and will enhance the strengths of western democracy and expose the weakness and sterility of Radical Islam. They can also, believe it or not, promote rational (scientific) thinking, diminish the rule of violence in societies, and make people smarter! (See   for details.)

Progressive critics have played an important role in the advance of western free-market liberal democracy. We need more of them. What we do not need, but will no doubt get, are radical "fellow travelers" who undermine our strength, limit our goals and create a noosphere conducive to surrender instead of victory.

These are folks like the professor, Jennie Traschen, at the University of Massachusetts who said the day *before* the 9/11 attack: "Actually, what the flag stands for is a symbol of terrorism and death and fear and destruction and repression." Or the environmental activist, Daniel Burton-Rose, who said he might have approved "taking down a Niketown or Starbucks" but as to 9/11— "Why couldn't they have done what they did on a Sunday? There are always ways to make allowances for people's lives." Or, in fact, the significant number of celebrities and ordinary citizens who claimed after 9/11 that, "We had it coming."

These Radical Islamic "fellow travelers" do not agree with the religious or the violent side of the terrorists, but they often do agree with the enemy's denunciation of western culture. In fact, Radical Environmental-ists today often agree with a good deal of Radical Islamic hatred of modern consumer culture. They call to mind the "new left" who used to

---

[46] June 8, 1982. The British House of Commons.

chant on elite campuses of the 60s, "Hey hey, ho ho/Western culture's got to go!"

Not so. We are living today at the dawn of modern history, not the twilight. Western culture's got to stay and grow. Make no mistake about it—western free-market liberal democracies are the good guys. Radical religions, whether secular or supernatural, are the bad guys. They are the ones that have to go, and we have to figure out how to hasten their exit.

In the long run, if we stick to what has proved to work so well in the past two centuries, in their last days Osama bin Laden and his radical Islamic brothers in arms will find their reward is not a bevy of virgins in heaven but the same ash-heap of history now occupied by so many tragically misled Marxist-Leninist fighters and supporters.

PART THREE

DEMOCRACY BASICS:

RELIGION, CAPITALISM, SCIENCE

"Better to marry than to burn"

Islam is not the only religion that is challenging
free-market democracy today. Christianity, too,
has a mixed report card when it comes to
supporting free market capitalism, as well as
liberal democracy. In my parochial school history
I remember well the moral admonitions in our
catechisms, but I don't recall nearly as vividly any
instructions to prepare us for constitutional
democracy or for free-market capitalism.

The moral and political lessons we were taught in
my parochial school experience broke down into
three major categories: dogma, bible stories and
sex.

As to sex, the lessons were mostly negative.
Avoid it at all costs and if you can't avoid it,
confess it and promise to do better in the future.
As St. Paul, the Apostle, said in Corinthians 7:9,
"It is better to marry than to burn." Best of all is
to bury your lust and be chaste like nuns and
priests. As for dogma, the important thing is to
say your prayers regularly, go to Mass every
Sunday, and obey all of the church's teachings
since the church is the Vicar of Christ on earth.
Above all, remember that if you commit mortal
sins, you are certain to suffer eternally in hell, but
if you follow the rules you will go to heaven and
live eternally in bliss with the angelic hosts.

I do remember, with some pleasure, the rituals and music that made the dogma and the bible stories more reassuring and powerful. First Communion day was a big deal, as was Confirmation. Confession was a sobering but freshening experience. Serving in the choir and as an altar boy was nice. I'm sure all of these made the dogmatic memes more stable and enduring. As some Jesuit (or was it Lenin or Stalin?) said, "Give me a child for the first seven years and I'll give you the man."

Bible stories also added memes that still linger today. Christ on the cross dying for our sins was the story that most moved and captivated me. When I did the Stations of the Cross in Lent, I used to imagine how painful those nails must have been. Once I actually tried putting my finger in the fire of a candle to test how painful hell might be. The stories with the most positive impact were lessons about being good, loving your enemies, honoring your father and mother, giving to the poor, forgiving those who hurt you—like the Sermon on the Mount, the Lord's Prayer, or the Ten Commandments. The truth is, I don't remember the details of most of the stories except for the crucifixion.

I was taught very little about democracy, though, or about free-market economics.

This is a bit unfair. We did have a civics class in high school where we were taught to honor the flag, George Washington, Abraham Lincoln and, in my day, Franklin D. Roosevelt. The dogma lessons, the Bible stories and the sex advice did not always fit well with free-market democracy.

My view today is that there are three basic pillars that undergird modern free-market liberal democracy: capitalism, science and technology, and humanistic religion. Before we lay out attainable means and end for the future of Free-Market Liberal Democracy, we need to examine just what the world history of these three basic pillars teach us, and how they operate in the modern world.

Let's go first to a primer on the rise of religion in general. I think the basics are worth repeating to help find the clues to address religious questions today.

Chapter 10

The Rise of Religion

NEARLY 3000 PEOPLE DIED on September 11, 2001. Their deaths caused by religious fanaticism. Islamic variety.

More than 300,000 people died in a Thirty Years War in northern Europe in the early 17th century.[47] Their deaths caused by religious fanaticism. Christian variety.

Untold millions died in wars and violent confrontations beyond counting over 10,000 years of recorded human history. Their deaths were due, often in large part, to Buddhist, Hindu, Confucian, Shinto, Christian, Islamic, Sikh, Mayan, Aztec and many hundreds of other varieties of religious fanaticism.[48]

ON THE OTHER HAND, most of the world's cultural treasures in art, architecture, music, sculpture, literature and dance were created from religious inspiration. All religious varieties.

Much of the world's compassionate history—moral codes, generosity, respect for fellow men, hospitals, relief for the poor, support for the downtrodden—arose out of religious motives and heritages. All religious varieties.

What about today? Is there a connection between religion and violence? Between religion and moral goodness? Between religion and sex? Between religion and democracy? If so, what are the connections?

---

[47] See "The Consequences of the Thirty Years War" by Nicole Smith on Article Myriad. Last accessed on 4/8/11.
<http://www.articlemyriad.com/thirty_years_war.htm>
[48] See *The History of the Medieval World* by Susan Wise Bauer for multiple examples on all continents.

HISTORICALLY RELIGION HAS been important, if not central to most human lives. It has also been at the center of many bitter conflicts. As it still is.

The Western world of Northern Europe, North America and Australia/New Zealand has been the pioneering leader in democracy. This Western world has also been mostly Christian in religion (Protestant for the most part) for many centuries. Southern Europe, Central and South America have also been Christian (Roman Catholic for the most part) for many centuries.

Much of the non-Western world of the Middle East, southeast Asia and northern Africa has been Islamic in religion since the early Middle Ages, 1,500 years ago. In the Far East, China and Japan have had a mixture of Taoism, Buddhism, Confucianism, Shintoism, Islam, and other folk religions for many centuries. India has had a mixture of Hinduism, Sikhism, Islam and other folk religions. Much of Africa, Oceania, and other more isolated areas of the world have long been polytheistic including a rich variety of nature religions.

In the early 21st century most liberal democracies are in countries that had a Christian history. Most, but not all, countries with a Muslim history are not liberal democracies. And most, but not all, countries with Hindu, Buddhist, polytheistic, or nature religions are not liberal democracies.

Is there a connection then between Christianity and democracy? Is there a disconnection between Islam and democracy? And what about the connections, if any, between Hinduism, Confucianism, Taoism, Judaism, polytheism and democracy? There are hints, but no certain answers.

WHAT IS RELIGION AND why is it so important, and so controversial, in almost every human society?

Religion, like capitalism, like science, and like democracy, had its origins in the remote past of the human species. Our *Homo sapiens* ancestors of 100,000 years ago lived in caves and rough shelters, and survived by hunting and gathering wild foods. Anthropologists and archeologists have been able to learn quite a bit about these ancestors by analyzing bones, tools and other remains in burial sites as well as by studying Stone-Age tribes still surviving today in remote regions of the Amazon, the South Pacific and Africa.

One thing they have found was that violence was the norm, not the exception. On average about fifteen percent of the people (twenty-five percent of the men) living in hunting/gathering societies died a violent death at the hands of other human beings. If modern humans in the U.S. and Canada had this same rate of violence, you could expect fifty million of us (eighty-five million men) would die from violence—and most before the age of 30.[49]

Partly because of this high rate of violence, but also because of high rates of starvation, malnutrition, disease and accidents, the average life expectancy was less than 30 years.

Homo sapiens individuals of 100,000 years ago had minds pretty much like ours today that could think, make subtle connections between events, make decisions and create.

Or did they?

IN A FASCINATING, if perplexing and controversial book, a modern psychologist from Princeton University put forth a novel hypothesis a few decades ago. Consciousness itself was only born a few thousand years ago, claimed Julian Jaynes, around the time humans learned to read and write. He presented his idea and his evidence to support it in a best-selling and well-reviewed book, *The Origin of Consciousness in the Breakdown of the Bicameral Mind.*

By consciousness, Jaynes meant introspection—the inner world in our minds that distinguishes between I and me. The central core that we recognize as our innermost self. A world where abstract thought goes on. A world where decisions are made when confronted with novel situations or difficult choices. A world where our conscience, our sense or right and wrong, resides. That inner world some have called the soul.

---

[49] For details on war in hunting/gathering societies see *War in Human Civilization* by Azar Gat. Data on deaths, p. 75.

Jaynes distinguishes this kind of consciousness from other mental activities like sensing, perceiving, problem-solving, communicating and learning, which are common to other animals. Only humans, though, are able to "be aware" of their own selves. We can use not just language, which is common in some form in many animals, but metaphorical language, which is special to human beings. It is this metaphorical language, abstract thought, introspective thinking that is special to modern humans, claims Jaynes, and even now, may not be that common among illiterate and uneducated humans. (See discussion of abstract thought and its connection to violence, intelligence and democracy in Chapter 15, pp.   .)

In the millennia before consciousness evolved (probably, speculates Jaynes, as a response to catastrophic environmental challenges in the Mediterranean basin four or five thousand years ago) humans had bicameral minds. In those prehistoric days one hemisphere in the brain, the right one, often literally "spoke" to the left one. There was an auditory hallucination whenever there was a need for choice. The voices people heard in their heads were very real and would almost always be obeyed. People interpreted the voices as coming from the gods or from some other authoritative source standing in for the gods—like monarchs, chiefs, medicine men, or village seers. Modern schizophrenia, possession, hypnosis and even religion itself, according to Jaynes, are leftovers from those pre-conscious days when everyone heard voices of authority inside their own heads.

Today we all carry around with us remnants of more primitive pre-consciousness ways of thinking, especially when it comes to religion, secular or supernatural, and in making important decisions. But also, in a perhaps diluted way, when it comes to believing in and following authorities—priests, parents, scientists, presidents, dictators, heroes.

Many people today, for instance, are convinced that God speaks to them sometimes.[50] Most people today, even those who don't hear the

---

[50] See "The Worst Corruption" by Arthur M. Schlesinger Jr. *Wall Street Journal*, Nov. 24, 1995.

voices, believe in some form of a supernatural world that governs the natural world, even though the connections are not obvious, rational or predictable. Prayer is seen as a way to influence that supernatural world so that it benefits our natural private world. Baseball players pray to get a hit, football teams pray to win the big game, lovers pray to win their true-love, mothers pray for their children's safety and welfare, nearly everyone with cancer prays for a miracle cure, and many citizens pray for world peace.

Jaynes would say all of these prayers are futile. He would also point out that not getting a satisfactory answer is rarely, if ever, seen as evidence for their futility. This is because we still believe the "voices" in our heads (which may still be the most powerful memes of all), even when the voices are faint or inaudible.

Jaynes' hypothesis, of course, is just that, an hypothesis. Since he first proposed the hypothesis it has been heavily criticized, but it has also been gaining some scientific support from new evidence in neurology in the late 20th and early 21st century. It does seem to make sense of many hitherto puzzling facts: the prevalence of violence, for instance, in prehistoric as well as historic centuries; the ease with which mass psychology can take over in political demonstrations, rock concerts and religious rituals; the irrational behavior of so many people especially when it comes to major decisions.

When Achilles, in Homer's epic poem *The Iliad,* hears voices that tell him he must fight and kill Hector, he does not hesitate. He fights and kills Hector. And he is not troubled with any remorse. When Abraham, the ancient Biblical godfather of Judaism, Christianity and Islam, hears God's voice telling him to sacrifice his beloved son, he goes to the mountain obediently and raises his knife to do so.

So today, when Stone-Age villagers in the Amazon or New Guinea attack a neighboring village, rape and kidnap all the women, kill all the men and then eat them, anthropologists report that they do so with no second thoughts and no remorse.[51]

---

[51] See *Dinner with a Cannibal* by Carole A. Travis-Henikoff, pp. 154-157, 238-239, 256.

Was it that different for the Native American "Anasazi, thought to be the ancestors of living Pueblo Indians," in Arizona who routinely killed and ate their enemies?[52] Or the people who slaughtered so many millions of human beings in past religious wars like the Crusades, the Thirty Years War in Reformation Germany? Or the Iran/Iraq war a few decades ago? Or the churchgoers who watched as heretics were tortured and burned at the stake in front of fascinated crowds? Or the Klu Klux Klan, who led crowds that lynched African-Americans in front of carnival-like crowds of the American South? Or the church-going SS troops who sent so many Jews go to their death in the Holocaust? Or just last month the crowd that cheered and threw rose petals at the feet of a man who assassinated a Governor in Pakistan just last year, because the Governor had tried to soften the punishment of a Christian woman who was condemned to death for insulting Mohammed.

OF COURSE THE VOICES have not always been hateful. There was also a New Testament where Jesus preached a peaceful message of love, compassion and forgiveness. And fortunately, too, there was an Enlightenment where philosophers like Baruch Spinoza, John Locke and David Hume made rational thought more respectable.

The voices today may also direct people in loving, unselfish ways. This was the case with Mother Teresa. Born in Macedonia to Albanian Catholic parents, she became a nun when she was eighteen years old and left for a missionary life in India. In 1946 she went for her annual retreat in Calcutta, and said that while there she heard "the call within the call" that told her, "I was to leave the convent and help the poor while living among them. It was an order. To fail it would have been to break the faith."

See also *The River of Doubt: Theodore Roosevelt's Darkest Journey* by Candice Millard for more insights into Amazonian primitive societies.
[52] See Research News, "Archeologists Rediscover Cannibalism" by Ann Gibbons in *Science* magazine, Vol. 277, 1 Aug. 1997. p. 635.

For the next forty-five years she obeyed the voices; begging for food and supplies, she became a nurse, an advocate and a friend to thousands of desperately poor, handicapped, homeless, orphaned, sick and dying people in Calcutta. She won the Nobel Peace Prize for her work in 1979.

WHEN THE AGRICULTURAL Revolution began some ten thousand years ago, religions that had their beginnings then still do survive today. Judaism, Buddhism, Taoism, Hinduism all had origins in early agricultural civilizations in the Middle East and Asia.

Then a little over two thousand years ago, the two monotheistic religions with the most worldwide adherents today had their beginnings. Christianity came first and about six hundred years later, Islam was born.

All of these religions have blossomed into many variations, and all of these variations have changed significantly over thousands of years. They are still changing today.

Religions of Asia like Buddhism, Taoism, Confucianism, Hinduism and all their variations tend to either be polytheistic (have many gods) or, like Buddhism and Confucianism, to dwell more on thought and behavior rather than on faith in a god or gods. They center on the eternal cycles of life, contemplation, moral codes, ways to cope with desire, disease and death.

Christianity and Islam, with their strong roots in Judaism, also stress moral codes and ways of coping with desire, disease and death. But in addition, they promote ideas like justice, progress, a personal God, individual rights, individual salvation and a promise of life after death. All of these differences mattered then and matter today.

Agricultural civilizations had a rigid class structure. A tiny minority (less than two percent of the total population) was at the top, and the huge majority was at the bottom. The tiny elite at the top included kings and queens, priests, warriors, artists, intellectuals, architects, engineers, storytellers and bureaucrats. The huge majority at the bottom were peasants, serfs or slaves. The elite's job was to govern, to enhance and to protect the society. The mass of people at the bottom, the peasants, serfs and slaves, did the agricultural, animal husbandry and artisanal work needed to provide food, shelter, weapons, and indeed all the material needs of the society.

Jaynes would say that one of the ways these ancient civilizations were bound together was the god-like powers that elite rulers were able to assume. Religion and the arts played major roles in all of these class-ridden societies, serving to reinforce the class structures, humanize them, unite the kingdoms (they also unfortunately sometimes acted to splinter the kingdoms), defend them against enemies, assure plentiful offspring and, only too often, be a key part of the motivation to attack perceived enemies.

Religion also played other roles, some positive and some not. On the positive side, religious belief, as with Mother Teresa, was a prime mover in caring for the sick, in founding hospitals, in softening the harshness of serfdom and slavery, in providing comfort to survivors, in restraining lusts (at some times and in some places, encouraging lust in order to get more babies), in providing moral codes, in inspiring art and architecture, and in general in promoting a more humane and just society in societies that were for the most part not very humane or just.

On the not-so-positive side the voices (or memes, if you prefer) of religious zeal often led to extreme emotional passion in support of bloody wars, as well as fiendish torture and terrible death for people of a different religion, or of heretics within a given religion.

A king of England, Charles I, for instance, claimed that, "The true glory of princes consists in advancing God's glory, in the maintenance of true religion and the church's good." Unfortunately Charles, a Catholic, had his head chopped of by Protestant rebels precisely for his insistence that his, and only his, was the "true religion."

Philip II of Spain said of a man accused of heresy, "If my own son were guilty like you, I should lead him with my own hands to the stake."

Sir Thomas More, celebrated as Saint Thomas More in the Catholic Church today, when he was Chancellor to King Henry VIII in England condemned at least six Protestants to burning at the stake when they refused to acknowledge the supremacy of the Pope. Then when England changed sides, More lost his head when he refused to acknowledge the supremacy of the Protestant King.

RELIGION WAS ALSO OFTEN a force opposed to trade and to inquiry, rejecting contacts with the enemy and rejecting reasoned inquiry into nature (science, that is) in favor of revelation and tradition (sacred books and inherited lore).

An early 6th century Christian bishop and philosopher in North Africa, later canonized as Saint Augustine, cautioned his followers:

> There is another form of temptation, even more fraught with danger. This is the disease of curiosity. ... It is this which drives us to try and discover the secrets of nature, those secrets which are beyond our understanding, which can avail us nothing and which man should not wish to learn.[53]

The Christian religion had its most dramatic growth when the Roman Empire dominated the lands around the Mediterranean Sea. At the beginning Christians were a tiny minority. The Roman elite persecuted them. In 325 AD the Roman Emperor Constantine converted to Christianity, made it the state religion and vastly increased the number of communicants.[54]

Once Christianity became a state-sponsored religion, it became richer, more bureaucratic, less mystical and more subject to corruption. Not too long after Constantine's conversion, the Roman Empire itself collapsed. Some historians think the change of religion had a major role in that collapse.

---

[53] From *Confessions* by St. Augustine. Quoted often by atheists and other secularists, as in *The God Delusion* by Richard Dawkins. p. 159.
[54] For detailed accounts of religion and state in late Roman and early Medieval times in Europe, the Middle East and Asia see: *The History of the Medieval World: From the Conversion of Constantine to the First Crusade* by Susan Wise Bauer.

The collapsed Roman Empire splintered into a multitude of small feudal states often at war with one another. There followed a serious decline in living standards—for the elite rulers. The peasants, serfs and slaves had always had a subsistence life, but even that life became more precarious in what followed, the Medieval Time of Europe from the 5th to the 13th century.

Around the Mediterranean and in Europe during that long period there were slow, very slow, changes in economics, in politics, in science and in religion. One of the most important changes in religion came in the 7th century when Mohammed founded the new monotheistic religion called Islam. His followers became known as Muslims.

Actually Muslims do not consider Islam a *new* religion. Muslims then and now consider Mohammed to be the true and final prophet in a series of prophets going back to Abraham, Moses and Jesus. They believe that the Jewish Old Testament and the Christian New Testament reveal true words of God. But they also believe that God (Allah) revealed his final words to his final prophet, Mohammed. These words are preserved in a sacred book called the Koran.

After Mohammed died in 632 AD, Islam split into two often-warring factions, Shiite and Sunni. The split was caused by a dispute as to who was the rightful successor to Mohammed. The split led to bitter wars between the two Islamic factions, wars that still go on today in Middle Eastern countries like Iraq, Iran, Egypt, Saudi Arabia, Syria and Palestine.

The Christian world as well had a major split (called the Great Schism) in the 11th century. Eastern Christians, centered in Constantinople (Istanbul in modern Turkey), and mainly Greek-speaking, split away from western Christians (mainly Latin-speaking), centered in Rome. The Schism centered on the role of the Pope, whom western Christians revered as the successor to St. Peter and the supreme ruler of all Christianity. The eastern Christians (called Orthodox Christians) revered the Pope but denied his supremacy.

From the 11th to the 15th centuries, the Christian world and the Muslim world fought each other in a series of wars, called Crusades in the West.

These wars still have strong echoes today. Led by Mohammed (and his followers after Mohammed's death), Islam spread its message by both pen and sword. The Christians wanted to regain control of territories lost to aggressive Muslim invaders, especially the Holy Land of Israel, a land that was sacred to both Christians and Muslims.

The Muslim world from its inception was aggressively expansionist and not only defended its territories, but in return attacked Christian communities all around the Mediterranean. This went on for hundreds of years. Much of Spain as well as much of Eastern Europe were for a time brought under Muslim rule.

Similar splits, disputes and wars were common in Buddhist, Hindu, African, American and Asian religious kingdoms throughout agricultural ages of the past ten thousand years.

In all of these bloody disputes, religion was important, but it was not the only issue. In all agricultural societies the economy was for the most part a zero-sum one, with rigid class structures dividing the population into haves and have-nots. Since there was only a limited amount of wealth (land, animals, serfs and slaves), the only way for one group to get wealthier was to steal from another group. The Crusaders (and the Muslims) were not ignorant of these facts, nor were they shy about taking advantage of them. Nor were the elite in other agricultural societies in Asia, Africa, the South Pacific and the Americas.

Genghis Khan, for instance, was a warrior prince from eastern Asia.[55] He led a fierce group of Mongolian warriors on horseback in a series of savage wars that eventually conquered territories larger than the Roman Empire in the 13th and 14th century. Like all groups, the Mongolian warriors had a religion (they worshipped a "sky god" in the "eternal blue heaven") that unified and motivated them, but the opportunity for increasing wealth through conquest was of greater, importance. Unlike most religious societies, they did not discriminate against people with other religions. They were also indiscriminate in their massacres when

---

[55] See *Genghis Kahn: and the Making of the Modern World* by Jack Weatherford.

they conquered a city, Christian or Muslim, killing all the men and raping all the women.

Genghis Khan himself could have been speaking for warriors of all persuasions in zero-sum agricultural societies, when he is reputed to have said, "The greatest joy a man can know is to conquer his enemies, and drive them before him. To ride their horses and take away their possessions. To see the faces of those who were dear to them bedewed with tears, and to clasp their wives and daughters in his arms."

It has been shown through DNA studies that a surprisingly large percentage of people in Asia, the Middle East and Eastern Europe still today carry genes that give tell-tale signs of having been descended from Mongol warriors. Many millions from Genghis Khan himself!

RELIGION, ESPECIALLY THE CHRISTIAN variety, has often been puritanical and opposed to sexual pleasures and activities. "Better to marry than to burn," is the best St. Paul could do for any positive side to sex.

Muslims have been more ambivalent about sexual ethics over the centuries. In some ages past—in Persia, Egypt and India—sexual pleasure was celebrated in stories like those in *The Arabian Nights*. Poems like the *Rubaiyat of Omar Khayyam* were popular and much imitated.

Devout Muslims today are more puritanical. A man is permitted to have four wives if he can afford it, but his wives must remain cloistered in their homes, not go to school, or drive cars. Really devout Muslims demand that women cover their bodies in robes so that only the eyes show, and above all, they must obey their husbands in every particular. If a woman were to commit adultery, in some Muslim countries still today, she would be stoned to death.

Both the Christian and the Muslim worlds of medieval days were only marginally less violent and brutal than Genghis Khan in their warfare and atrocities. Beside the battles of the Crusades against Islam, feudal communities of Christians in western Europe engaged in bloody wars with fellow Christian communities, often over land and wealth, but sometimes also over doctrinal disputes. Was the mother of Jesus a virgin without sin? Was Jesus equal to the father or not? Was God unitary or a trinity?

Heretics (those who believed differently than the current orthodoxy) were usually not tolerated. To put it mildly. Sometimes they had their tongues cut out to keep them from spreading the heresy any further. They might be tortured or burned alive. The rationale for the burning was that since heretics were certain to burn forever in hell, perhaps during the burning on earth they would repent and escape eternal damnation.

To me the apparent acceptance of these events by the general population gives credibility to the Julian Jaynes theories of pre-conscious voices that must be obeyed, and being obeyed do not lead to guilt or remorse. It's not my fault; it is the gods who decreed it. In modern times people have puzzled about the Nazi atrocities. How could an SS officer send Jews to the gas chamber and then come home that night and be a gentle father and loving husband? I don't think there is much evidence that the SS officers actually heard voices from God, but they surely did hear voices from Hitler and his minions.

In Christian communities of medieval times and later, Jews were persecuted and often driven from one community to another, denied rights, and sometimes murdered when they resisted or refused to convert. One of the crimes traditionally attributed to Jews was that they killed and ate Christian babies.[56]

Many Islamic communities treated infidels much the same. Some Islamic scholars taught that the Koran itself recommended killing infidels if they did not convert and acknowledge the supremacy of Allah. In medieval times, however, Muslims—especially Muslims in India and Persia—were more tolerant of Jews and Christians in their midst than Christians were of Muslims and Jews in their midst. Muslims called Jews

---

[56] In many primitive societies, even today, cannibalism is common, and for many tribes, children and babies are considered a delicacy. For many examples, see *Dinner with a Cannibal* by Carole A. Travis-Henikoff, especially pp. 196-201.

and Christians "people of the book," since they came from the same Judaic Biblical tradition.

This difference in tolerance may also have been due to a richer cultural life among the elite of the Muslim World during much of medieval time. While most of Christian Europe was illiterate, Muslim scholars in Africa, in the Middle East and in Asia, were doing important work. They were the ones who translated classic Greek and Roman writers into Arabic, saving them from extinction. Muslim countries in North Africa, Spain, India and the Middle East also had more schools, more hospitals, and a higher level of art and science than was achieved in the chaotic blend of Christian, Roman and barbarian culture that was early Medieval Europe.

Unlike the classical civilizations of Greece and Rome, and unlike most Asian, African and American civilizations, both Muslim and Christian religions at their best did teach the dignity of the individual, whether rich or poor (even if they often did not honor this teaching in practice). This emphasis on individual dignity would have important consequences for future political evolution in the world.

More thoughts on religion and sex

Thinking about Bible stories, dogma and sex again, what about the resurgence of religion today in the United States? Europe seems to have left Christianity behind, but in America, Christianity has never been more widespread and powerful. Non-Christian and secular religions have also proliferated at impressive rates.

So far in this narrative, sex has not seemed very relevant. Everyone in the world, of course, knows that in our personal lives sex is always relevant. In a fascinating, well-researched book *Dinner with a Cannibal,* anthropologist Carole A. Travis-Henikoff points out that while sex may not be number one in the living world, it is certainly in the top four. She lists the top four instincts in all living animals as the four "F's."[57] In order they are: Flee, Fight, Feed and Fuck. The first three have already played major parts in our narrative. Except for an aside about prostitution in Cuba, the fourth major instinct, fuck, has not played much of a part.

Religion to me means many things, but above all, as I said before, it means Bible stories, dogma and sex. Both the Bible stories and the dogma have contributed I think to a Christian moral tone that has been a base for both social-democratic and

---

[57] Ibid. pp. 74-75.

radical socialist memes in all of our lifetimes. As
for sex, the Christian tradition has not been a
particularly happy one.

I was taught by a faculty of all nuns, brothers and
priests, first in elementary school, then in an all-
male high school. Presumably none of my
teachers had experienced sexual intimacy. We
know today, of course, that despite their vows of
chastity, many priests, nuns and brothers were
not as innocent in sexual matters as we were led
to believe in those naïve school days of the
1930s and 1940s.

As a teenager I experienced the usual combination of lust, fascination and repression, all as
refracted through an orthodox Catholic lens. You
can read James Joyce's novel *A Portrait of the
Artist as a Young Man* for a vivid appreciation of
what it was like to grow up as a young man in
Catholic schools, with one eye on girls and the
other eye on eternal damnation. I can look back
now on my experiences and experiments with
sex with humor and understanding, but at the
time it was as confusing as it was sinfully exciting.

Theodore Dalrymple (a pseudonym for Anthony
Daniels), a compassionate conservative psychia-
trist and prison physician in Great Britain, has a
heart-rending article[58] that contrasts in a striking
way the differences and the historic likenesses

---

[58] "When Islam Breaks Down," *City Journal*, Spring, 2004.

between Islam and Christianity in regards to sex. He tells the story of his first visit to Afghanistan, back in the days when it was still a kingdom and Iran was governed by the Shah. He was part of a small troop of student thespians who performed parts of *Romeo and Juliet* before an elite audience that included the then crown prince in the deserts of Afghanistan.

Capulet's [Juliet's father] attitude to his refractory daughter, Dalrymple writes, is precisely that of my Muslim patients' fathers:

> Look to't, think on't, I do not use to jest.
> Thursday is near, lay hand on heart, advise:
> And you be mine, I'll give you to my
> friend;
> And you be not, hang, beg, starve, die in
> the streets,
> For by my soul, I'll ne're acknowledge thee,
> Or what is mine shall ever do thee good.'

In fact, claims Dalrymple,

> The situation of Muslim girls in my city is even worse than Juliet's. Every Muslim girl in my city has heard of the killing of such as she back in Pakistan, on refusal to marry her first cousin, betrothed to her by her father, all unknown to her, in the earliest days of her childhood. The girl is killed because she has impugned family honor by breaking her fa-ther's word, and any halfhearted official in-

quiry into the death by Pakistan authorities is easily and cheaply bought off. And even is she is not killed, she is expelled from the household ... and regarded by her community as virtually a prostitute, fair game for any man who wants her.

In the past (as Shakespeare's play shows) Christianity, too, was often intolerant and addicted to some of the same things that Radical Islam is today. Twenty-first Century Radical Muslims sometimes still sentence adulterous women to be stoned to death, and cut off the arms of thieves in accordance with Sharia law.

Christians in the Middle Ages were as bad, or worse. Thousands of heretics, for instance, (especially young women) were paraded naked through the streets, spit upon, often raped and then burned at the stake, all before a carnival-like crowd where parents held up their children to get a better view of the spectacle.

Philip II of Spain, where the Inquisition was at its worst, said, "I would rather sacrifice the lives of a hundred thousand people than cease my persecution of heretics."

Fortunately that does not happen in Christian countries today. But yes, sex is relevant to politics.

Communism preached a mixed vision when it came to sex. On the one hand, communists had a popular reputation as being in favor of "free love." On the other hand, when in power in the Soviet Union and China (or today in Cuba and North Korea), I read that communists can often be as repressive as Jesuits. Leaders like Stalin and Mao had harems that would put an Ottoman prince to shame, but like Muslim autocrats, communist bureaucrats often demanded puritanical codes for their citizens.

The Soviets, immediately after the revolution, made divorce and abortions legal and easy to get. At the same time, they demanded that women enter the industrial work force in large numbers (they still were expected to have babies and do all the housework in an age and economy that had very little mechanized help in the house-hold). Later the Soviet government realized that the population was declining, and they changed the laws to make abortion and divorce more difficult, and began a campaign to encourage births.

Communist parties in the west have often joined with progressives and liberals to lead in the fight for women's liberation.

Conservatives want relations between the sexes to remain as they have been in what they see as the conservative past. No sex before marriage, the woman subservient to the man, responsible for keeping the house, taking care of social and philanthropic matters, and satisfying their husbands in the bedroom.

In America today abortion is a burning issue. The Catholic Church stubbornly maintains its demand that there be not only no abortion, but no birth control. Conservative Catholics and Christians of all denominations also preach abstinence before marriage and oppose sex education in the classroom. These teachings are often more honored in the breach than in the action. The voices, in other words, at least when it comes to sexual practices, are getting fainter and are often ignored.

Many, if not most, Catholics today do not follow the Church's admonitions about sexual ethics. Likewise, Christians today do not support the burning of heretics. However, bombing of abortion clinics and murder of doctors does happen in America. And abortion rights, sexual ethics, women's liberation are still at the forefront of political life in America today.

Christians, like non-Christians in America, split roughly into two major camps—conservative and liberal. Not surprisingly, conservative Christians tend to favor conservative sexual ethics. They are strongly anti-abortion and pro-life and also tend to oppose social engineering by the government, except where it favors their causes—like punishment for abortion, rejection of birth control help in underdeveloped countries, opposition to condom distribution and birth control pills, etc.

Liberal Christians tend to favor social engineering, when it favors their causes. Programs like universal health care, welfare, unemployment insurance, social security, birth control in foreign aid programs, and governmental subsidies for agriculture and hospitals and mental health all get their support. Many activist liberal Christians also form the backbone of peace groups.

When you look beyond the past fifty years, you find the past was not always as religiously conservative as conservatives imagine. Nor was it as Christianly liberal as the liberals imagine. Be that as it may, what does any of this have to do with the future of free-market democracy?

Chapter 11

Religion in the Modern World

THERE WERE AND ARE DIFFERENCES in the two dominant monotheistic religions, Islam and Christianity. Despite the chaos and poverty, in medieval times, the Christian world of Western Europe had things the Muslim world did not have (nor did any other religiously dominated culture of that time).

Both slavery and polygamy were accepted practices in the Islamic world, sanctified by the Koran. Feudal Muslim, Buddhist and Confucian societies in China, Japan, Africa and Southeast Asia were also known for brutal slavery, for huge harems, for castrating males to serve as slaves, and for routine subjugation of women. The world of Hinduism in India favored sexual pleasures for the elite, but it also had slavery and polygamy, sanctioned child brides, supported an especially rigid caste system, and approved the burning of widows.

The Christian world inherited the practice of slavery from the Roman Empire. Spurred by Christian doubts, slavery was gradually abolished. For the most part, it disappeared in Western Europe by late medieval times. Like all feudal societies, the medieval Christian world was male-dominated. However it did not sanction or practice polygamy, child brides, burning of widows or extreme subjugation of women. (It did, however, allow the castrating of young males to provide tenors for the choir.)

The Christian world of medieval days fostered the beginnings of an important new idea—the separation of church and state. Jesus had said, "Give unto Caesar the things that are Caesar's, and to God the things that are God's." In matters of religion, the Pope was supreme. But in matters of all else, the feudal king or queen (even though ruling by "divine right") was supreme. And the king's law owed as much to the precedents of Roman law as it did to Christian church law.

In Islamic countries there was no distinction between church and state. Like the secular religion of Communism, Islam taught that church and state were the same thing. In Islam, these were the laws of Sharia, as written down in the sacred book, the Koran, and codified and interpreted by Islam's clerics.

Another great divide between the two monotheistic religious cultures opened up in the 14th to the 18th centuries. The western Christian world went through a Renaissance, a Reformation and the Enlightenment. The Islamic World did not. This western road led eventually to modern free-market capitalism and liberal democracy. The Islamic road has made only limited progress in moving beyond feudal economies and clerical-dominated states.

Hindu, Buddhist, Confucian and other religion-dominated societies in Asia, are today tending to follow the Christian world into modern free-market capitalism and democracy, often with remarkable ease and efficiency.

What happened in the Renaissance, Reformation and Enlightenment that was so important to democracy today?

DIFFERENCES BETWEEN ISLAM and Christianity widened in 14th-century Italy in the Renaissance, when the Christian world brought back some of the ancient heritage of Greece and Rome. Scientists like Galileo, Copernicus and Vesalius made dramatic progress in astronomy, physics and medicine. Merchants in Venice, Genoa, and Milan made progress in trade and financial management. Artists like Michelangelo, Botticelli and Leonardo da Vinci made progress in the visual and architectural arts. Writers like Dante, Cervantes and Shakespeare laid foundations for modern western literature.

Paradoxically, they made this progress both building upon and in spite of their Christian backgrounds. I say "building upon," because they inherited a rich medieval Christian tradition of individualism, of technology advances, of separation of church and state, of respect for women, of rejection of slavery, of advances in logic and reasoned argument in the universities, and the beginnings of a kind of Christian capitalism in the monasteries of medieval Europe.[59]

I say "in spite of," because often the church hierarchy was intimately entwined in feudal politics, was a major player in the dominant elite class, was the major landowner in feudal Europe, was often corrupt, was usually opposed to trade with enemies, and was in favor of the status quo. The church was also content to have the people illiterate, and thus dependent on the clergy for knowledge and guidance in all religious, scientific and political matters. The church, with its emphasis on sexual restraint, was also responsible for a decline in genetic pools when so many of its leaders became nuns or priests, and did not leave progeny. Fortunately a substantial number of priests and nuns did not follow the strict rules on sexual restraint. That number included a healthy batch of cardinals and popes.

In 1517 the church hierarchy received a severe jolt when a learned monk named Martin Luther nailed his "95 thesis" onto a church door in Germany. It was the beginning of the Reformation. Rebelling against what they considered enormous corruption within the Catholic Church, leaders and groups all over northern Europe split away from the Roman church and established what came to be called Protestant churches.

In reaction, the Roman Church launched a counter-reformation and the stage was set for long-lasting violent conflicts. Over the next century northern Europe, especially, was savaged in a long series of religious wars between Protestant and Catholic villages, cities, and feudal kingdoms. One of the worst was a Thirty Years War in what is now northern Germany. Mercenary armies, some on the Catholic side, some on the Protestant side, brought death to one-third of the population as well as catastrophic devastation to cities and countryside.

---

[59] See Rodney Stark. *The Victory of Reason: How Christianity Led to Freedom, Capitalism, and Western Success.* Other sources are Thomas Cahill and Michael Novak.

This Reformation, violent as it was, brought some new ideas into the western world. It also found a new way to get them distributed. That new way was the invention of movable type and the printing press.

Before the printing press, Bibles (indeed all books) were rare and treasured items, only available in a few monasteries, churches and universities. A book cost more than a house. Cambridge University, one of the richest universities in the world, owned a total of 122 books in 1424.[60] Before the printing press, most people in Europe (and elsewhere), including kings, queens, priests and nobles, were illiterate.

The first book printed on the new invention was the Christian Bible. Within a few years there were printing presses in more than 110 European towns and cities. Protestant reformers distributed large numbers of Bibles, taught people to read the Bible for themselves. Protestantism's central message was a return to the early days of Christianity where it was the individual's relationship with God that mattered, not his or her relationship with the traditional church.

Along with this religious message, Protestant thought and practice eventually led to a gospel of individual authority and a work ethic that encouraged the further development of nationalism, of humanism and of capitalism in the western world.

This message was especially potent in the new world of the United States and Canada, as were the messages that came in the Enlightenment.

The Enlightenment was centered in the British Isles and northern Europe, and then a little later in the new world of what would later become the United States of America. It was led by a new breed of intellectuals: philosophers like Voltaire, Baron de Montesquieu and Rousseau in France; Thomas Hobbes, David Hume, Adam Smith and John Locke in Britain; Baruch Spinoza in Holland; Immanuel Kant in Germany (he was the one who coined the term "enlightenment"); and Benjamin Franklin, Thomas Jefferson, Thomas Paine and Alexander Hamilton in the new world of America.

---

[60] *Cambridge University Library: a Historical Sketch* by J. C. T. Oates, 1975.
<http://www.lib.cam.ac.uk/history/>

These radical thinkers disagreed about many things, but were united in their rejection of feudal politics and of otherworldly religions as guides to human governance. They put their confidence in human experience and in natural reason as the keys to happiness and to a just society. If you choose to believe in Julian Jaynes' theory of "voices," you could say they were among the first to break away from the ancient subservience to the voices of the bicameral mind. If you believe in memes and the noosphere, you could say the memes were mutating and the noosphere was permanently changed. (See Chapter 15.)

"We hold these truths to be self-evident," wrote Thomas Jefferson in the Declaration of Independence in 1776, "that all men are created equal, that they are endowed by their Creator with certain inalienable Rights, among these are Life, Liberty and the pursuit of Happiness."

Like the English Enlightenment philosophers who were Jefferson's mentors, this was religion still, but it was a radical new variation of Christianity called Deism. Deism, while acknowledging a supreme being, and staying in the Christian tradition, stressed human rights and humanitarian values, and rejected theological dogmas. This was the religion of most of America's founding fathers, including Benjamin Franklin, George Washington, James Madison, Alexander Hamilton and Thomas Jefferson. It heavily influenced both the Declaration of Independence and the Constitution, particularly in the first ten amendments to the Constitution called the Bill of Rights.

All of these men attended Christian church services. Their religious beliefs differed from those of earlier Protestants. Influenced by the English Enlightenment, they believed strongly in humanistic Christian values like love thy neighbor as thyself, do unto others as you would have them do unto you, help the poor and downtrodden, comfort the afflicted, do good and avoid evil, forgive your enemies, nourish and protect the family, etc. These moral memes, many of them derived from Christian roots and stories, still play a large role in Christian countries today.

Other memes that were just as important in the past do not have the same power today. Fortunately. For instance, few if any Christians today believe that heretics should be banned or burned.

Our founding fathers, though Christian, did not promote the idea that only one religion was the true religion, or had a privileged path to God. They did believe in prayer and in life after death (they rarely mentioned heaven or hell), but they did not stress these aspects of Christianity. They believed strongly in freedom of religion and in tolerance for all beliefs, including atheism. Jefferson was accused of being an atheist, and Thomas Paine in his early years was an acknowledged atheist. Jefferson also made his own translation of the New Testament in which he omitted parts that referred to miracles, life after death, etc., stressing instead the moral lessons of Jesus, such as his Sermon on the Mount.

Deists also believed in separation of church and state, and wrote it into the First Amendment of the Constitution. "Congress shall make no law respecting an establishment of religion, or prohibiting the free exercise thereof; ..." Jefferson went further in his writings, recommending a "wall of separation" between church and state.[61]

Not everyone in the new United States, of course, shared this Deist religion and philosophy.[62] Although many settlers originally left England and Holland to escape religious persecution, many of these same settlers were intolerant of Christians from denominations other than their own. Congregationalists did not approve of Baptists. Anglicans did not approve of Methodists. And all Protestants were deeply prejudiced against Catholics, who they thought were not just heretics—they were Antichrist. A few years before the Revolution there was a mass event called the *Great Awakening*, when charismatic revivalist preachers roamed the countryside, the villages and the cities awakening the religious spirits in thousands of

---

[61] Worthy of mention here is the fact that the Constitution of the United States does not mention God. See "Jefferson, Madison, Medow?" *The New York Times*, Mar. 24, 2004. <http://www.nytimes.com/2004/03/26/opinion/jefferson-madison-newdow.html>

[62] See Thomas S. Kidd, *God of Liberty: A Religious History of the American Revolution*. Also Philip Hamburger, *Separation of Church and State*.

Americans. Some scholars think this awakening had a great deal to do with powering the American Revolution itself.

Probably most of our pioneer ancestors thought of religion as more than humanistic moral codes. Many had a tenacious and abiding faith in divine providence. God would provide. God was on our side. This faith was not exclusively Christian, but more transcendental, more non-denominational, and most of all, more significantly and exceptionally American. This was the faith that Abraham Lincoln invoked when he claimed in the Gettysburg Address that, "this nation, under God, shall have a new birth of freedom." And in the Second Inaugural, "With malice toward none, with charity for all, with firmness in the right as God gives us to see the right. ... "

That kind of fearful, stubborn, unshakeable faith in divine providence and mercy is still common today among many Americans, as it was among our pioneer forefathers. It does not, however, usually involve much, if any, theological baggage. That is, while strong and comforting, the faith in divine providence, does not carry with it dogmatic guides to practical action. As Lincoln said of the prayers of both North and South in the Civil War, "It may seem strange that any men should dare to ask a just God's assistance in wringing their bread from the sweat of other men's faces, but let us judge not, that we be not judged. The prayers of both could not be answered. That of neither has been answered fully. The Almighty has His own purposes."

The wall of separation—and freedom of religion—has led to a remarkable flowering and an incredible variety of religious belief in the United States throughout its history, including today. There are still strong Roman Catholic churches, many varieties of traditional Protestant churches, new mega-churches of non-denominational theology but charismatic and evangelical persuasion, Jewish synagogues, Muslim mosques, Hindu temples, Scientology meeting places, Native American sweat lodges, and more.

The slippery word "more" serves to indicate that I am aware of some of the many cults that stretch the meaning of the word "religion." Like the thirty-nine members of "Heaven's Gate" cult who, on March 26, 1997, when the comet Hale-Bopp was at its brightest, committed suicide. Their cult taught them that the earth was about to be refurbished and it was time for them to "enter the next level" themselves. "It is also possible that part of our test of faith is our hating this world ... to the extent to be willing to leave it without any proof of the Next Level's existence."

Then there were the more than 900 followers of Jim Jones in Jonestown, Guyana who in 1978, obeying the "voice" of their leader, committed mass suicide by drinking poisoned Kool-Aid.

The 20th and early 21st centuries have also seen the birth of many "near-religions" or "quasi-religions" you might call them. That is, individuals and groups who believe passionately in causes they look on as all-important, causes that for true believers, like traditional religion, permeate, color and influence all their thought and behavior.

Among these secular "near-religions" of the 20th and 21st centuries I would include Nationalism, Communism, Nazism, Racism, New Age religions of many varieties, Scientology, Radical Feminism and Radical Environmentalism. Like major religions of the past, at their best each of these new "religions" offer grains of truth. But like major religions of the past, at their worst they tend to foster absolutist beliefs that brook no disagreement, dogmas often so all-encompassing that they cripple thought and lead to major tragedies.

"The worst corruption," wrote the Protestant theologian Reinhold Niebuhr "is a corrupt religion." He added that "religion is so frequently a source of confusion in political life, and so frequently dangerous to democracy, precisely because it introduces absolutes into the realm of relative values." And by "religion" he did include secular near-religions like Communism, Fascism, Racism, Radical Environmentalism, etc.

The 19th-century novelist Nathaniel Hawthorne warned of the danger from both secular and religious fundamentalists. A character in one of his novels says, "They have no heart, no sympathy, no reason, no conscience. They will keep no friend, unless he make himself the mirror of their purpose; they will smite and slay you, and trample your dead corpse under foot, all the more readily, if you take the first step with them, and cannot take the second, and the third, and every other step of their terribly strait path."

IN 1787 THE UNITED STATES was the first and the only liberal democracy on earth. To be sure, it was seriously flawed. Slavery, in the western world, seemed to be extinguished in the Christian late Middle Ages. It made a brutal comeback in the 17th and 18th centuries as Africans were kidnapped, crammed into the holds of sailing ships, and sold into slavery in Asia, Europe, and in North and Latin America. The U.S. Constitution was ratified with a provision that slaves only counted as three-fifths of a person.

Some Christian groups, like the Quakers in Pennsylvania, had long fought against slavery as an abomination against God. Other Christian groups, however, argued that slavery had support in the Bible and was a part of the natural order of things.

And so it was with other social issues of the 19th and 20th centuries in the United States and in the rest of the liberal democratic world.

Where laissez-faire capitalism might allow callous exploitation of workers, Christian-derived values would curb this exploitation and encourage laws to protect workers, to provide social security, unemployment insurance, and welfare benefits to the poor. Where laissez-faire capitalism might allow discrimination, Christian-derived humanistic values have intervened to outlaw discrimination by race, color, creed, or sexual orientation.

Communist theorists like Marx, Engels and Lenin denounced Christianity, and indeed all religions, as the "opiate of the people." In practice socialist reformers in Europe and America often joined with Christian leaders in promoting some of these social-democratic policies.

Just as some religious groups in the 18th and 19th centuries supported slavery, so some religious groups in the 20th century have supported racial segregation using arguments from the Bible. For the most part, few

Christian groups still support racial segregation today. However, many Christian groups still support discrimination based on sexual orientation and many still adhere to a Biblical view of male supremacy.

There is a also a resurgence today in the United States of far-right religion-based cults that promote and plan violence to stop abortion, to punish sinners, to "bring America back," to combat socialism, to keep out immigrants, or to keep America pure and white.

As for science, some religion-derived humanistic values support scientific investigation of the unknown even if it does not seem to have any practical economic or spiritual value. On the other hand, many traditional Christians oppose areas of science that challenge Biblical authority. Evolution is one important example. New work in biotechnology is also coming under attack from religious fundamentalists —as well as from radical environmentalists (some of whom also oppose Darwinian evolution theory!)[63].

THE NATIONS WITH PROTESTANT Christian backgrounds are for the most part democracies today. The United States, Canada, United Kingdom, northern Europe, Scandinavia, Australia, New Zealand, and South Africa. All of these nations came to democratic political structures with their accompanying electoral politics, civil liberties and civil rights, liberal values and free market capitalist economies through the historical paths cited in this book.

The nations with Catholic Christian backgrounds are also, for the most part, democracies today, though they came to democratic ways of life later and many are still shaky in their commitment to democracy. These countries include Spain, Portugal, Italy, and most of Latin America.

Some democratic countries today, like Germany, Spain, Italy, Chile, Argentina and Portugal, suffered through desperate periods in the 20th century under Fascism and Nazism in which religious values, indeed all decent human values, were trampled upon. Sad to say, Christian religious

---

[63] See "Oppressed by Evolution" by Matt Cartmill. *Discover* 19(3): 78-8, March, 1998, pp. 78-83.

leaders in many of these countries did not distinguish themselves in defending human dignity.

Some other Christian countries, like Russia, Cuba, Poland, Romania and Hungary, suffered through equally desperate times in the 20th century when a secular religion, Communism, came to power and rejected humanistic religious values.

The United States, as well as all the countries of Latin America, had to pass through shameful times before they abolished slavery and gave equal rights to African-Americans. The United States and Canada were guilty of repressing and in many cases exterminating indigenous tribes of North America.

Leaders like Abraham Lincoln, the many abolitionists in the 19th century, Martin Luther King and his followers in the 20th century were motivated in great measure by strong religious beliefs.

Religious leaders also have pioneered efforts at reconciliation, reform and repentance for crimes of the past against Native Americans.

THERE ARE SOME LIBERAL democracies today, however, that do not have a Christian history. Two major non-Christian countries, Japan and India, are vibrant free-market liberal democracies today. Many smaller non-Christian countries in Asia, Africa and Southeast Asia also have liberal democratic governments today. And all of these countries join in varying degrees of commitment and enthusiasm for free-market globalization.

Some analysts think the largest non-Christian country of all, China, is moving in that same direction. China has embraced free-market capitalism, and is progressing economically at an unprecedented pace. It is still governed, however, by a dictatorial party committed to a secular religion that is neither democratic nor liberal.

Muslim countries, for the most part, are not democracies, though there are exceptions. Indonesia has more Muslims than any other country and is democratic today, even if shakily so. Turkey is Muslim and democratic. Pakistan, Bangladesh, Iraq and Afghanistan are Muslim in religion and haltingly moving toward democracy. India has a large Muslim population and today is solidly free-market democratic.

Why has free-market liberal democracy proved so powerful and why is it spreading so rapidly in the late 20th and early 21st centuries? Even to countries that had little or no experience with Christianity, nor with the Renaissance, Reformation or Enlightenment?

Good questions. No one knows. Here is one answer.

Democracy has three principal supports: science, capitalism and humanistic religion.

Democracy has flowered when the humanistic moral versions of religion (like our founders Deism) have been stronger and the absolutist versions, often based on literal readings of books like the Bible, the Koran, or Marx's *Das Capital* have been weaker. "Absolutist versions" includes secular "religions" like Marxism-Leninism, Nationalism, Radical Islam, Nazism, Fascism and Radical Environmentalism. Worthy of note, most, if not all, of these secular religions arose out of monotheistic religious cultures, Christian or Islamic.

Who and which will prevail in the 21st century? No one can say.

The weight of evidence from the past seems to point to the eventual worldwide triumph of humanistic religion, free-market capitalism and liberal democracy. But the weight of history also shows it will not be simple or easy, and may take a while. Without question there could be serious and long-lasting reversals, as there were in the past century when secular religions like Communism, Nazism and Racism brought such hate and misery. In this century a newly aggressive Radical Islam is challenging the west, and the outcome is far from certain.

Who will triumph?

No one can be sure. Military power may be needed, but modern tools of communication are more likely to be the key agents of change. Just as the printing press played a major role in the birth of liberal democratic ideas in the Reformation and Enlightenment in Europe, so the revolution in communication technology today—radio, television, computers, cell phones, satellites, Internet—seems to have favored democracy in the past century and will in the long run favor the spread of science, of capitalism, of humanistic religion and of democracy in the 21st century.

Fairness, freedom and money

I go back to my childhood in the depression when I could not understand why the president, or the banks, did not give us the money we needed. Some left-progressives seem to think that way today. Is there a limit on how far democratic countries can or should go in fighting poverty and promoting equality? Is there a limit in how wide the safety net should stretch?

Is good health care a right or a privilege? Are a decent house, a full plate of food, a good job, a powerful car, a healthy dose of entertainment, a working computer, a stylish wardrobe, rights or privileges? How about clean air, pure water and healthy soil? How about freedom from crime, clean streets, electric power, Internet access, health club membership, etc. etc.? The answers, of course, are *yes*. And *no*.

At times in my life I thought the answer to all of these questions should be yes. As an adolescent, when I looked around me at some of my richer friends, I was envious and thought life was not fair. I worked just as hard and deserved just as much as they had. I also remember when I was just out of college and my parents asked me what kind of "work" I was planning to do. At the time I was reading up a storm and writing poetry that would never get published. But I was offended by their question. I thought I was "working" as hard as anybody. I just was not getting paid for my work.

It took me quite a few years before I realized that people would only pay you for your work if it resulted in some goods or services of at least equal value for them. Preferably more. That is, in any free trade transaction (the basic transaction in the capitalist world), both sides should gain. Ideally it should always be a win-win trade. And when you add up all the win-win trades, in the long run society as a whole profits, and society grows in wealth and prosperity.

Socialism downplays the freedom side and stresses the equal and the fairness side. If my neighbor gets a new computer, I deserve a new computer. If my neighbor gets a new car, I deserve a new car. If my neighbor is rich, I deserve to be rich.

In some cases today, the socialist idea makes good sense. If my neighbor gets protection from robbers, I deserve protection from robbers. If my neighbor gets clean air, pure water and paved streets, I deserve clean air, pure water and paved streets. It's only fair, right and sensible, even if I cannot or do not pay any taxes in return for these benefits.

In other cases the choices are more difficult. If my neighbor gets an expensive heart transplant, do I deserve a heart transplant even if I cannot offer anything in return? If you answer yes, okay, but what if I am 95 years old, do I still deserve a heart transplant?

Where does "right" end, and "privilege" begin? And in particular cases, who decides?

Our Declaration of Independence claimed that all people have the right to "Life, Liberty and the pursuit of Happiness." Our Constitution says we have the right to expect the government to pursue "a more perfect Union, establish Justice, insure domestic Tranquility, provide for the common defence, promote the general Welfare, and secure the Blessings of Liberty to ourselves and our Posterity."

In the years since 1787, the U.S. government has used the "Justice" and "promote the general Welfare" clauses to expand considerably what we can deem our "rights".

Franklin Roosevelt, our 32nd president, made the biggest expansion when he added "freedom from want" and "freedom from fear" to the rights that governments should guarantee to all its citizens. Taken literally, these freedoms are impossible to achieve at any price. Everyone's "wants" are elastic. If I have a nice Chevy, maybe I want a Mercedes. If I have a hamburger, maybe I want a porterhouse steak. If I feel free from crime, maybe I don't feel free from getting cancer.

Since Roosevelt's day his Democratic Party has
generally been in favor of following his lead and
enacting legislation to assure that freedoms from
want and fear become reality. The Republican
Party has gone along with some of the legislation
needed to assure these "rights," but at times has
balked at extending them too far, preferring to
honor the capitalist free market dictate, that
every trade should be to the benefit of all parties.
In other words, you have to pay the piper to call
the tune.

It is an ongoing dispute with no clear answers.

Looking closer at the history of capitalism can
help clear up some of these questions, or at a
minimum provide a factual base to discuss
possible answers.

Chapter 12

The Rise of Capitalism

The golf links lie so near the mill
That almost every day
The laboring children can look out
And see the men at play.

THAT'S HOW SARAH CLEGHORN, a turn-of-the-19th-century Quaker pacifist and socialist, looked at capitalism.

A 20th-century scholar, Francis Fukuyama, on the other hand, claims that we may be approaching the "end of history" now that free-market capitalism and liberal democracy are spreading so rapidly around the entire world.

Who is right? Is capitalism good or bad? Is it necessary for democracy or opposed to democracy?

Scholars and citizens disagree. Many scholars in western democracies today would agree that capitalism is necessary for democracy, but not sufficient. Let's look at the evidence.

Despite the sophisticated mathematical analyses of modern economists, the basic truths of economics are surprisingly simple. What is capitalism?

In the broadest sense capitalism is an economic system based on three simple ideas:

(1) An individual human being's self-interest is a good thing.

(2) Private property is a good thing.

(3) Specialization of labor and free trade is a good thing.

IT GETS MORE COMPLICATED in the modern world, especially when it comes to artificial individuals called corporations, but these three basics still hold true today.

How did capitalism get started?

In a sense the ideas behind capitalism are as old as the human species. Our prehistoric ancestors lived in caves and crude shelters and had to survive by hunting animals and gathering wild foods.

They knew one's survival depended on looking out for oneself as well as one's fellow tribe members. In other words, they had *self-interest.*

The tools to do that (spears, bows and arrows, knives, as well as cave paintings, shelter materials and fire) had to be produced and kept safe from animals, and from other human beings. In other words, they had *private property.* (Private, in their case, was not necessarily or always individual private property. Land, for instance, was "owned" and fiercely defended by a tribe rather than an individual.)

They learned that one human (or one tribe) could trade with another human, or tribe, so that both could profit. The warrior got a better spear; the spear maker got a better cut of the mammoth. One tribe got beads; the other got baskets. In other words, they had *specialization of labor* and they had *trade.*

When hunter/gatherers made trades they were the pioneers in what we can call win-win transactions, rather than zero-sum ones. In other words, it was not like a baseball game or a boxing or tennis match, where one side wins and the other side loses. In free trades both sides gain, both sides win.

One interesting example of a hunter/gatherer tribe engaging in trade that was not zero-sum, gives clues to further progress in win-win transactions many centuries later. It comes from the Shoshone Indians of western North America. Robert Wright points out in his book, *Nonzero— the Logic of Human Destiny,* the Shoshone Indians had a problem. They lived in small family-sized units in a desert-like environment where animals were scarce. Most of their food was secured by roaming the desert landscape with sticks to find roots and seeds. There were no large animals, but there were jackrabbits aplenty. The problem was, it was difficult for a single individual or family to catch a rabbit. Some Shoshone genius in the past figured out a way that worked, a triumph of technology. Here is how Wright describes the way it worked.

To harvest [the jackrabbits], the Shoshone employed a tool too large for one family to handle—a net hundreds of feet long into which rabbits were herded before being clubbed to death. On such occasions, the requisite social structure would materialize. More than a dozen normally autonomous families would come together briefly and cooperate under a "rabbit boss." Though the Shoshone spent most of their time with the "irreducible minimum" of organization, the sudden appearance of non-zero-sumness brought latent social skills to the fore, and social complexity grew.[64]

Not only did all of the Shoshone families win food in this early win-win transaction, they won in social democratic ways that would serve them well in the future transactions. (Am I stretching the idea too far to claim that this discovery of "social complexity" in primitive times anticipated the discovery of corporate structure in industrial times?)

From these primitive beginnings, capitalism, in fact all systems of economics, evolved over the past 100,000 or more years. About 10,000 years ago some people in some parts of the world learned how to grow food and domesticate animals. Eventually this agricultural revolution spread to all the continents of earth, and brought with it big changes in economics as well as in culture.

Economically the agricultural revolution was a mixed blessing for most people. With a more reliable food supply, populations increased dramatically. There was now enough surplus wealth to allow a few people to escape the day-to-day struggle for existence and to specialize—to become kings and queens, priests, warriors, engineers, architects, bureaucrats, artists, story-tellers and to found the world's first cities and civilizations.

---

[64] *Non-Zero—the Logic of Human Destiny.* p. 21-22.

(If Julian Jaynes is right, the agricultural revolution also led eventually to the most momentous change of all, *The Origin of Consciousness in the Breakdown of the Bicameral Mind,* as was discussed in the chapter on religions. According to Jaynes, people in early agricultural societies, even up to ancient Greece of Homer's day, were not really conscious. That is, they did not and could not introspect. They listened, like modern schizophrenics, to voices in their heads when they had to make a decision. Which lack may explain many of the traits of these early agricultural cities and civilizations. See pages 113-115.)

The agricultural revolution also led to new kinds of economic and social systems that featured strong class differences, tyrannical governments, bloody wars, and severe restrictions on freedom for everyone.

Because agriculture and animal husbandry demand more heavy sustained labor than hunting and gathering, it not only cut back on leisure, it led to peasantry, serfdom or slavery for most people. The strongest exploited the weakest both within the tribal, ethnic, religious and political group and between tribal, ethnic, religious and political groups. Most people lived a subsistence existence where bartering was common, but free trade and private property were severely limited.

In ancient Rome texts on agriculture recommended that a master would need at least twelve slaves to operate a small farm. Roman emperors, senators, philosophers, artists, writers, warriors and assorted nobles, like the Greek, Persian, and Egyptian nobility before them, got their wealth from rent on farmland worked by slaves. With such widespread slave labor, there was little incentive to improve technology or economic organization.

In China, India, Southeast Asia, Africa, Polynesia and North and South America the picture was similar. The ruling elite laid heavy taxes on the peasants or simply enslaved them and used this agriculturally-based wealth, not to make more wealth, but to construct forts, castles and palaces for the rulers and his or her followers. These forts, castles and palaces (along with plentiful warriors and armaments) were needed to defend the societies' wealth from potential thieves and aggressive neighbors, as well as to wage aggressive war on nearby kingdoms in the effort to get more wealth (land, animals, slaves).

Since wealth in all of these agricultural kingdoms was a more or less fixed quantity, one person or one group could only become wealthier by taking from another person or group. If I win, you lose. If you win, I lose. Net result, zero increase in total human wealth. It was by and large a *zero-sum economy*.

Although there were many differences between them, in all agriculturally based societies there was a strong class distinction between the elite rulers (typically less than one or two percent of the total population) and the working peasants, serfs or slaves (typically over ninety-eight percent of the population.).

As could be expected in zero-sum economies, wars were extremely common. Like never-ending. There was no way to get more wealth other than stealing it, and that almost always meant war.[65] As late as the 17th century there were over fifty major wars in northern Europe alone. It was much the same in Africa, in the Americas, in Asia and in the South Pacific.

All of these feudal societies also nurtured and shaped religious beliefs and practices to help unify and justify their economic and political structures. Buddhism, Hinduism, Taoism, Confucianism—many varieties of polytheism—and then later the two monotheistic religions, Christianity and Islam, grew from, supported, modified and sometimes also made these agricultural civilizations more humane.

For thousands of years this kind of mutual interdependence with class-defined obligations, gargantuan wealth gaps, religious zeal, zero-sum economies, frequent wars and subsistence living was the norm in agriculturally based societies. Progress was rarely considered a possibility. People as well as kingdoms grew up, grew old, prospered or not, and died.

---

[65] If you want to read an account that almost makes you laugh at the horror of its the constant violence and war in agricultural societies around the world see *The History of the Medieval World* by Susan Wise Bauer.

Life was cyclical, like nature. In both the Christian and Islamic worlds the only "progress" would come in another world, life after death. In many Asian Buddhist and Hindu societies "progress" could only come for the individual by conquering desire and achieving nirvana, the extinction of earthly desire.

This zero-sum mentality (along with its wars, poverty, class and religious differences) was, and is, so powerful that it has lasted right up to the 21st century in many parts of the world. Fortunately, not in all. Even in the industrialized western world, however, where zero-sum economics no longer need apply, many people still cling to memes founded and fostered in zero-sum days.

Consider the average person. Fifty thousand years ago he or she lived less then thirty years, in almost daily fear of disease, starvation or violent death. For more than ten thousand years past (the agricultural ages) there were more people, but the average human being still lived only slightly more than thirty years as a peasant, serf or slave. He or she could not read or write, saw most of their children die before the age of two, rarely traveled more than a few miles from their place of birth, and were still always and everywhere in daily fear of disease, starvation and war.

And then suddenly ("suddenly" in historical perspectives) in the last two hundred years there has been a change. An enormous change—for people living in an industrial society that is. The average person today lives two or three times as long—over seventy years. He or she can read and write, travels thousands of miles a year, rarely see their children die, are healthier, wealthier, and freer than ever before in human history. They rarely find themselves in daily fear of violence, starvation and death.

How did it happen? History is not like science. There are no ways to conduct controlled experiments that yield definitive answers. Nevertheless I think most modern scholars would agree that the weight of evidence supports the following story.

What makes much of the modern world different is the combined power of science and technology, free-market capitalism, and liberal democracy. Some would add humanistic religion, especially when it comes to explaining the present popularity and dominance of welfare-state democracies. Instead of zero-sum economies, we now have (in many parts of the world, not all) win-win economies, based and driven not by serf or slave labor, but by the creativity and innovation of free labor, free markets, and free trade. By what we call modern capitalism.

LET'S BACK UP AND QUALIFY and quantify. Past agricultural societies were not totally zero-sum. In agricultural societies, as well as in hunting/gathering societies, there was *some* progress. All human societies, for instance, have engaged in trade. Some scholars think that reading and writing arose out of merchants' need for accounting in trade deals.[66] In agricultural societies in Asia, Africa, Europe, South and North America and in the classic Egyptian, Greek, and Roman empires around the Mediterranean, this trade increased. Aided by energy-rich innovations like sailing ships, a slow-growing merchant class managed to buy goods in one place and sell them in another, profiting from the exchange.

This merchant class was small in agricultural societies. It was usually looked down upon, and sometimes suppressed, by the land-rich elite rulers. These rulers, however, often used the merchants' services to get luxury goods from far-off places and to borrow money, usually to finance wars.

Local markets were common in all agricultural civilizations. Markets where local farmers could bring their fruits, vegetables and livestock, and exchange them for locally produced cloth, leather belts, pottery and metal pans. Again, you had the basic elements of win-win free trade, where both partners in the transaction benefited.

Merchants, like the famous Marco Polo, traveled what was called the Silk Road from Europe to the Middle East and China in medieval and Renaissance times. They took wool, gold and silver from Italian city-states

---

[66] See "Out First Words, Written in Clay, in an Accountant's Hand" by Alberto Manguel in *The New York Times*, Science Section, April 20, 2003. <http://www.nytimes.com/2003/04/20/weekinreview/ideas-trends-lost-iraq-our-first-words-written-clay-accountant-s-hand.html>

like Venice or Genoa and traded them for silk, beautiful ceramics, jewels, carpets and rare spices. These win-win exchanges were the precursors of modern capitalism.

This early merchant capitalism was important to the elite, but was not the basic life supporting structure that kept the vast majority of people alive, nor it did not greatly increase the net wealth of any society.

The feudal world, of course, was not the same everywhere. The feudal world, like the industrial world and the modern world, was shaped and colored by the religion, by the technology, by the culture, and by the geography of the given society.[67]

Many historians today argue that the most important of the differences that led to modern capitalism and democracy came out of the chaotic Christian world of Western Europe.[68]

In medieval times in Europe (unlike the more geographically far-reaching empires in China, Japan, Southeast Asia, Africa and South America, as well as the Middle Eastern World of Islam) there were literally thousands of feudal estates, along with hundreds of small city-states—all of them relatively independent of one another—often at war with one another.

While serfdom was still the rule in the Middle Ages, slavery (universal in the Islamic and most other societies at that time) was for the most part abolished in Europe by the late Middle Ages. The lack of slaves, along with a disaster known as the Black Death that killed a third of the population in Europe, left feudal estates and city-states with a severe

---

[67] The popular scientist, Jared Diamond, claims that geographical factors were the overwhelmingly determining ones that lead to the rise and fall of societies in agricultural ages. He extrapolates freely in predicting that environmental factors will determine the rise and fall of civilizations today. I will have more to say about Diamond's theories in the final chapters of this book. Suffice to say here that, like the agricultural biologist Trofim Lysenko in the Stalin era, and for that matter Marxism-Leninism, theories that rely exclusively on environmental determinism are as suspect as ones that rely exclusively on genetic, racist or cultural determinism.

[68] See *The Victory of Reason: How Christianity Led to Freedom, Capitalism, and Western Success* by Rodney Stark. More insight from books in the bibliography by Thomas Cahill, Peter Jay, David Landes, Michael Novak and Peter Spofford.

shortage of workers. This shortage acted as a stimulus to innovation. People had to find ways to get necessary work done with fewer workers. And they did. The first steps were taken to move away from a static zero-sum society.

New kinds of plows, as well as new methods of field crop rotation, greatly increased agricultural output. New horse collars were invented that enabled horses to do twice the work of Greek and Roman horses without choking themselves. Sailing ships were improved. The compass, clocks, eyeglasses and water wheels were invented. In 1080 there were over 5,624 waterwheels in Great Britain alone, used for grinding flour and sawing wood.

Many of these innovations were invented in China, and slowly passed on to Europe over the Silk Road. As often happens in the modern world, the inventors were not the people who most profited from the inventions. People in Europe for some reason (some think the printing press played a major part) were more efficient and effective in developing, using and popularizing the inventions.

In Europe Christian monasteries sometimes managed to escape the chaos of division, ignorance and war of medieval times. Some of these monasteries became seedbeds for scientific and technological invention, as well as an early kind of religious capitalism.

Trade in agricultural kingdoms was limited mainly to luxury goods, and did not produce any great accumulations of capital for future profit. Few people even thought of the idea we call progress. Things just happened. Civilizations rose and fell. Good happened. Bad happened. Life was zero-sum.

Some monasteries in the European middle ages, on the other hand, began to experiment with new forms of economic organization that did emphasize investment for future profit. Motivated in part by their Christian faith, dreams of progress began to spread in the European noosphere. Trade began to flourish as one monastery specialized in making wine, another in woolen goods, and still another in cheese making. That was just the beginning.

Monasteries developed some of the first banks, lending money to other monasteries as well as to princes, kings and the Pope. In England alone there were over 500 banks in 1200, most of them branches of Italian banks. These banks also lent money at interest, even though Christian morality and law had traditionally prohibited such usury, as Islamic morality still does.

After the invention of the printing press in 1450 and the Protestant Reformation a few years later, literacy became more common in Europe than anywhere in the world.

These trends eventually led to modern capitalism and democracy. They were accelerated in the late Middle Ages and the Renaissance (13th to the 15th centuries) in northern Italy by merchant capitalists and bankers in fast-growing prosperous city-states like Venice, Genoa, Pisa and Milan. They were aided by new innovations in science and technology like compasses, better sailing ships, better mathematics, and better maps and atlases.

This new kind of merchant capitalism moved a few decades later from Italy to northern Europe and to the British Isles. Amsterdam and London became the vibrant centers of a rapidly expanding worldwide trade as larger sailing ships began to explore and expand trade and markets to all corners of the world. The profits from this merchant capitalism as well as imperialist ventures in Africa, Asia and North and South America soon made England and the Netherlands the richest countries in the world.

Imperialism itself was an interesting amalgam of new capitalist economics alloyed with zero-sum feudal economics. In the cases of Holland and England, the imperialistic ventures often had a saving grace. Settlers lived, and developed farms and industries, in the colonies. This in turn led to trade, and the transfer of both goods and memes that eventually led to free-market liberal democracies in former colonies like the United States, Canada, India, South Africa, Australia and Indonesia.

On the other hand, explorers and settlers from France, Belgium, Spain and Portugal still adhered to the feudal zero-sum memes—you could only become richer by conquering other countries and stealing their resources and wealth. Mexico and many countries in Africa, South America, the South Pacific and the Caribbean Islands are still lagging behind in the modern world, due in large part to this zero-sum feudal heritage of reactionary memes.

The real explosion of capitalism, industry and science that is dominant in our 21st-century world happened just a little over 200 years ago.

Cal Coolidge, Woody Guthrie, and Mother Theresa

My wife, Jane, inherited a share of a family summerhouse in Vermont. Back in the 1920s, when she was a little girl, her family's next-door neighbor in Plymouth Township, Vermont was Calvin Coolidge, our 30th president. Jane had her picture published on the front page of *The New York Times*, with Mrs. Coolidge looking down benignly on her and her dog. Liberal progressives are fond of making fun of "silent" Cal. Like the time at a White House dinner when a woman sitting next to the President, said to him, "My friend bet me, Mr. President, that I couldn't get three words out of you." The story has it that Cal responded, "You lose."

His most-quoted statement, "the business of America is business," has come in for much ridicule. Recently I came across the actual speech in 1925, the year before I was born. He did use a phrase like that. But if you compare Coolidge's words in context, to more recent presidential speeches, I think you will be surprised how thoughtful, insightful and eloquent he was. Here is a bit more of what he said that day.

> After all, the chief business of the American people is business. They are profoundly concerned with producing, buying, selling, investing and prospering in the world. I am strongly of the opinion that the great ma-

jority of people will always find these are
moving impulses of our life ... Wealth is
the product of industry, ambition, character
and untiring effort. In all experience, the
accumulation of wealth means the multipli-
cation of schools, the increase of
knowledge, the dissemination of intelligence, the encouragement of science, the
broadening of outlook, the expansion of
liberties, the widening of culture. Of course,
the accumulation of wealth cannot be justified as the chief end of existence. But we
are compelled to recognize it as a means to
well-nigh every desirable achievement. So
long as wealth is made the means and not
the end, we need not greatly fear it.[69]

When I was a beginning teacher of physics in
Brooklyn, New York in the late 1950s, I had my
hands full to keep my small family above water.
My salary as a high school science teacher never
exceeded $3,200 a year. As for the environment,
I remember vividly the soot that collected daily
on our windowsills in the summer, the noise of
the subway I rode so often (I think that may have
been the cause of my hearing loss in later years),
the struggle in the winter to heat our small "cold-
water flat" apartment with kerosene heaters that
I wonder now did not suffocate us, the escape to
a New England camp in the summer where I

---

[69] Complete speech is at the Calvin Coolidge Memorial Foundation web-
site: <www.calvin-coolidge.org/html/
the_press_under_a_free_governm.html>

made extra dollars and enjoyed the great
outdoors in company with nine- and ten-year-old
campers who shared my delight with primitive
camping, canoe trips and rousing camp songs.

Among occasional visitors to this progressive
camp was Pete Seeger, the famous folk singer.
We all enthusiastically joined him in singing union
songs, Spanish Civil War ballads, and other
socialist-inspired folk songs. Among the favorites
was the Woody Guthrie song, *This Land is Your
Land*, Guthrie wrote the song as an answer to
Kate Smith's version of *God Bless America*, a song
he hated. Guthrie's song, I learned later, has
strong anti-capitalist lines that I don't remember
Pete Seeger including in his camp appearances.
Lines like . . .

> There was a big high wall there that
> tried to stop me:
> The sign was painted—it said Private
> Property
> But on the other side—it didn't say
> nothin'
> That side was made for you and me.

I think that some of this world-view, some of
these powerful socialist memes, have been
parents to much of the green movement today.
We interviewed one of the more prominent of
the green crusaders, Jeremy Rifkin, at a science
teacher convention in the 1990s. He confidently

parroted the green mantra, "The United States, with only six percent of the world's population, uses over thirty percent of the world's resources and generates *over* thirty percent of the world's pollution. ... We need a green life style. We need to realize that if we use more of the world's resources, others will have less."

Along the same line, I watched a good-looking older businessman on TV the other night who said he had had a good career, made a good deal of money and now it was time to retire. He was grateful to his customers, his city and his country, and he made a point of saying "now it was time to give back."

A curious phrase.

Unless he was a crook or crack-dealer, presumably he had made his money providing some useful goods or services to his customers. Apparently he had also unwittingly bought into a common opinion among socialists that profits are like stealing. And now it was time to "give back" some of the loot.

The reputed richest man in the world, Bill Gates, made his fortune pioneering the computer revolution. Yet today he receives more accolades for his philanthropic work than he does for his computer pioneering. And he himself seems to think the philanthropic work is more important than the wealth-creating work he did in the computer world. Without downplaying benefits his grants have no doubt brought to education and to health, especially in Africa, it seems to me that in comparison, the computer work wins the "net good for humankind" in a landslide. If he feels compelled to "give back," perhaps the people who bought his computers should also give back their end of the bargain—their computers. It was after all, like all free-market transactions, a win-win trade.[70]

Socialism has a better public image than capital-ism. The socialist vision is clear and inspiring, to have people work together unselfishly for the common good. Contrast that with the capitalist idea where the individual profits by providing useful goods or services in a win-win free trade. If the profit (or salary) gets too large, this is seen by many people as greed. Even when the profit (or salary) is more modest, many still consider this not as praiseworthy as volunteer or non-profit activities. The capitalist, in other words, works for self-interest. The philanthropist, volunteer or non-profit worker works for the greater good in an unselfish way.

There is a close association between Christian charity (and, for that matter, charitable memes from other religions like Islam, Hinduism and Buddhism) and modern liberal free-market

---

[70] See "Bill Gates's Charitable Vistas" by Harvard economic professor Robert Barro. <http://www.economics.harvard.edu/faculty/barro/files/Gates%20column%20WSJ.pdf>

democracy (as well as every other kind of government). Christian charity compliments the welfare side of modern liberal democracies, but sometimes clashes with the creative, productive side. The charity side is usually the more popular one, but in the long run it may not be the most progressive one. Good intentions only too often lead to unintended results that are not so good.

The humanitarian thing to do, for instance, is to enact generous minimum wage laws, on the theory that everyone should have a decent "living wage." The unintended consequences are that unskilled or poorly educated teenagers or young adults (especially minority group members) are denied jobs that could be steps up the ladder to the middle class, and in earlier times, were indeed steps up the ladder to the middle class.

The career of the famous Mother Teresa in Calcutta, India, is another case in point. She is celebrated as a hero of compassionate Christianity. She devoted her life to nursing and advocating for the poor and the downtrodden, the forgotten casualties of modern society. She won a Nobel Peace Prize for her work.

On the other hand, as many critics point out, she was also opposed to ending the caste society and did not support democracy. She was against birth control and abortion, but she supported forced sterilization of poor women. She was once asked, "Do you teach the poor to endure their lot?"

She answered, "I think it is very beautiful for the poor to accept their lot, to share it with the passion of Christ." She also contributed to a very misleading picture of modern India, one of the fastest growing free-market liberal democracies in the world. This misleading picture may, in the end, harm more people than were helped by her humanitarian efforts.

Chirita Banerji pointed out in a *New York Times* op-ed piece, "For Calcutta natives like me, Mother Teresa also evoked the colonial past— she felt she knew what was best for the third world masses, whether it was condemning abortion or offering to convert those who were on the verge of death ... Charity need not be inconsistent with clarity. Calcutta is a modern city where poverty and inequality coexist with measurably increasing prosperity, expanding opportunities, cautious optimism and, above all, pride in its unique character. Mother Teresa might have meant well, but she furthered her mission by robbing Calcutta of its richly nuanced identity while pretending to love it." [71]

---

[71] *The New York Times*, Sept. 5, 2007. See:
<http://www.nytimes.com/2007/09/05/opinion/05banerji.html>

Chapter 13

Free-Market Capitalism and Liberal Democracy

IN 1776, THE YEAR THE United States declared its independence from England, England was the richest country in the world. It was also the freest and the most democratic. Unlike its archrivals, Spain and France, England had a parliament that shared power with the king. It also had a tradition of relative freedom from arbitrary state and clerical power. More than most other nations it nurtured and protected a rapidly growing entrepreneurial and merchant class; and England was a leader in the radical intellectual revolution called the Enlightenment.

The Enlightenment happened in the 17th and 18th centuries. It was centered in England, France, northern Europe and the Low Countries of Holland and Belgium, and then a little later in the new world of what would later become the United States of America. It was led by philosophers like Voltaire, Montesquieu and Rousseau in France; Thomas Hobbes, David Hume, Adam Smith and John Locke in England; Immanuel Kant in Germany (he was the one who coined the term "enlightenment"); Baruch Spinoza in Holland; Benjamin Franklin, Thomas Jefferson, Thomas Paine, James Madison and Alexander Hamilton in America.

These radical new thinkers disagreed about many things but were united in their rejection of feudal politics and of other world-religions as guides to human governance. Instead they put their confidence in human experience and in natural reason as the keys to happiness and to a just society. The United States of America was the first major national state to put this philosophy into action. As such, it deserves the label of *exceptional*.

Central to that confidence was the progress and the example of science and technology that had taken such giant steps forward in the Renaissance, and now vastly increased its stride in the days of the English

Enlightenment.[72] This faith in science and technology was reinforced by the Protestant revolt and led to a new turn toward economic and political freedom as the only sure path to progress and wealth.

At the time of the American Revolution, the Catholic countries of Spain, Portugal and France, for instance, (despite the Enlightenment) had absolutist monarchies, with little freedom for any but the elite. Even more important for our subject they had feudal zero-sum economies through and through. (Like all other kingdoms and empires in Asia, Europe, Africa and South America.)

The history of the Americas is instructive. Pioneer families, some of whom brought with them memes of the Enlightenment, especially the English and Dutch varieties, settled North America in the early years of colonization. These settlers crossed the ocean at great peril and planned to stay and make their fortunes in the new world. Ordinary farmers were probably not conscious of Enlightenment connections, but they had enough common sense (the noosphere is, in a sense, what we call "common sense") to support the leadership of people like Benjamin Franklin, George Washington, Alexander Hamilton, John Adams, James Madison, Thomas Paine and Thomas Jefferson. The founding fathers *had* read John Locke, Adam Smith, David Hume and Baron de Montesquieu, and they believed what they read. And they had the right environment to put these ideas into practice. And they did.

Among the most important of these memes brought to North America were ones that fostered science, individualism, belief in the power of human reason, self-reliance, hard work, worldly progress and the separation of church and state.

Latin America, on the other hand, was not so much settled as robbed by explorers, and later by fortune-seekers and pirates, primarily from Spain and Portugal. These folks came not to settle, but to rob the natives and their land of its gold, silver and whatever other treasures they could find. They also brought with them memes that fostered religious

---

[72] See especially the book by Gertrude Himmelfarb, *The Roads to Modernity: the British, French, and American Enlightenment.*

orthodoxy, the primacy of the Catholic version of Christianity and, most important of all, belief in the traditional view of wealth that had been dominant in agricultural societies for thousands of years—that real wealth was in land, gold and slaves. In short, they brought with them a firm belief in zero-sum economics. If I win, you lose. If you win, I lose.

These differences have played a major part in the centuries since settlement, and still operate today. Latin American countries are only now learning that you cannot build a modern economy on theft or on printing money, which is much the same thing. For most of the 19th and the 20th centuries Latin American countries were often stuck in these outdated agricultural-age memes. A very small landowning class (as in the Middle Ages of Europe) cornered the wealth from land, gold and slaves (or peasants) and ruled from their rich haciendas. Industry languished, as did freedom. Entrepreneurship was not encouraged. Tradition was.

Revolutionaries sometimes challenged the oppressive landowners. On occasion the rebels were able to take power. The new leaders, in their zeal to right the wrongs of the past, soon found that while wealth can be stolen and then distributed to the poor, this does not bring lasting prosperity. Wealth must be continually and consistently created before it can be distributed if lasting progress is to happen.

Revolutionary leaders like Simon Bolivar, Jose Marti, Emiliano Zapata, Juan Peron, Toussaint L'Ouverture, Miguel Hildalgo and Jose de San Martin, failed over and over again to bring progressive change to their countries, in spite of their courage, charisma and zeal. Most of the time they ended up as dictators themselves after taking power, trying desperately to control inflation, as they tried to use the Robin Hood principle and steal from the rich and give to the poor. Soon they found that there was no more wealth to give. The net result, in most cases, was ruinous inflation and government collapse.

In the second half of the 20th century Latin American leaders like Fidel Castro, Salvador Allende, Che Guevara, Hugo Chavez and Luiz Lula da Silva have tried to apply some of the same outdated memes to solve the problems of poverty in their countries. The idea again was the Robin

Hood principle—take from the rich and give to the poor. Let the government produce goods and services for the welfare of all, and not for private profit. This plan is always doomed to fail because it is based on that same outdated agricultural-age view of wealth—a zero-sum one. If I get more, you get less. If I win, you lose.

Argentina is good example. It has alternated between socialist and capitalist memes for most of its history. One of the richest countries in the world a hundred years ago, it went into steep decline when it turned to excessive social welfare schemes under Juan Peron and later his wife, Eva Peron. It see-sawed back and forth between free-markets and socialist schemes throughout the 20th century. Now in the early 21st century, under a new president, Peron-follower Cristina Kirchner, "It [has] abandoned free markets, ostensibly in the interest of social justice. The predictable result has been greater injustice, more poverty, and increasing concentration of wealth in the hands of the political class and its friends. Efforts to make the economy competitive have repeatedly been defeated even as the standard of living declined."[73]

An exception in 21st century Latin America seems to be Lula da Silva in Brazil. Though he came to power with promises similar to the other Marxist leaders, he has surprised his critics by building a successful partnership with international capitalist powers and agencies. He has built upon, instead of abandoning, the policies of his conservative predecessor and has supported, not condemned, private enterprise in his own country. His support of these policies has lifted Brazil to a new level of wealth and power on the international stage. Instead of nationalizing industry and agriculture and then printing money to offer social welfare benefits to more people and on a grander scale than ever before, he paid the country's debts to the World Bank, become a trusted partner in free-trade agreements and in general put his country in the ranks of free-market liberal democracies. As a result, Brazil today is one of the most rapidly

---

[73] "Argentina's Warning to America" Mary Anastasia O'Grady in *Wall Street Journal,* Oct. 17, 2011

growing economies in the world. He left office in 2010. His hand-chosen successor, Dilma Mousseff, promises to continue his policies.

CHILE IS STILL ANOTHER STORY. In Chile the radical socialist Salvador Allende was elected in 1970 with ambitious plans and promises to redistribute wealth from traditional conservative landholders and industrialists to impoverished workers and peasants. Unfortunately, despite his high hopes and good intentions, his socialist measures led instead to widespread chaos and eventually to a ruinous inflation when he began to print money in an attempt to pay debts and carry through on extravagant welfare programs. As his cousin and ardent supporter, the popular novelist Isabel Allende, writes in her book of memoirs, *Paula*, "There was paper money to burn, but very little to do with it. ... a black market was inevitable. For my birthday, my friends at work gave me two rolls of toilet paper and a can of condensed milk ... Sometimes we stood in line only out of fear of missing something even if the reward was yellow shoe polish."

A friend of ours in Colorado was a high school principal in Chile in the Allende days and she described to us first-hand the chaotic condition of the country when the military under General Augusto Pinochet staged a coup in 1973 (with aid from the American CIA) to restore order. He did restore order. But the order came with a fearful price. As a dictator, Pinochet and his army ruled with an iron hand, suppressing trade unions, torturing and murdering hundreds (some claim thousands) of citizens in the process of restoring order.

On the plus side, Pinochet brought in American economic experts from the University of Chicago who advised and directed an economic recovery plan, featuring free-market ideas, that has led Chile to having today, next to Brazil, the highest per capita production and wealth of any Latin American country. As the free-market policies began to slowly, and at times erratically, work their economic magic, there also came a gradual loosening of dictatorial controls and oppression. Eventually, in 1990 democracy was restored, elections were held, and today Chile has an enviable record as one of the wealthiest and freest country in Latin America.

The hope is that the happy ending of the Chile story can be replicated in a much larger country, China, as well as in Vietnam, Cambodia, Laos, Afghanistan, Iraq, and other Muslim-dominated countries of the Middle East and North Africa.

FREE-MARKET CAPITALISM CAME along historically at about the same time that modern science was shaking up our noosphere with new views of the universe and huge leaps forward in technology. The next chapters will examine that story and its synergistic links to capitalism and democracy.

Supporting and accelerating developments in science and technology, another Enlightenment philosopher, the Scotsman Adam Smith, laid an intellectual base for this industrial revolution and the accompanying leap forward from zero-sum feudal economics to modern free-market capitalism. Smith wrote and had published a book in 1776, *The Wealth of Nations*, a book that is still used today in defining and defending capitalism.

Adam Smith returned to simple principles. Capitalism, he wrote, was based on three simple ideas:

Self-Interest, Specialization of Labor, and Free Trade.

If societies adhered to these principles, he said, an "invisible hand" would lead to a win-win economy rather than a zero-sum one. In other words, so long as there was freedom—free labor, free markets and free trade—wealth for all was bound to increase.

To make sure there was free labor, free trade and free markets, Smith realized that civil order was necessary. This meant that government had a part, an essential part. The government must make and enforce effective laws to protect private property, enforce contracts, prevent crime, and protect against foreign threats. Other than that, however, for the most part the government should stay out of private affairs and let the "invisible hand" do its work. Some call it "laissez-faire" capitalism.

As capitalism and industry exploded on the world stage in the 19th century, Smith's optimism seemed to bear fruit. Never in the long history of the human species had the world seen such an enormous growth in wealth and human populations, power and prosperity. And not for just the elite, but especially for the ninety-eight percent who had been desperately poor and cruelly exploited as peasants, serfs and slaves.

Coal and iron, capitalism, and the invisible hand made the nineteenth century a century of rapid population growth, impressive new cities and ostentatious new wealth.

The 19th century, however, also became famous for urban poverty, worker exploitation in dangerous factories and mines, industrial pollution and bloody wars.

Poverty, exploitation, pollution and wars were nothing new. For thousands of years, ninety-eight-plus percent of the people who lived in low-energy agricultural societies had lived always and everywhere with poverty, disease, slavery, infanticide, cannibalism, pollution and wars.

Even the elite few who escaped poverty—the kings and queens, the bishops and nobles—could not escape pollution, wars, disease and death. For even the wealthiest human beings, the average life span was still only a little more than thirty years and no one on earth could be free from want and fear.

In the nineteenth century Industrial Revolution, however, all this changed. The sudden enormous new increases in energy, useful knowledge and wealth meant that many more people could now live richer lives. They could travel more, eat better, read and write, and had many more choices about what they could do with their lives. The average life span increased to over forty years.

In the United States, capitalists like John D. Rockefeller, Andrew Carnegie, Cornelius Vanderbilt and J. P. Morgan pioneered whole new industries in oil, steel, railroads and finance. They were often bitterly resented and called "robber barons" by labor leaders and intellectuals. And true, they did use aggressively harsh methods and they did become "obscenely" wealthy. True also, in many cases they benefited from government help in the form of tariffs, loans, subsidies and new infrastructures. Despite this *help*, the basic rules that were the foundation stones of these new industries were market-oriented and were the offsprings of Adam Smith's "invisible hand."

In their defense, it is also true that the workers in their refineries, steel mills, railroads and offices were paid two and three times as well as workers in similar European industries or peasant farms. They were paid these higher wages not out of charity or management goodwill, but because the workers were two and three times as productive as the workers in Europe in creating new wealth. And they were more productive because of greater incentives, technological change, more innovation, and the large profits that came with the win-win free-market system.

These new industrial workers of the 19th century were, in fact, so much better off than European farmers and workers in that same century that people from Germany, Poland, Russia, Italy, Ireland, Scandinavia and eastern Europe emigrated to America in record numbers. Those immigrants were the great-grandparents of *most* people in the United States and Canada today.

THERE WAS A BIG EXCEPTION to this good news. Slavery got a new lease on life in western societies after having been all but abolished in the Christian Middle Ages. Slave-traders in Africa, Europe and Middle and Far Eastern countries bought or kidnapped hundreds of thousands of African natives and sold them as slave-workers for plantations in North and South America, as well as the Caribbean Islands. These slave-powered plantations played a major part in the growing profits of the new capitalist world of Western Europe and North America.

In the middle of the 19th century Karl Marx wrote his powerful critique of this new industrial capitalist world, *Das Kapital*. Instead of the invisible hand promoting the welfare of all, Marx claimed that it promoted only the welfare and wealth of the capitalists, the owners of industry, the bourgeoisie. It left the workers—he called them the proletariat—as *wage* slaves. They would, he claimed, inevitably sink deeper and deeper into poverty until they revolted and took power for themselves. They would then establish true socialist utopias where the workers themselves owned the means of production, and production was not for profit, but for the welfare of all.

It sounded like a good idea to many people in western and non-western countries. It never worked out as Marx and Engels predicted. The prediction that workers would sink deeper and deeper into poverty turned out to be mistaken. Due to the dynamics of capitalism itself, along with struggles of free-trade unions and humanistic religious reformers in western countries, instead of sinking deeper and deeper into poverty, workers became richer, not poorer. Wealth did "trickle down." It trickled down so much that by the middle of the 20th century workers had became middle class, bourgeoisie, the very class Lenin wanted to "wipe off the face of the earth."

At the same time that workers were getting richer, industrialized countries were also slowly and haltingly becoming more democratic. Free trade, free labor and free markets may not have demanded democratic governments, but they were a good fit with freedom of speech, freedom of religion and free elections. And that is what began to happen in Western Europe and North America. In the 19th century, this partnership of capitalism and democracy (with help from religious reformers, moral leaders, and the violence of the American Civil War) led to the final extermination of serfdom and of slavery in the western world.

The free markets and the civil freedoms that new liberal democracies like the United States offered their citizens has an interesting and important twist in the win-win economies of capitalist progress. In any given free trade transaction, the theory says that both sides gain or else the trade would not have happened. However, as Robert Wright points out in his book *Nonzero: The Logic of Human Destiny*, there is often a significant zero-sum component in an otherwise win-win free trade.[74]

---

[74] *Nonzero: The Logic of Human Destiny.* p. 25.

When the customer, for instance, bargains with a car salesman to buy an automobile, in the end both sides win. The customer gets his car and the salesman get his commission. However, within the bargaining itself, there is a zero-sum component. That is, there is a gap between the most the customer would offer, and the least the salesman will take. Within that gap, the partners engage in zero-sum bargaining. In that bargaining any gain to one comes at the expense of the other.

The same principle applies to larger transactions in free-market liberal democracies. When a worker agrees to work for a factory or office, both the worker and the factory or office owners win. But as with the car sales, there is a gap between what the worker will take and what the company will give. Here, the worker often joins a union to get greater power in his or her salary transactions with the company. The income and profits of the enterprise, in other words, are the new wealth that management, owners and workers (and government) have produced. This income and these profits are the lifeblood of economic progress. But how to divvy them up?

Socialists would say the workers deserve all the income and profits since they did all the work. Communists would say the government should take all the income and profits and then distribute them equably to the whole population. Liberal democracy says let the owners, management, unions and government bargain it out. Since unions, management, owners and government have all contributed to the income and profits, so each should have a say in how to distribute them.

Like the car salesman and the car customer, all parties will end up winners in these bargainings, but it is true that some will win more than others. The trick in a free-market liberal democracy is to try to manage things so that all parties have roughly equal power and skill in the bargaining. That, of course, is the ideal, and is never quite reached in practice. The net result is often a wide gap, which does lead to income inequality.

Income inequality in capitalist societies has gone up and down over time.[75] In the 19th century, the owners and management usually had the most powerful hand in the bargaining, and income inequality was very great. Rich industrialists like John D. Rockefeller, Andrew Carnegie and Cornelius Vanderbilt took a much larger share of the national income than the richest people today. Corrected for inflation, for instance, Rockefeller (in the much poorer 19th century) had twice the net worth of Bill Gates, the Microsoft pioneer who was once reputed to be the richest man in the world today.

The ordinary workers in 19th-century factories, in turn, got a smaller percentage of the national income than workers today. Worthy of note, however, these workers in 19th-century American factories were much richer and had a much larger percentage of national income (a much bigger piece of the "wealth pie") than their parents and grandparents who had worked as peasants and servants on European farms and estates. Everyone gains in capitalism, in other words, though some gain more than others.

In the 20th century, unions, humanitarian religious reformers and social-activists combined to pass progressive income tax laws and other government reforms that have tended to reduce income inequality. In the last quarter of the 20th century, income inequality has increased again, though it is still far short of the 19th and early 20th century rates.

Capitalism, in other words, does give "trickle-down" benefits. The rich get richer, but the poor also get richer. The principal alternative of the 20th century, Marxist "trickle-up" command-economy, has not worked nearly as well for the poor. Instead of win-win, these economies typically ended up zero-sum stagnations where no one benefits (with the exception of high government officials and their friends).

THE MORAL SEEMS TO BE that free-market capitalism does benefit all, but it benefits some more than others. The ones it benefits the most are entrepreneurs like Rockefeller, Carnegie, Vanderbilt, Steve Jobs,

---

[75] See "What Wealth Gap?" by Michael Novak. *The Wall Street Journal*, July 11, 1995.

Warren Buffett and Bill Gates, who take the greatest risks in pioneering new industries. It also brings handsome rewards to hundreds of thousands of small business people and indeed to millions of creative workers in all industries, trades and services.

Few people, for instance, have heard of a rich man named Brandon Fisher. He is the founder and president of Center Rock Inc., a small company in Berlin, Pennsylvania with 74 employees. It was his company that supplied the drill bits for the shaft that saved the miners in Chile after a 2010 cave-in. Schramm Inc., another small company in West Chester, Pennsylvania, supplied the drilling rig. Brandon Fisher and the other executives of Center Rock Inc. as well as the founders, owners and executives of Schramm Inc. no doubt make handsome profits in their productive businesses.

So, too, did Catherine Clark, who turned her recipe for all-natural whole wheat bread into Brownberry Ovens, a national bakery in the small town of Oconomowoc, Wisconsin. She made a profit of $59 her first year in 1946. By 1979 sales were $25 million and thousands of jobs had been created. She became a very wealthy woman when she sold the company a few years before for five and half million dollars.

Free-market capitalism also generously rewards plumbers who figure out more efficient and effective ways to stop dripping drains or fix balky washing machines. Or businessmen who design and produce better gadgets to efficiently move energy from windmills and solar panels onto the electric grid. Or chemists who research and produce pills that will slow Alzheimer's or Parkinson's diseases; factory workers who figure out more efficient ways to install gaskets in new cars; teachers who find better ways to teach physics, or English, or history to gifted students—or ones who find better ways to do the same for below-average students.

All of these creative people find ways to do more with less and create the new wealth that is shared by all workers, from the lowliest janitor to the highest manager, artist, professor or doctor. They also create the wealth that is needed to support citizens who do not produce goods or services of enough value for win-win transactions. These non-producers include: children, students, retirees, the handicapped, the injured, the lazy, the criminal, and the incapacitated for whatever reason.

A SECOND MORAL IS that we should appreciate but be cautious, when it comes to the government side in the bargaining process. The government has the power of taxation, near unlimited credit and overwhelming force on their side. They can only too easily dominate the bargaining. If the government becomes too powerful, the result is fascism—or communism—and misery for all sides, rich and poor.

Short of that, zero-sum bargaining involving the government can also create imbalances that threaten future growth and prosperity. In recent years, for instance, government unions have become stronger in all western democracies. Democratic governments often take the line of least resistance when it comes to bargaining with government employee unions over wages and benefits. Not having to worry about making a profit or avoiding bankruptcy, as private companies must, the government often gives in and grants excessive increases in wages and benefits. Over time this can lead to serious problems as it has today in the early 21st century.

In many European and American welfare-state democracies, for instance, teachers, police officers, prison guards, librarians, diplomats, as well as thousands of other professional, technical and office workers for the government can retire in their early 50s with generous retirement benefits. These pension costs, as well as health care and other benefits, are mounting to dangerously high levels as average life spans increase and the number of young workers to support the retirees decreases. This imbalance has already led to street riots in France, Greece, Spain and Italy, massive protests in Great Britain and the U.S., and severe restrictions on new infrastructure projects. It also leads to higher rates of taxation, especially on the rich, which in turn leads to lower investment rates in new industries and more unemployment as old industries cut back and fewer new industries are founded.

These trends can go to the extreme, and, as Friedrich Hayek pointed out, can and have led to virtual serfdom. In the 20th century, in the wake of World War I, a revolution in Russia did lead to serfdom in the first totalitarian state, the Soviet Union, where the government took all power and made all the decisions as to how to produce, distribute and manage economic exchanges. After World War II communist parties in China, in Korea, in Vietnam and Cuba followed suit and took power and established totalitarian states. All these intellectually led communist parties took power in the name of the workers and the peasants. All were dedicated to economic memes where freedom was denied, profit was forbidden, and zero-sum exchanges were the norm. As a result, all became the most unproductive, oppressive and totalitarian regimes in the long history of the human race. Instead of welfare for all, these 20th-century experiments with communism led to stagnation, boredom, declines in living standards, and savage gulags where eighty to one hundred million people were enslaved or murdered.

By the end of the 20th century only a very few communist states still survive to carry on the communist cause. Rulers in Cuba and North Korea are probably the only true believers. The Soviet Union is no more. All the former communist states of Eastern Europe are now free, democratic and capitalist. China, like Vietnam, is still not free or democratic, but it is strongly capitalist in its economy and is rapidly recovering from decades of economic decay under communism. Whether it will gradually become more democratic, freer and more respectful of human rights remains to be seen.

DESPITE THE SEEMING TRIUMPH of capitalism and democracy as well on the world stage, there is strong opposition to capitalism in many parts of the world, including the western world where it originated.

One of the major problems of capitalism is that it does not foster romantically utopian hopes and dreams. Instead, to many sensitive and intelligent people, it smacks of crudity, selfishness, greed, and a ruthless competition that rewards the bully and punishes the weak. And it fosters, some claim, an environmentally and morally destructive hedonism and consumer driven excess.

Socialism gets a better press. In practice, however, full-blown socialist societies like the Soviet Union, China, Cambodia, Cuba and North Korea have been the most brutal and ruthless tyrants. They have also been the world's worst polluters.

Many capitalist countries in Europe, especially in Scandinavia, have experimented with a modified version of capitalism that emphasizes strong government interference in distributing the accumulating wealth of a capitalist economy via an expanded welfare state. In fact, most western democracies, including the United States and Canada, do not rely on an "invisible hand" to equably distribute wealth. Social security systems, national health systems, unemployment insurance, welfare payments, etc. are common throughout Europe, North America and Japan. All of these liberal democratic states today, however, do rely on the private ownership of productive industries to produce the income, profits, and wealth that democratic governments then help distribute, softening some of the inequities and harshness of the "invisible hand."

All of these welfare-state liberal democracies, including the United States, have to cope with serious problems described a few pages back— older populations, rising benefits, higher taxes, larger deficits, soaring crime rates, etc.

Some countries of South America today, notably Venezuela, Bolivia and Ecuador, are flirting with more radical socialist ideas like government ownership of key industries in the hopes that they can make faster progress in overcoming poverty. Already, however, there are signs of run-away inflation in these countries. Cuba was kept solvent for many years by the generosity of the Soviet Union. Venezuela is for the moment kept solvent by huge sales of its non-renewable resource, oil. Cuba is also a police state with massive poverty and scant respect for human rights and civil liberties, and Venezuela is fast going that direction.

In large modern states the "invisible hand" of Adam Smith works well in increasing a society's wealth, but it also makes serious mistakes that have in the past led to booms and crashes. These recessions and depressions have caused suffering for many hard-working people. Many individual companies, and sometimes entire industries, are destroyed in the competition for efficiency and innovation. Analysts call this "creative destruction," but that does not make it any more pleasant for those whose jobs or companies are destroyed.

There is also deepening concern in the 21st century about non-economic goods like the environment and human rights. How does capitalism, with its unprecedented power of wealth creation deal with non-economic goods (what economists call "negative externalities") like clean air, clear water and productive soil? How does it deal with racial, sexual, religious and gender discrimination? How does it deal with "fairness?" In all of these issues, religion and the arts come into play as well as capitalism and science. Private organizations, both secular and religious, and a free press have acted in the past as powerful and effective restraints to correct problems brought on by the "free hand."

WHAT ABOUT GLOBALIZATION? As modern liberal and capitalist democracy becomes ever more powerful and ever more common around the world, some activists object strongly. In both the western world and the underdeveloped world they claim that globalization harms both worlds by letting giant multinational corporations profit generously, while doing little or nothing about poverty in the underdeveloped world. Instead, they claim, globalization results in frivolous and environmentally harmful wealth in the western world, and increased poverty in the underdeveloped worlds of Africa and Asia.

This charge, say most economists and scientists who have studied poverty and wealth, is simply false. Globalization does lead to change, as capitalism always has. Uncontested statistics, however, show enormous overall gains in countries as diverse as India, China, Korea, Taiwan, Malaysia, Brazil and South Africa. The Index of Economic Freedom consistently finds that free markets and entrepreneurship are the keys to prosperity. The results of the *2010 Index* demonstrate a significant positive correlation between higher economic freedom scores and reduced poverty as measured by the Human Development Index (UNDP), as well as improved democratic governance and political stability as tracked by the Economist Intelligence Unit's Index of Democracy."[76]

The *Financial Times* writer Martin Wolf wrote in his recent book *Why Globalization Works*: "Never before have so many people or such a large proportion of the world's population enjoyed such large rises in their standard of living."[77] The World Bank noted a "spectacular" decline in poverty in East and South Asia. Recent reports showed that, with the exception of sub-Saharan Africa, world poverty as a whole has declined dramatically.

Many of these underdeveloped countries were written off as hopeless just a few decades ago. There have also been solid gains in income, agriculture, health, life expectancy, pollution control and almost every other measure of progress in countries that were formerly communist in Eastern Europe, as well as in poorer countries in South America, Central America, Africa and Southeast Asia. If the old zero-sum dogma were true, how could this happen? With all of the gains in wealth and the explosion of natural resource use and population growth in the developing countries, you would expect the gains to be offset by losses in the rich industrialized countries of Western Europe, North America, Japan and Southeast Asia.

But they, too, have gained! Contrary to the critics of globalization, the Congressional Budget Office (CBO)[78] reported that average wages in the United States rose between 1991 and 2005, the period of greatest expansion in global trade and the period when China and Mexico were blamed for taking American jobs and income. Dividing the level of income in the U.S. into five parts, the gains between 1990 and 2005 for the wealthiest fifth were indeed large, 50%. But contrary to what many think, the gains for the lowest fifth, the poorest in the U.S., were even larger. They increased by 80%! (The gains for the three in-between

---

[76] For 2011 report from The Index of Economic Freedom see:
<http://www.heritage.org/index/>
[77] *Why Globalization Works*, by Martin Wolf, pp. 43-44.
[78] See report by CBO: <http://www.cbo.gov/ftpdocs/76xx/doc7693/12-04-LaborForce.pdf>

middle-class fifths increased by around 20%.) In the end, globalization not only resulted in truly astonishing increases in world-wide prosperity, but it has also added around $10,000 a year to the average American household income!

The recent history of China is even more dramatic and gives more powerful evidence for the virtues of capitalism and globalization. In the days of Mao Zedong a zero-sum command-economy was the rule. In a new book *Red Capitalism*, Carl Walter and Fraser Howie relate a telling tale. In the late Mao days in 1974, the future reformer Deng Xiaoping was chosen to lead a large delegation to the United Nations in New York. When they went to the Chinese treasury to finance the trip they found to their dismay that they could "muster only $38,000 in foreign cash."[79] The egalitarian command-economy of the entire nation had apparently made a "profit" of $38,000 from 30 years of trying. That "trying" also cost over thirty million Chinese their lives, when they starved to death or were otherwise murdered during the Great Leap Forward from 1958 to 1961.

That same Deng Xiaoping later became the leader of China and radically changed the command-economy of socialism to a variation of the free-market of capitalism. (Unfortunately he did not change the political system to liberal democracy, but that is another story.) After just a few decades operating with the new free-market economic system, China had foreign exchange funds of over three trillion dollars (much of it invested in the United States to prop up our lagging economy). China is not only well fed now, but in 2011 is the best customer of what used to be our largest corporation, the bankrupted General Motors.

SOME COUNTRIES, IT IS TRUE, seem to have been left out of this progress so far. Many of these are Muslim, oil-rich but industrially and ideologically disadvantaged countries, in the Middle East and northern

---

[79] See review article in Wall Street Journal by Edward Chancellor, Mar. 14, 1011: last accessed on web site 4/11/11.
<http://online.wsj.com/article/SB10001424052748704132204576190864046071514.html?mod=googlenews_wsj>

Africa. These same countries are misleadingly "rich" like feudal Spain and Portugal were with their gold and silver, and handicapped in the same way by illiteracy, religious and ethnic memes and differences inherited from a thousand years ago.

Some of the countries in sub-Saharan Africa have also been slow to progress, handicapped by corrupt governments, poor education and endemic health and environmental problems. And finally, the few still-communist countries like Cuba and North Korea, handicapped by a perverse and tyrannical economic and political system.

If capitalism is rapidly expanding its reach around the world, what about freedom and democracy? Is there a natural partnership between free-market capitalism and liberal democracy?[80]

At the beginning of the Industrial Revolution and the beginnings of modern capitalism in the late 18th century, the only countries that were relatively free, democratic and capitalist were England and the United States. All other countries in the world were authoritarian feudal states or still in hunting/gathering tribal societies.

By 1900, there were a few more democratic and capitalist countries in Europe, North America and on the Pacific Rim (Australia, New Zealand).

By 2011, capitalism and democracy are not only more common, they are the norm. Worthy of note, too, is that many smaller countries in Asia and Africa are capitalist in economy, but not democratic in politics. The same is true of China and Russia. There are no countries today that are free and democratic, but not capitalist.

Countries in Europe, especially in Scandinavia, are sometimes claimed as exceptions because of their strong commitment to social welfare policies. Their basic economy is firmly capitalist, however, as most of the productive sphere that creates their wealth is privately owned.

---

[80] A good summary article detailing the connections between economic freedom and prosperity in particular countries and regions and be found at the web-site listed below. Last accessed 4/11/11.
<http://www.heritage.org/index/PDF/2011/Index2011_Chapter3.pdf>

Some might claim Venezuela is an exception. While still relatively free and democratic, under the leadership of Hugo Chavez it is moving rapidly in the socialist direction, and in the process restricting important liberal democratic rights, like freedom of the press and enforcement of private contracts. It is also putting severe restrictions on private property. Chavez has openly boasted of his admiration and desire to follow in the footsteps of Fidel Castro's Cuba. Considering Cuba's near total lack of freedom and abundance of poverty, insofar as Chavez is able to carry through on his plans it is rapidly becoming a dark day for his country.

In conclusion, we can answer the question posed at the beginning of this chapter with some confidence. Yes, capitalism is necessary for democracy—but not sufficient. A healthy regard for self-interest, for private property and for free trade, combined with humanistic religious values and strong support for science and technology, seems to be the story of past economic success as well as human prosperity and freedom.

It may or may not be the end of history, but it does seem to be the wave of the future.

"Wonders are many . . . "

I was a science teacher in high schools in
Colorado, New York and Wisconsin. I'm not
sure I was a good science teacher because I was
always more interested in the philosophic, social
and historic side of science than I was in details of
the technology side. For certain kinds of students
that was probably good, but for other kinds—the
kinds of students who are more fascinated by the
razzmatazz technology side of science—it was
not so good.

George W. Bush is not wildly popular nowadays.
It was not always so. I am republishing here a
Hawkhill News that I wrote just after Bush's 2nd
Inaugural Address. I think it still has relevance
today.

> President Bush used the word "freedom"
> 24 times in his 2nd Inaugural Address.
> Whether you agree with his means or
> not, it is hard to disagree with his end, a
> world of free nations. A world of free
> people. To my thinking one good way to
> pursue this end is through a dramatic
> expansion and improvement in science
> education, worldwide. As a wise man
> once said, "Ye shall know the truth, and
> the truth shall make you free." What hu-
> man activity has a firmer grasp on truth
> than science.

Ah! There is the catch. Truth with a capital T (whether it comes from religion,
politics or science) is just the kind of truth
we don't need. This is the kind of truth
that for many sad centuries people have
been killing one another about. One
group thinks they have *The Truth*, while
their adversaries are just as certain that
they have *The Truth*.

Question: what kind of truth does make
us free?

Answer: the kind of truth (with a small 't')
that science at its best gives and promotes.

Science has two sides. One side I call the
power part, technology that is. This is the
side that can lead to power (and wealth).
Unfortunately it can also ally itself with,
and support tyrannical governments.
That's what happened in the 20th century
in Germany, in the Soviet Union, and it is
happening today in the Middle East.

But technology is only half of science. The
other half I call the wonder half, the *Soul
of Science*.[81] This is the side of science that
promotes tolerance, wisdom, freedom

---

[81] See *The Soul of Science*, a DVD program from Hawkhill Associates, Inc.
available on <www.hawkhill.com> as well as in many college libraries.

and democracy. This is the side of science that the jurist Learned Hand was thinking of when he said "the spirit of liberty is the spirit that is not quite sure it is right." Or that the Nobel prize-winning physicist Richard Feynman was talking about when he said that we should above all teach "doubt."

In Feynman's book, *What Do You Care What Other People Think?* he explains the relation of science to democracy this way.

"Through all ages of our past, people have tried to fathom the meaning of life. They have realized that if some direction or meaning could be given to our actions, great human forces would be unleashed. So, very many answers have been given to the question of the meaning of it all. But the answers have been of all different sorts, and the proponents of one answer have looked with horror at the actions of the believers in another—horror, because from a disagreeing point of view all the great potentialities of the race are channeled into a false and confining blind alley. In fact, it is from the history of the enormous monstrosities created by false belief that philosophers have realized the apparently infinite and wondrous capacities of human beings. The dream is to find the open channel.

"If we take everything into account—not only what the ancients knew, but all of what we know today that they didn't know—then I think we must frankly admit that we do not know.

"But, in admitting this, we have probably found the open channel.

"This is not a new idea: this is the idea of the age of reason. This is the philosophy that guided the men who made the democracy that we live under. The idea that no one really knew how to run a government led to the idea that we should arrange a system by which new ideas could be developed, tried out, and tossed out if necessary, with more new ideas brought in—a trial-and-error system."

How best to teach this soul of science to young students in high school and college is the tough part. Certainly one way not to do it is the way many schools in Islamic countries choose. They hope to teach and get the benefits of science on the technology side without letting the wisdom of science challenge their fundamental religious dogmas. In the worst of their schools the students study only the Koran. Unfortunately this approach is also present to a lesser degree in some fundamentalist schools in the west, including the United States, where the Bible is considered the final authority not only on moral questions, but on scientific questions as well.

One of my own modest suggestions for all schools is to spend more time teaching the history of science than we have in the past. All three of the major science curriculum projects— *AAAS Project 2061, NSTA's Scope, Sequence* and *Coordination of Secondary School Science* and *The National Science Education Standards*—strongly urge this path.

The more students learn about how we found out about atoms, about stars and galaxies, about germs, about genes, about weather and climate, about animals, plants and ecosystems, about our own bodies and brains and emotions, the less susceptible they will be to people and to movements that claim to know it all. The more they will respect the power of evidence. The more they will respect the virtues of tolerance, of doubt, and of ignorance. The more they will realize the power of free inquiry. And finally, the more they will appreciate the value of freedom.

Humanistic religion and free-market capitalism are essential to democracy. What about the third of the essential ingredients, science?

Chapter 14

The Rise of Science

"BLESSED IS HE WHO LEARNS how to engage in inquiry, with no impulse to harm his countrymen or to pursue wrongful actions, but perceives the order of immortal and ageless nature, how it is structured."

The words are those of a poet named Euripides. They were sung in 400 BC by the chorus in a play performed in an outdoor theatre built by citizens of the world's first democracy in ancient Greece.

"The general spread of the light of science has already laid open to every view the palpable truth that the mass of mankind has not been born with saddles on their backs, nor a favored few booted and spurred, ready to ride them legitimately, by the grace of God."

The words are those of Thomas Jefferson, Enlightenment philosopher and one of the founding fathers of the first modern democracy in the United States of America.

This "light of science," this "blessed inquiry," is indeed central to the blessings of democracy. How so?

Science got its start at the same time religion and capitalism got their start, in prehistoric times. As explained in earlier chapters, our *Homo sapiens* ancestors lived in caves and rude shelters and survived by hunting, fishing and gathering wild foods.

Partly because of a high rate of violence, but also because of high rates of starvation, malnutrition, disease and accidents, anthropologists have found that the average life expectancy was less than 30 years. And yet, surprisingly enough, they found that people then may have had more leisure than most people do today!

Homo sapiens individuals of 100,000 years ago may or may not have had minds pretty much like ours today. Julian Jaynes has a strong argument that they did not. According to this late Princeton psychologist, *Homo sapiens* of 100,000 years ago were not conscious! (See discussion in Chapter 10, pages 113-115.)

As Jaynes points out, consciousness, in the sense of introspection and abstract reasoning, is not necessary for many mental operations like sense perception, language, problem-solving and learning. As animal psychologists (and pet owners) know, animals do have good sense perception. They also have a kind of language and they can solve problems and learn.

HOMO SAPIENS INDIVIDUALS had a good brain and a good hand with an opposable thumb. They used brain and hand to invent tools like fire, spears, bow and arrows, better kinds of shelters, and new and better ways of hunting, fishing and gathering wild foods. And so in the broadest sense science and technology were born.

In some parts of the world around 10,000 years ago some humans made a major advance using these same science and technology skills. They found ways to grow food and husband animals. The agricultural revolution began and over the next few thousand years spread to all the continents.

This agricultural revolution has lasted 10,000 years. In many parts of the modern world (though not all) it has been replaced by an industrial revolution that began only a few hundred years ago.

During this long 10,000-year time many civilizations in Africa, Asia, Europe, the South Pacific and the Americas rose and fell. During their ascendancy and their fall, all of them made advances in what we would today call science and technology.

Weather, seasons, soils, sun and stars, are all of prime importance in agriculture as well as in navigation on land and sea. All agricultural kingdoms on all continents made discoveries important to the beginnings of earth science, astronomy and chemistry.

All agricultural kingdoms by necessity also learned more about the natural living world of plants and animals, and so laid a factual base for what would come to be called today the life sciences of biology, ecology and agriculture.

All agricultural civilizations fought frequent wars and in the process laid a base for much of what would today be called physical science, engineering and metallurgy.

Similarly, all agricultural kingdoms learned more about the human body and about disease and health. Even though much of this knowledge (like their knowledge in earth science, astronomy and biology) was compromised with magic- and religion-based error, it was the beginning of what we would today call medicine.

The Chinese people created a rich civilization that for many centuries surpassed all others in science, in the arts, in organization and in trade. The first printing presses, the first magnetic compasses, the finest ceramics and metal work, gunpowder, porcelain, silk and paper, the largest and best sailing ships all came to the world first in China.

Similar advanced agricultural kingdoms flourished in India. One of the most important scientific ideas from India was the invention of what came to be misnamed "Arabic" numerals, 1, 2, 3, 4, 5, etc. including the most important numeral of all, 0 (zero).

All of these agriculturally based ancient civilizations had political systems that featured strong class divisions, powerful religions, slave labor, frequent wars and tyrannical governments. Unfortunately, most of these traits worked against more rapid progress in what we today call science and technology.

Reliance on slave (or peasant or serf) labor, universal in all agriculturally based civilizations, made for little incentive to improve technology. Why bother when there were plenty of slaves, peasants or serfs to do the work?

Powerful religions usually did little to encourage unbiased inquiry into the mysteries of the natural world. A god or gods made the world the way it is, and they govern its ways. Humans can do nothing about it—except perhaps pray to the gods to bring peace and prosperity and to take away pain and adversity. We should not puff up ourselves to complain, or to fight what must be. Since tyrannical governments relied on religious myths to enhance and uphold their power, science and invention were again the losers.

Frequent wars were one of the few places where need was the mother of invention and there were strong incentives to improve weaponry. This was a boon to science and invention.

AT LEAST ONE AGRICULTURALLY based civilization in the ancient world did more to encourage unbiased inquiry into the natural world—as well as to introduce a new way of governing. That rare combination of natural science and political innovation was in ancient Greece, and it turned out to be a powerful model for civilizations of much later times, especially our own western civilization.

A few hundred years before the birth of Jesus, in small city-states like Miletus, and later in larger city-states like Athens, a new idea for governing based on reason and experience was tried. The Greeks called it "democracy."

In Athens all citizens would gather in the center of town to pass laws, make judgments on disputes, assess taxes, and vote for war or peace. The duties and offices of government were assigned by lot. Every citizen was free to pursue his own interests so long as they did not interfere with others. Every citizen had the right to his own private property.

This direct democracy of the ancient Greek city-states had severe limitations. While citizens of the city-state were free and equal, citizens did not include women, nor did it include slaves.

At the height of Athens' democratic glory, out of an estimated population of 400,000 people, there were only about 40,000 citizens. Even for these citizens, it was a democracy of majority rule, with little attention paid to the rights and civil liberties of minorities. One of their most illustrious citizens, a philosopher named Socrates, was sentenced to death for "corrupting the youth."

The Greek democracy did nourish an environment that encouraged rational inquiry. Natural philosophers like Thales, Anaximander, Plato, Aristotle, Pythagoras and Hippocrates were among the first humans to look at the natural world and to construct theories to explain why and how it worked the way it did, without invoking supernatural forces. Probably because of their reliance on slave labor for most manual work, these early natural philosophers never quite made the solid connection between theory and experiment that characterizes modern science. But it was a start. A poem sung by the chorus in a popular Greek play of the time gives a good sense of the power and the pride of the creators of this first democracy.

Wonders are many, and none is more wonderful than man;
the power that crosses the white sea, driven by the stormy south-wind,
making a path under surges that threaten to engulf him; and Earth,
the eldest of the gods, the immortal, the unwearied, doth he wear,
turning the soil with the offspring of horses,
as the ploughs go to and fro from year to year.

And the light-hearted race of birds, and the tribes of savage beasts,
  and the sea-brood of the deep, he snares in the meshes of his woven
  toils,
he leads captive, man excellent in wit.
And he masters by his arts the beast whose lair is in the wilds,
who roams the hills; he tames the horse of shaggy mane,
he puts the yoke upon its neck,
he tames the tireless mountain bull.

And speech, and wind-swift thought,
and all the moods that mould a state, hath he taught himself;
and how to flee the arrows of the frost,
when 'tis hard lodging under the clear sky,
and the arrows of the rushing rain;
yea, he hath resource for all;
without resource he meets nothing that must come:
only against Death shall he call for aid in vain;

but from baffling maladies he hath devised escapes.

Cunning beyond fancy's dream is the fertile skill
which brings him, now to evil, now to good.
When he honours the laws of the land,
and that justice which he hath sworn by the gods to uphold,
proudly stands his city: no city hath he who, for his rashness,
dwells with sin. Never may he share my hearth,
never think my thoughts, who doth these things!

Sophocles, *Antigone*, 442 B.C. Translated by R. C. Jebb.[82]

ROME, FOUNDED AS a city-state in Italy, began as an aristocratic republic. Rome borrowed and built on some of the cultural riches of Greece and in some important ways advanced its democratic ideas as well as improving some technologies and advancing science.

In the process of founding and governing their empire, for instance, the Romans developed a system of Roman law based on nature and reason that has had great influence in the Western world. Romans were also the first to separate the government into executive, legislative and judicial branches.

Romans were the world's greatest engineers when it came to roads, water supply, sanitation systems and civic architecture, as well as the world's greatest bureaucrats when it came to administering their empire.

The enduring ideas that led to these achievements have had great influence in the Western world of today. We still speak of senators, consuls, constitutions, and republics—all words derived from their Latin Roman roots. Many of our democratic government buildings use designs derived from Greek and Roman architecture.

As Rome prospered it became more imperial and tyrannical. It grew into an empire that eventually included most of the land around the

---

[82] For complete text of *Antigone* see:
<http://classics.mit.edu/Sophocles/antigone.html>

Mediterranean Sea, and went as far north as Great Britain, as far east as Persia, and as far south as North Africa. Slavery also increased as liberty was crushed under the boots of the marching imperial legions.

During this long period, science made some advances in the Western world, though it lagged behind the Islamic, Indian and Chinese civilizations for many centuries.

What the Western world did have that the other civilizations lacked was a culture that gradually abandoned slavery; a culture that gradually came to respect women (more so than other non-Western cultures did); and some scholars think most important of all—a culture that began to accept reason as an important route to understanding and truth. Reason was not the only route, to be sure. Divine revelation was still given first place as it was in almost all agricultural kingdoms, but reason to medieval philosophers was a valued and necessary virtue.

Respect for reason was not absolute by any stretch. Thomas Aquinas, considered the greatest of the Roman Catholic philosophers of medieval times, struggled to reconcile the natural reason of Greek philosophers like Plato and Aristotle with divine revelation from the Christian Bible. Philosophers a few hundreds years later in the western Enlightenment would build on his work with natural reason, but, for the most part, discard the need to reconcile reason with revelation.

For most everyone, life was a desperate struggle for survival in the Middle Ages. Christian monasteries, and later the first universities in Europe, sometimes managed to escape the worst of the chaos, poverty and ignorance. In these early universities logic, reason and a respect for learning were kept alive. In the monasteries slow progress was also made in technology and science, and an early form of capitalism was invented.[83]

Wheelbarrows, rotation of crops, the spinning wheel, heavy plows, better horse collars that enabled a medieval horse to do ten times the work that a Roman horse could do without choking himself, water wheels and windmills.

---

[83] See Rodney Stark, *The Victory of Reason: How Christianity Led to Freedom, Capitalism, and Western Success.*

Monasteries also stimulated a closer contact between work and thought, where the power of practical invention could be yoked with the wonder of God's world. Monks believed it was a world one could understand with the gift of reason if one worked at it. It was in these monasteries as well as in the universities of the later medieval times that scholars like Gerald of Cremona spent their lives translating works of ancient authors like Aristotle, Euclid, Ptolemy and Archimedes, translating them from Arabic into the scholarly language of the West, Latin.

Monasteries began to experiment with production for profit and with free trade. They were becoming some of the world's first capitalists and bankers. They lent money to the Pope as well as to other monasteries, and to nobles and kings.

All of this scholarly and technical progress in Christian monasteries and universities laid a base for the remarkable flowering of human invention and progress in what is called the European Renaissance. It was in 16th- and 17th-century Renaissance Europe that modern science was born.

In northern Italy Galileo Galilei was one of the most important of the new natural philosophers, who for the first time did combine natural reason with experimental observation. We call him today one of the world's first scientists, though that name was not used while he was alive. Galileo, along with other pioneers like Nicolas Copernicus, Johannes Kepler, Francis Bacon, Rene Descartes, and later, Isaac Newton, changed radically the way human beings looked on the world, and began a revolution that is still going on today.

Before Galileo's time everyone in the world *knew* for certain the obvious truth that our earth was the center of the universe. Everyone *knew* that the sun and stars were out there, some fixed and some revolving around our central stationary earth.

The thought and experiments of these first scientists proved that what everyone knew for certain, was not true.

The earth is not standing still, nor is it at the center of the solar system, much less the universe. Instead, the earth, they proved, was moving! And fast! It was, in fact, spinning around once every day on its own axis.

And instead of being at the center, it was also moving around a central sun, taking 365 and 1/4 days to make a complete circuit.

(Later astronomers proved that this solar system of ours is only a tiny part of the wider Milky Way Galaxy that has billions of stars. Still later astronomers proved that this Milky Way Galaxy is itself moving, as only one of billions of galaxies in the universe!)

Quite a change from what everyone knew was true just a few hundred years ago.[84]

If all of that were true, and their experiments and reasoning were convincing to anyone who took the trouble to investigate, it was a serious challenge to all religions of that day.

Religions had always assumed we on earth were special, central to God's plan. Galileo was brought before a church court of the Inquisition and convicted of heresy, for claiming that the earth was not the center of the universe. Faced with such a serious charge (that could lead to his being burned at the stake), Galileo recanted, and was let off with house arrest, on the condition that he refrains from making such absurd claims again.

The Catholic monk Giordano Bruno refused to deny his scientific convictions and *was* convicted of heresy. He was brought to a central Roman market square, his tongue in a gag (to prevent him from spreading his heretical views), tied naked to a pole, and burned at the stake on February 17, 1600.

Despite the efforts to suppress it by the Church, the interest in this new way of thinking, science, began to spread over the next centuries. First throughout Europe, and later throughout the entire world. This

---

[84] "Nothing could be more obvious than that the Earth is stable and unmoving, and that we are in the center of the Universe. Modern Western science takes it's beginning from the denial of this common-sense axiom." Daniel J. Boorstin, *The Discoverers*

interest and its consequences were, and still are, powerful for two major reasons.

(1) Science works. That is, it leads to new knowledge and to new technologies that are of obvious benefit to people.

(2) Science has a powerful way to spread its working knowledge—in early days that was the printing press, today it is the electronic revolution as well.

The work of Galileo, Copernicus, Kepler, and especially of Isaac Newton led to the discovery of the first basic force in the universe—gravity. Once this was understood and described with mathematical precision, the way was clear for the physical scientists and engineers who followed to construct better calendars, better maps, better artillery, better vehicles, better mines, better sanitation, better machinery of all kinds, and eventually huge increases in available energy that would power automobiles, airplanes and earth satellites.

When scientists of the 19th century discovered the second basic force in the universe, electro-magnetism, the way was clear for electricity, radio, television, computers, cell phones and the Internet.

When Albert Einstein and quantum physicists in the 20th century discovered the third and fourth of the basic forces, the weak and strong nuclear forces, the way was clear for nuclear power.

Similarly, the work of life scientists like Andreas Vesalius in Italy, William Harvey in England, Anton van Leeuwenhoek in Holland, Louis Pasteur in France, Robert Koch in Germany and Charles Darwin in England led to better health, less disease, better crops, less pollution, better understanding of the human body and brain, an enormous increase in life span from less than thirty to more than seventy years of life for the average human being.

In the case of Charles Darwin, it led to a revolution in the way educated humans viewed the natural organic world, a revolution fully as profound as the one initiated in the physical world by Galileo, Copernicus and Newton.

None of this remarkable progress would have happened had it not been for that late medieval invention—the printing press.[85] Had it not been for printing, the insights of Copernicus might have gone unnoticed for centuries by the world at large. That was the fate of many of the insights and inventions of Chinese, Islamic, Mayan, African, Indian and Japanese thinkers and inventors of earlier centuries and civilizations. After the printing press ideas and inventions could be shared comparatively quickly and widely throughout the literate world with printed publications after 1450. And so they were.

---

[85] See the *Gifts of Athena: Historical Origins of the Knowledge Economy* by Joel Mokyr. "The main thing I'm interested in is how societies can end up knowing more and how that changes us."

"I seem to be a verb ..."

In my science classes, and later in my filmstrip, video and DVD productions, I often used quotes to make a point. Here are a few favorites:

"I live on Earth at present, and I don't know what I am. I know that I am not a thing—a noun. I seem to be a verb, an evolutionary process." *R. Buckminster Fuller.*

"I wouldn't have seen it if I hadn't believed it." *Marshall McLuhan.*

Green's Law of Debate: "Anything is possible if you don't know what you're talking about."

"In ten years all important animal life in the sea will be extinct. Large areas of coastline will have to be evacuated because of the stench of dead fish." *Paul Ehrlich on Earth Day, 1970.*

Lieberman's Law: "Everybody lies; but it doesn't matter since no one listens."

"A mouse is miracle enough to stagger sextillions of infidels." *Walt Whitman.*

"Hell, if I could explain it to the average person, it wouldn't have been worth the Nobel Prize." *Richard Feynman after winning the Nobel Prize.*

"Don't follow the crowd. Nobody goes there anymore. It's too crowded." *Yogi Berra.*

"No matter how much evidence exists that seers do not exist, suckers will pay for the existence of seers." *J. Scott Armstrong.*

"It has been for me a glorious day, like giving sight to a blind man's eyes, he is overwhelmed with what he sees and cannot justly comprehend it." *Charles Darwin, on first seeing tropical forests.*

"A dog is a dog except when he is facing you. Then he is Mr. Dog." *Haitian proverb.*

"Ben Wattenberg's new book is a compelling reminder that we must learn to bear the truth about our society, no matter how pleasant it may be." *Jeanne J. Kirkpatrick.*

"Any idiot can face a crisis. It's the day-to-day living that can wear you out." *Anton Chekhov.*

"I ran into someone I hadn't seen for twenty years last week and he'd changed so much he didn't even recognize me." *Piers McBride.*

"We all know that no proposition is so foolish or meretricious that at least two Nobel laureates cannot be found to endorse it." *Walter Gratzer.*

"The spirit of liberty is the spirit that is not quite sure it is right." *Judge Learned Hand.*

"I have been rich and I have been poor. Rich is better." *Sophie Tucker.*

"How do you tell a communist? Well, it's someone who reads Marx and Lenin. And how do you tell an anti-Communist? It's someone who understands Marx and Lenin." *Ronald Reagan*

Chapter 15

Science and Democracy in the Modern World

WHEN GALILEO LIVED and worked, Italy and the rest of the world were still living and working in an agriculturally based feudal system. This feudal system was built on the labor of peasants, serfs and slaves and the authority of nobility and clergy. It was about to radically change As the Enlightenment philosopher and politician, Thomas Jefferson, wrote a few centuries ago, "... the mass of mankind has not been born with saddles on their backs. ..." Stirred by the beginnings of merchant capitalism and experimental science, things did change.

Merchant capitalism and modern banking, begun in late medieval monasteries and now blossoming in Renaissance Italy, were beginning to eat away at the economic foundations of the feudal system. Now the beginnings of modern science in this same Renaissance Italy were further eroding the feudal system by undermining faith in traditional religious authority.

These trends were further advanced in northern Europe in the Protestant Reformation, and still later in the European Enlightenment.

The Protestant Reformation was centered in northern Europe in the 16th and 17th centuries when men like Martin Luther and John Calvin led religious revolts that denied the supremacy of the Pope and the authority of the Church. Martin Luther translated the Bible into German, a crime punishable by death. Protestants encouraged people to make their own compact with God, to do away with indulgences, and what they considered other corrupt practices of the Roman Church.

A century later in the Enlightenment, secular philosophers in France, Germany, the Netherlands and England, and later in the newly formed United States of America, went further. They discarded revelation altogether and instead put their faith in natural reason and human experience as better guides to progress.

One of these Enlightenment philosophers, Thomas Jefferson, wrote in the Declaration of Independence, "We hold these truths to be self-evident, that all men are created equal and that they are endowed by their Creator with certain Inalienable Rights, that among these are Life, Liberty and the pursuit of Happiness."

Like the other founding fathers, Jefferson was a Deist. That is, he believed in God but did not believe in the literal truth of so-called divine revelations of the Bible, or for that matter, any other holy book. Jefferson went so far as to rewrite the New Testament, removing passages about miracles and ones that dwelt on heaven and hell, but retaining the moral and compassionate parts of the gospel of Jesus.

This new faith in natural reason and human experience was a direct outgrowth of the growing faith in science that had such a notable and dramatic beginning in the Renaissance.

At the same time science was making such dramatic progress in understanding and controlling the natural world, merchants and entrepreneurs were dismantling the feudal economic system, and turning it into an economy of free labor, free trade, and free choice. Science and capitalism worked side by side to make peasants, serfs and slaves unnecessary. They worked to make zero-sum economics a thing of the past, and they challenged the power of aristocratic and clerical rule.

All of these events and thoughts seriously undermined a feudal system that had lasted over ten thousand years everywhere in the civilized world. It is not surprising such enormous changes brought with them serious violence. The American Revolution, followed closely by the French Revolution,[86] were only the first, and not the most bloody, of the conflicts that eventually led to the radical change from feudal to modern times.

THE HUGE CHANGE IN intellectual understanding of our world begun in the Renaissance by scientists like Nicolas Copernicus, Galileo Galilei and Isaac Newton gathered force and became a tsunami about the

---

[86] The Chinese communist Zhou Enlai may have had the last word about the French Revolution. When asked about its impact today, he answered: "It's too early to say."

time of the American Revolution in the late 18th century. It was then that the power of the scientific revolution joined with the power of the industrial revolution to give birth to the modern world.

The industrial revolution began in England in the middle of the 18th century. Newly invented machinery to spin thread and weave cloth soon made England the center of the world's textile industry. An engineer, James Watt, perfected a new steam engine that would soon power the world's railroads, factories and ships. In Coalbrookdale, iron-makers were learning how to make iron in stronger, larger batches, strong enough to build the first Iron Bridge in the world over the River Severn, and plentiful enough to provide rails, locomotives and iron steamships to connect the world.

Consider the scope of the changes brought on by this scientific and industrial change. Before the industrial revolution ninety-eight percent of the population everywhere in the world were peasants, serfs or slaves. The average life span was less than thirty-five years. Over half the children in England in 1600 died before the age of six. Starvation, plagues, dreadful diseases like smallpox, tuberculosis, malaria and childbed fever led to disfigurement, disability or early death for millions of otherwise healthy young adults. Almost everyone was illiterate. Books were rare and extremely expensive. Only a very few people traveled more than a few miles from their place of birth. Wars were so common that few people escaped their horrors.

Today the lives of men and women in the industrialized democratic world have been transformed. The average life span is over seventy-five years. Most people can read and write. Most people travel thousands of miles in their lifetime. Most people rarely experience violence except vicariously in movies, games or on television. Most people are healthy for most of their lives. And most children survive to become productive adults, able to retire at an age when their grandparents were long dead.

Before the industrial revolution a small farmer needed at least twelve slaves to operate a small farm. Today everyone in the industrialized world has the equivalent of one hundred slaves working for him or her in the form of energy-rich machines.

All of this change can be traced to the synergy of humankind's revolutionary advances in science and technology, free-market economics, humanistic religious values and liberal democratic ways of life.

It was in the 19th century that these revolutionary advances in science, religion, capitalism and democracy spread rapidly throughout Europe and North America. In the 20th century these same advances in religion, science, capitalism and democracy went global, shaking up and replacing feudal societies almost everywhere on earth with new forms of government, new ways of making a living, and new ways of organizing societies.

These new ways spawned by science and capitalism were not always democratic, nor were they always capitalist in the strict Adam Smith formula. Nor were they always an improvement in the lives of ordinary humans. Especially in the 19th century and the early 20th century the new ways included child labor, homeless people, unemployed people and, for those who did have work, long hours of grinding labor in unsafe factories and mines. All living creatures also had to cope with polluted air and water in the new cities, as well as the old countryside. The contrast between rich and poor became ever more obvious.

IN THE MIDDLE OF THE 19th century the German-born scholar Karl Marx claimed to have discovered the scientific key to curing the ills of the new industrial societies.

Marx admitted that free-market capitalism was the most powerful system yet found to increase wealth in a society. His analysis also showed that free-market capitalism contained contradictions that would inevitably lead to its destruction.

His new "science" appealed to many people, especially since many educated people in both Western and non-Western countries distrusted both religion and capitalism. Unfortunately the so-called "scientific" solution of Marx and Engels never worked out as predicted. In fact this secular, scientific solution to human problems turned out to be, if anything, worse than the traditional religious solutions to human problems of ancient and medieval days.

IN THE 20TH CENTURY STILL another challenge, as serious as the communist one, arose in Europe, also claiming scientific foundation. This was the challenge of fascism. Fascists like Benito Mussolini in Italy, Francisco Franco in Spain and above all, Adolph Hitler in Germany, gained dictatorial power with an agenda of racial and ethnic superiority. Hitler, the most powerful of the fascists, claimed that Jews and other non-Aryan people were inferior and the cause of wars and depressions of the early 20th century. The solution was to rid the world of Jews and other unfit people (homosexual, retarded, crippled), and let the superior races, the Aryans, rule. Hitler promised that the new world of Nazi control and supremacy would lead to a utopia—for Aryans at least. Inferior peoples would have to fend for themselves.

Like communists, fascists worked to gain total control of the society. In practice this meant a command-economy and iron-fisted suppression of dissident individuals and groups. In the case of religion, Hitler, like communists before him, made his own fascist dogma into a secular religion, one that supplied answers to any and all questions, and brooked no dissent.

Like communists, fascists today are opposed to liberal democracy. While they support some kinds of physical science (like ancient tyrants, they support weapon research, schemes for genetic purity and grandiose architecture), they reject and suppress much of biological and social science.

The most destructive war in human history destroyed Nazism and crippled Fascism in the middle of the 20th century. By the end of the 20th century there were still some semi-fascist states. Some would list former communist states like Russia and some of the smaller communist countries in Asia that used to be a part of the Soviet Union. Some would classify China as semi-fascist today, though it still claims to be communist.

Other semi-fascist states include Muslim countries in the Middle East and North Africa where religion and ethnic loyalties are dominant and poverty is the rule, not the exception. These countries prize science when it contributes to weaponry or to political power, but suppress it when it challenges religious or political power.

Most scholars today would say that just as capitalism is necessary for democracy, but not sufficient, so science is necessary for democracy but not sufficient. It is surely no accident that both capitalism and science thrive on freedom. In the former case, free labor, free markets and free trade. In the latter case, free inquiry, free speech and a free press.

Within democracies today, the power and validity of science are being challenged from both the radical right and the radical left. On the right, religious fundamentalists refuse to accept findings of scientists in fields like evolution, genetics, climatology and reproductive health—and more important, deny that science has any right to inquire into some of these fields.

On the left, environmental fundamentalists denounce findings of science in fields like biotechnology, genetic engineering, intelligence testing, using live animals for research, industrial growth and sometimes evolution.

Politicians and groups from both far-right and far-left have also been active in opposing immigration reform. Immigration has a little-known but important influence on both scientific and economic progress. Before, during, and after the Second World War, the United States allowed a few hundred world-class European scientists, whose home countries had been devastated, to immigrate and take up residence and citizenship.[87] Some claim, with good evidence, that this humanitarian help made an enormous difference in the U.S. economy, and in our scientific and technical leadership in the 20th century.

---

[87] *New Scientist*, 16 November. 1976, pp. 642-644.

Thomas L. Friedman, in a recent *New York Times* column,[88] pointed out that if we want to create more jobs today in our recession handicapped economy, we need to open our borders to high-aspiring risk-takers from abroad. Plentiful new jobs, he points out, rarely come from established companies or from government-funded construction projects. Overwhelmingly they come from high-tech start-up companies who "have been in business for five years or less." And "roughly 25% of the successful high-tech start-ups over the last decade were founded or co-founded by immigrants."

Despite these political challenges from the right or from the left, science today is for the most part accepted, admired and encouraged throughout the civilized world. No matter what the political stance, countries around the world aspire to leadership in science and technology. However, only in democratic countries is science likely to find bedfellows that nurture the free inquiry and free press that are so necessary for the scientific quest to succeed.

One of the wisest of our fellow citizens, the late physicist Richard Feynman, summed up one case for science, for capitalism and for democracy by calling attention to a not-usually noted feature of free-inquiry science, of free-market capitalism, of humanistic religion and of liberal democratic practice, when he called for "a satisfactory philosophy of ignorance, and the progress made possible by such a philosophy, progress which is the fruit of freedom of thought."

"I feel a responsibility," Feynman wrote, "to proclaim the value of this freedom and to teach that doubt is not to be feared, but that it is to be welcomed as the possibility of a new potential for human beings. If you know that you are not sure, you have a chance to improve the situation. I want to demand this freedom for future generations."

---

[88] "Start-Ups, Not Bailouts," *The New York Times*, Apr. 3, 2010. <http://www.nytimes.com /2010/04/04/opinion/ 04friedman.html?ref=thomaslfriedman>

THE VALUE OF FREEDOM, whether in science, religion or society has still another side, also not often acknowledged. Stephen Pinker points out in a new book, *The Better Angels of our Nature: Why Violence Has Declined*, that the rise of rational science-based thinking along with the freedom of religion has been a major force in not only reducing violence in human societies. It has also led to an increase in average intelligence! People are not only getting more peaceable, they are getting smarter.

On the average citizens worldwide are gaining around three points of IQ every decade. This means that a teenager today with an average IQ of 100 would have scored at the gifted level of 130 back in 1911, superior to 99% of the population.

PART FOUR

THE SECOND COLD WAR

Al Gore and carbon footprints

In the 20th century, communist and fascist memes were the most threatening challenges to free-market liberal democracy. In the 21st century, Radical Islamic memes are the most obvious ones. But there are other memes burgeoning today in Western countries that also pose serious challenges to free-market liberal democracy. These include: multicultural activists, new-left leftovers, environmental, anti-corporation and anti-globalization radicals. I call the synergetic sum of these disparate but related challenges the Second Cold War.

One of the most popular is the "green" move-ment. One of the leaders of this movement is Jeremy Rifkin, president of *The Foundation on Economic Trends.*

Jane and I interviewed Mr. Rifkin when he was speaking at a science teacher's convention in New Orleans a few years ago. He is an impres-sive speaker. At the conclusion of his speech he agreed to answer questions in front of our camera. I asked Mr. Rifkin to explain the rationale of the green movement.

"Our U.S. population," said Rifkin, "are the main users of resources on the planet. With 6% of the world's population we are using a third of the resources of this earth and we are responsible for 28% of global warming, so that the beginning track for any discussion on addressing global warming is to change our lifestyles in this country. We need to develop a green lifestyle. We have to realize that the planet is an organism and that we need to treat it with respect and dignity. And finally we have to learn that the more we consume, the less resources are available for other human beings and other creatures. So if we want to steward this planet for our children's generation, we are going to have to develop a green lifestyle, a green cultural movement. We are going to have to learn to use our fair share of resources and no more."

This is a widely held view today. It harks back to zero-sum days of agricultural ages. However popular with the public and with some well-publicized scientists, the majority of working scientists today do not share it. These main-stream scientists agree that we have resource, population and pollution problems. But to solve them their approach is more like U.S. Navy Seabees in World War II. "The difficult we do immediately. The impossible takes a bit longer."

The "green" (also called the "sustainable development") movement promotes three claims: (1) that natural resources are running out and will soon be exhausted; (2) that the world is grossly overpopulated and this is a major cause of imminent disaster; and (3) that world-wide pollution is crippling today and getting worse year by year (especially the carbon dioxide emissions that have the potential to cause catastrophic climate change).

Leftist political activists often add a fourth meme: the greed of giant corporations and the capitalist drive for globalization are the major cause of resource, population and pollution problems. In summary, modern worldwide capitalist industrialization is leading the world to an unprecedented collapse in the near future.

A few years ago a left-leaning friend in the state of Washington sent me an academic journal article, "The Coming Collapse of the Age of Technology" by a Professor of Biology at Rutgers University, David Ehrenfeld.[89] In this article Ehrenfeld writes movingly in promoting the Radical Environmental Green agenda. His conclusion is that we will almost certainly have an unprecedented worldwide collapse in the near future. The only hope for aware individuals is to create as soon as possible a "shadow system" of organic farming, corporate suppression and green technology that is ready to take over when the present system collapses.

His final two sentences eloquently summarize his hopes and his vision.

---

[89] *Tikkun Magazine*. Vol. 14. January-February 1999, No. 1

What is arising—I hope in time—is a
new spirit and system rooted in love of
community, and love of the land and nature that sustain community. And the
greatest challenge will be to make this
spirit and system truly new and truly enduring by finding ways to develop our
love of nature and community without
returning to destructive nationalisms,
without losing our post-Enlightenment
concern for the common good of the
rest of humankind and nature.

A more well-known author with similar views but
a wider following is the geographer Jared
Diamond, who made a splash a few years ago
and won a Pulitzer Prize with his book *Guns,
Germs and Steel: The Fates of Human Societies*. His
contribution was to provide what he claimed was
strong historical evidence to back up the claims
of the environmental movement. The success of
western civilization, Diamond claimed, was due
not to any cultural or racial differences, but was
founded almost solely on environmental accident.
We in the West simply had a better evolutionary
deal. We lucked out, in other words, when it
came to what continent (Europe and the Middle
East) our ancestors inhabited, and how relatively
easy it was for them to cultivate plants and
husband animals.

He followed this book up with one even more
deterministic and one-dimensional, *Collapse: How*

Societies Choose to Fail or Succeed. Like religious
fundamentalists who take delight in predicting
that the end of the world is nigh, Diamond and
his fellow environmental doomsayers seem to
take a peculiar pleasure in telling us we are going
to collapse erelong. If current events look
gloomy, as they often do, these warnings are
popular. If we don't collapse and things look
better, like religious fundamentalists predicting
the end of the world, they find it easy to adjust
the timetable.

Doomsayers like Diamond and Ehrenfeld typically
oversimplify and consider only the narrowest
range of variables in their attempts to find *The
Truth* about human history. With Marx and
Engels, it was the class war. With Radical
Islamists, it is straying from the Koran. With
Radical Environmentalists, it's the environment,
stupid.

Sometimes it sounds convincing. But I wrote back
to my Washington friend that his article (like
Diamond's books) was interesting, but it
reminded me of the response Abraham Lincoln
gave to the "popular sovereignty" issue in the
famous Lincoln-Douglas debates: "The argument
of Judge Douglas is about as thin as homeopathic
soup that was made by the boiling the shadow of
a pigeon that had starved to death."

In my personal experience, the people most in
favor of a radical "green" lifestyle are usually well-

to-do people with the best of intentions. They are often the same people who have their own cabin in the woods in Vermont, ski in Colorado in the winter, spend winters in Florida or on a bareboat cruise in the Caribbean, own a new Toyota Prius, and travel often in Europe. They are people who read and heap praise on "serious" books like those of Jared Diamond. People like the writer Stephanie Mills, who has a chapter in the Roger Rosenblatt consumer-bashing book *Consuming Desires: Consumption, Culture and the Pursuit of Happiness*. She writes that she bought thirty acres of land adjoining her own land because, "I didn't want to see the smoke from my neighbor's cabin."

In due obeisance to the new religion, some of these green enthusiasts hasten to confess their sins and get indulgences for their energy profligacy and large "carbon footprints" by buying carbon credits. The most common "credits" are supporting the planting of trees in some developing country—similar to the way rich people in the 19th century supported missionar-ies to Africa to atone for their greed.

Al Gore, who came within a whisker of being president of the United States, is a good example. Recently he bought a second home on

the Pacific coast.[90] It is apparently quite luxurious
with six fireplaces, a spa and swimming pool, five
bedrooms, nine bathrooms, fountains and an
ocean view. This second home adds to his villa
with spa and swimming pool in Tennessee. And
to "pay for it," he no doubt bought more carbon
credits.

I know. I know. It is all too easy to make fun of
the elite rich and upper-middle class (rarely the
middle class or poor) who, like puritanical priests
and ministers, often fail to practice what they
preach. But what about the real issues? Are we
threatened by resource depletion? Is the world
dangerously overpopulated? And what about
pollution? Al Gore claims we "face an unimaginable calamity requiring large-scale, preventive
measures to protect human civilization as we
know it." Jared Diamond claims western
civilization is collapsing due to our environmental
sins.

Are these claims true? Is climate change the
world's most serious problem? Does globalization
of the world's economies threaten disaster for
the world's living environment? Does growing the
economy mean shrinking the ecosystem? Is Jared
Diamond right when he predicts the western

---

[90] "Al Gore's New $8.875 Million Montecito Villa." *The Huffington Post*,
May 17, 2010. <http://www.huffingtonpost.com/2010/05/17/photos-
al-goree-new-8875_n_579286.html#s91230&title=undefined> Last
accessed 02/17/2011

world will crash and fail like so many civilizations before because it ignores environmental realities?

Finally, the core subject of this book, is the future of free-market liberal democracy seriously constrained, if not doomed, by environmental realities?

Chapter 16

Environmental and Globalization Challenges

THE MOST POPULAR NEW secular religion in the Western world today is Radical Environmentalism. One of America's leading environmental historians, William Cronon at the University of Wisconsin–Madison, agrees that it is indeed a new religion that offers "a complex series of moral imperatives for ethical action, and judges human conduct accordingly." And I would add that, like communists of old, many of its communicants abandon common sense, claim scientific certitude, and brook no deviation "in the slightest degree"[91] from its imperatives.

Radical Environmentalists see excessive consumption as a mortal sin against the goddess earth. One of their mottoes is "A growing economy means a shrinking ecosystem." They view climate change much the same way Christians once viewed tampering with God's creation. Deuteronomy says this kind of abomination against the almighty will "bring infections, plague and war. He will blight your crops, covering them with mildew. All these devastations shall pursue you until you perish."

Al Gore says "global warming will bring unimaginable catastrophe," and goes on like Deuteronomy to detail the devastations it will bring. Jared Diamond claimed in a Sierra Club interview that, "The United States has long thought of itself as the land of infinite plenty, and historically we did have abundant resources. But now we are gradually exhausting our fisheries, our topsoil, our water. On top of that, we're coming to the end of world resources."

Instead of the traditional Ten Commandments, Radical Environmentalists have their own version. Their versions include commands to Save Energy, Save Water, Recycle, Refrain from Excessive Consumption, Save

---

[91] See Vladimir Lenin. "To belittle the socialist ideology in any way," wrote Lenin, "to turn aside from it in the slightest degree *means to* strengthen bourgeois ideology."

Species, Reduce your Carbon Footprint, Eat Organic, Travel Less, Respect Wilderness and above all, Put Earth First.[92]

It has its own version of communion wafers—organic foods grown within 100 miles of your home. It has its own version of confession and indulgences—if you must travel and use resources and energy, you should confess and buy carbon credits. The most popular penances are supporting the planting of trees in developing countries, much like rich people in the robber baron era of the 19th century supported missionaries in Africa.

The movement also has its version of Noah's Ark. Preserve all species no matter how small, no matter how insignificant, or even how harmful to man. One of the high priests of the new religion, the pediatrician Dr. Helen Caldecott, in an interview an environmental activist friend gave me, claimed, "Bacteria have as much right to live as we do."

It has its own version of Easter, Earth Day. It does not have as yet a single bible, but Rachel Carson's 1962 book *Silent Spring* comes close. Close seconds are Jared Diamond's *Guns, Germs, and Steel: The Fates of Human Societies* and *Collapse: How Societies Choose to Fail or Succeed.*

Green missionaries are often noted as much for their fall from grace as they are for their preaching. Sixty thousand delegates came to a 2002 United Nations World Summit on Sustainable Development convened in South Africa. According to chef Desmond Morgan, "money was no object" when it came to feeding this green multitude. Delegates dined on 5,000 oysters, 1,000 pounds of fresh lobster, 4,400 pounds of chicken breasts and filets mignons, 450 pounds of salmon, and more than 1,000 pounds of bacon and sauages. This Summit conference happened when quite a few million people in sub-Saharan Africa faced starvation.

One of the VIPs at the conference, Zambian President Levy Mwana-wasa, was understandably concerned over nearly three million of his citizens who were on the verge of starvation. But he rejected a gift of U.S.

---

[92] "Earth Day is the new Easter." Column by Robert H. Nelson, senior fellow with the *Independent Institute* in Oakland, CA., *Wisconsin State Journal*, Apr. 16, 2010, p. 12.

corn because some of it might be contaminated by genetic engineering, and he was worried that his people would be "poisoned."[93]

Former Vice-President Al Gore is one of the most famous and outspoken advocates of green lifestyles. In his book *Earth in the Balance: Ecology and the Human Spirit,* he argues that Western Civilization itself has been on a destructive track for much of the past two centuries. Science and its handmaiden technology have combined with capitalism to rape our environment, wasting resources and causing populations to explode. To be fair, Gore is approving and enthusiastically promoting some new technologies—"green" ones like solar cells, windmills, etc.—that he sees as possible technological fixes for our energy, environmental and climate problems. (In fact, he has heavy personal investments in companies that research and produce some of these technologies.)

Surely everyone is in favor of green living and sustainable development, right? Well, no. Not all of us. Some of us are against fouling our nest with harmful pollution, yes. Some of us are for common sense and frugality, yes. Some of us are for birth control and stabilizing populations, yes. But some of us are also for vigorous economic development on a global scale, and for an increase in energy production, and an increase in freedom for ourselves and for all others in this fast-developing and increasingly prosperous world. And some of us think we can have all of these things, not by locking away our natural resources, cutting back on populations, cutting back on energy use, recycling plastic cups and using paper bags instead of plastic ones. We can have all of these things by expanding free-market liberal democracy.

There are at least two sides to the green sustainable movement. One, let's call it the "light green" side, promotes efficiency, doing more with less. This side is progressive. The other, call it the "dark green" side, promotes the opposite, doing less with more. This side is regressive.

The never-ending search for greater efficiency, doing more with less, is the story of the industrial revolution and free-market capitalism. It has led

---

[93] "Food Crisis in Zambia." PBS Newshour, Posted 12/18/02.
<http://www.pbs.org/newshour/extra/features/july-dec02/zambia.html>

us to our incredible leap forward in wealth and prosperity the past two hundred years. It continues today with ever-increasing power to improve our world. Insofar as the green movement promotes more efficient ways to heat our homes, light our streets, produce our energy, manufacture our goods and deliver services we want and need, it is a strong positive.

The dark green side, however, is not progressive. Dark green proposes to cut back on goods and services and to spend more to get less. It advises us to use fewer natural resources, have fewer children, not waste wealth on new gadgets and frivolous luxuries. It says we should live in smaller houses, abandon the suburbs for denser life in the central city, restrict the import of food and goods from other countries and buy food only from local farmers and manufacturers, use public transportation more and private vehicles less. It counsels us to travel less, restrict trade, discourage competition, encourage government regulation, put moratoriums on oil exploration, mining ventures, nuclear power construction and genetic crop use. It suggests increases in government control, command-economy planning and in general counsels us to be satisfied with a lower standard of living so that the rest of the world can have more resources.

Green activists make common cause with more traditional left-wing activists resisting globalization and bemoaning the materialistic bent of free-market capitalism. In the early and mid 20th century the communist challenge was alive and expanding year by year. The communists claimed to be leading the way to a future where poverty would be eliminated and abundance, peace and universal happiness would come with the death of private property, free trade and the bourgeois world of free-market liberal democracy.

It never worked out that way. Their way collapsed. Our way succeeded. Ironically, today we have Russian and Chinese officials lecturing us on the virtues of private property and suggesting better ways to promote capitalist banking and industry![94]

---

[94] "Chinese officials lecture Paulson." Greg Dyer, *Financial Times*, Dec. 5, 2008. <http://www.ft.com/cms/s/0/44f2eca4-c26d-11dd-a350-000077b07658.html#axzz1EFkKcxCj>

Communists promised worldwide prosperity once the worldwide revolution succeeded. The communist solution won power but failed to bring prosperity. Miserably. The capitalist one has brought worldwide prosperity. Spectacularly. Yet today we find progressive-leftists in Western countries of Europe and North America making common cause with green-obsessed environmentalists to complain now that our worldwide abundance is a curse!

As an anonymous writer for the *New Yorker's* "Talk of the Town" column wrote in 1992, "Almost everyone now agrees that if people in the South tried to live the way we do in the North, the results would be ecological disaster."[95]

Marx hated capitalism because it denied affluence to the masses. The new prophets of sustainable development hate capitalism because it has brought affluence to the masses.

As Kurt Vonnegut might say, "So it goes."

IN 1969 A WORLD-FAMOUS biologist, Paul Ehrlich, and a world-famous physicist, John Holdren (currently the science advisor to the president of the United States), invented a special equation in honor of the first Earth Day. Their equation was simple. I=PAT. "I" stood for environmental Impact. "P" stood for Population. "A" stood for Affluence. "T" stood for Technology.[96] As people get more numerous, get wealthier and use more technology, the earth suffers. The moral of the equation is that so far as the earth goes, it would be better to have fewer people, less wealth and less technology. In other words, a growing economy means a shrinking ecosystem.

The clear implication was also that traditional free-market capitalism has to go, presumably to be replaced by a more humane form of socialism that would work to reduce populations, decrease wealth, and curb, regulate and control new technologies to make sure they are "green" and "sustainable."

---

[95] *The New Yorker*, June 29, 1992, p. 26.
[96] See " Population Growth and Migration," on the web site of Gaia Watch of the UK: <http://www.population-growth-migration.info/essays/IPAT.html>

To put it in another way, they are recommending we go back to a new version of zero-sum economy—or worse. If you follow their drift to a logical extreme, they are recommending we consider a pre-agricultural hunting/gathering lifestyle! At least that seems to be the drift of one of the most renowned environmental leaders, Bill McKibben, in his books *The End of Nature* and his latest one, *Eaarth* (not a misprint).

In 1980, a scholarly study commissioned by President Jimmy Carter, *The Global 2000 Report to the President*, echoed the same moral by concluding that, "if present trends continue, the world in 2000 will be more crowded, more polluted, less stable ecologically and more vulnerable to disruption than the world we live in now. Serious stresses involving population, resources, and environment are clearly visible ahead. Despite greater material output, the world's people will be poorer in many ways than they are today."

In 2007, an international panel of scientists, The Intergovernmental Panel on Climate Change (IPCC) warned that increasing levels of carbon dioxide in the atmosphere would bring on global climate change. This, they claimed, would lead to worldwide catastrophes in the 21st century as sea levels rose, rain patterns changed and climate-brought-on diseases became pandemic. The recommendations that many Radical Environmentalists took from this report were that we needed to rapidly and drastically cut back on energy use, reduce populations, conserve resources and move to a simpler, greener lifestyle.

These claims and predictions have been blessed with such wide media publicity (though not with such wide actual acceptance in practice) that many people today do not know that there is substantial disagreement about all of them within the scientific world. In fact, according to many experts, most of these claims and predictions are exaggerated, many are seriously misleading and others are simply false. As that comic song from the Gershwin opera *Porgy and Bess* goes, "It ain't necessarily so."

Let's take the big issues one at a time. (1) Resources. (2) Population. (3) Pollution and Climate Change …

Julian Simon, Paul Ehrlich, and Bjørn Lomborg

One of the experts we interviewed for some of
our video programs, was the late economist from
the University of Maryland, Julian Simon. His
lifetime work on resources and population issues
was often not well received in establishment
circles. A world-famous biologist at the Smithson-
ian Institute, Thomas Lovejoy, bristled when I
brought up his name at an interview. Lovejoy got
noticeably red in the face and snapped, "Criticisms
from somebody like Julian Simon are utterly trivial.
I mean the man does not understand biology at
all. He is the guy who says you can do it with
mirrors."

On the other hand, Simon had supporters at
prestigious places like the independent nonprofit
liberal institute *Resources for the Future*. And since
his death in 2001 he has gained increasing
credibility.

Bjørn Lomborg, a Danish statistician, environmentalist, "man of the left," and former Greenpeace
supporter, had a low opinion of Simon's work
when he first heard of it in a visit to California. He
had read that Simon claimed the world was better
off environmentally today than ever before. Simon
also claimed that resources were more plentiful,
and were likely to become even more plentiful in
coming decades. He claimed that pollution was
decreasing, and would likely decrease still more in

coming decades. And he claimed that populations were stabilizing, and in many places would decline in coming decades.

Lomborg didn't believe it. He thought Simon must be a crank. Or crazy.

But he did think it would be an interesting challenge for himself and his students to check up on Simon's arguments, and the data he used to support them. His expectation was that the check-up would show how misled and unscientific Julian Simon was. After careful study, he and his students in Denmark were stunned. They found that most of the time Simon was quite accurate. His well-documented data did show conclusively that the world is not running out of resources, the world is not becoming more polluted and the world is not overpopulated.

Lomborg published his own findings in a meticulously documented book, *The Skeptical Environmentalist: Measuring the Real State of the Earth.*

That isn't the end of the story. Furious environmentalists demanded a retraction. In an effort to refute the book's claims, they brought a complaint about Lomborg to The Danish Committee on Scientific Dishonesty (DCSD). The DCSD sided with the environmentalists, proclaiming in good bureaucratic prose, "Objectively speaking, the publication of the work under consideration is

deemed to fall within the concept of scientific
dishonesty."[97]

A few months later, Lomborg and his book were
vindicated by a higher-level Danish government
commission, The Ministry of Science, Technology
and Innovation. Among a long list of criticisms, the
ministry reported that, "the DCSD has not
documented where [Dr. Lomborg] has allegedly
been biased in his choice of data and in his
argumentation, and ... the ruling is completely
void of argumentation for why the DCSD finds
that the complainants are right in their criticisms of
his working methods. It is not sufficient that the
criticisms of a researchers' working methods exist;
the DCSD must consider the criticisms and take a
position on whether or not the criticisms are
justified, and why."[98]

As Ronald Bailey argued in a review of Lomborg's
book in *Reason Online*, "Only economic growth
will allow, for example, the 800 million people
who are still malnourished to get the food they
need. But will they get it? Not if the anti-
Westerners win out. As *The Skeptical Environmentalist* makes clear, those who hate modern
industrialized societies, whether they are Islamic
radicals or radical environmentalists, threaten the

---

[97] See reviews of the book and the controversy
<http://www.amazon.com/Skeptical-Environmentalist-Measuring-
State-World/dp/0521010683>
[98] See report in *The Economist*, Dec. 20, 2003. P. 115.

hopes of the poor and imperil the natural world as well." [99]

---

[99] *Reason Online*, Oct. 2, 2001.
<http://reason.com/archives/2001/10/02/dire-predictions>

<u>Chapter 17</u>

Resources

NATURAL RESOURCES ARE NECESSARY for wealth, but not sufficient. In fact, while natural resources in the narrow sense are necessary, in the long run they are for the most part irrelevant when it comes to wealth. Many of the richest countries in the world, for instance—Japan, the Netherlands, Belgium, Switzerland, Taiwan—have few natural resources. Many of the poorest countries in the world—Nigeria, North Korea, Burma, Pakistan, Afghanistan, the Congo, Ecuador, Russia—have rich natural resources. What, then, is the connection between natural resources and wealth?

Many people today ("many people" does not include most scientists and economists) still think that resources and wealth are a more-or-less fixed quantity. In other words, the world's natural resources and accompanying wealth are like a large pie. If I get a bigger piece, you will have to be satisfied with a smaller piece. If a few get rich, the majority will have to be poor. If we in the United States use too many resources, others in the rest of the world will have to do with fewer. This is called a zero-sum world.

In past agricultural ages—before the scientific and industrial revolutions a few hundred years ago—this view made sense. Wealth then was usually measured in three all-important natural resources—land, gold and the muscle and brainpower supplied by slaves, serfs or peasants.

Countless wars were fought over land, gold and slaves because the only way one group could get wealthier was to steal from another group. Countries often resorted to imperialistic expansions to gain more "living space," more resources, more power. Many still do. They believe that it still is a zero-sum world.

But it is not.

THE DEATH OF ZERO-SUM economies came a few hundred years ago, when humans learned that natural resources and wealth are *not* the same thing. Natural resources are usually, in fact, the least important ingredients of the wealth pie. Coal and oil, for instance, are natural resources, but it is energy that is wealth. Soil and sun are natural resources, but it is food and lumber that are wealth. Sand and metal ores are natural resources, but it is reinforced concrete, powerful machines and fast computers that are wealth. Newborn human beings are natural resources, but it is mature creative muscles and minds that are wealth.

In other words, it is what you make of nature, the contributions of the creative human muscle and mind, which are the most important ingredients of what we call wealth. That contribution is limited only by the number and creativity of the muscles and the minds. From this point of view, an expanding population is not a curse, but a blessing. As Julian Simon pointed out in his classic book *The Ultimate Resource*, "the source of improvements in productivity is the human mind, and a human mind is seldom found unaccompanied by the human body." Of course that is only so if the new humans are educated and creative, and are then free to work, invent and contribute.

Energy, for instance, can be obtained from natural resources like coal and oil. But it can also be obtained in other ways. Like nuclear fuels, solar panels, windmills, fusion reactions, geothermal heat, ocean waves, biomass, natural gas from shale, and who knows what new ways we may discover tomorrow.

Food and lumber can be obtained from natural resources like crop plants, farmed animals and tree plantations, but they can also be multiplied almost indefinitely by improved agricultural, animal husbandry and forestry practices. Improvements like using better fertilizer, better seeds, better irrigation, genetically engineering crop plants, animals and trees, and who knows what new technology we may come up with tomorrow. Some think that tomorrow we may even be able to produce food and lumber in factories once we learn the secrets of nature's own photosynthetic and stem cell technology.

When that day comes, we can use the same raw materials—water, carbon dioxide and a few common minerals—that crops and trees use today. These simple basic chemicals would be the only natural resources needed to produce all the food and lumber a growing world population will need. In 2010, J. Craig Venter and his associates took a giant step in that direction when they created the first living thing, a bacterium, from scratch.[100] That is, starting with simple common chemicals like water, carbon dioxide and minerals.

Reinforced concrete, machines and computers are a little different. The natural resources needed here are so widely available that they offer no limiting factors in the creation of wealth. We are not likely to ever run out of the principal ones, sand and ocean water. One glass of seawater, for example, has significant enough quantities of most metallic and non-metallic atoms that new technology is the only limiting factor in harvesting them.[101]

In computers the value resides in the knowledge that goes into their construction. The advancement of that knowledge is unlimited, so long as you have free markets and free trade in a rational-thinking globalized world, where you can produce computers without limit, using educated minds and skilled hands.

The wealth of the world today, in other words, is no longer like a big pie where a few fat cats get the big pieces, leaving the crumbs to the poor. Instead, the pie is being multiplied over and over again every hour, every day, every month, every year. Potentially all can have a big piece.

THIS NEW VIEW OF RESOURCES and wealth did not take root in most people's minds, however, until quite recently. Unfortunately it is still not widely accepted by many people, including political and intellectual leaders. New "ecological economics" and "dark green" activism are

---

[100]See TED web site: video speech, "Craig Venter unveils 'synthetic life'"
<http://www.ted.com/talks/craig_venter_unveils_synthetic_life.html>
[101] See Water Encyclopedia web site "Mineral Resources from the Ocean:":
<http://www.waterencyclopedia.com/Mi-Oc/Mineral-Resources-from-the-Ocean.html>

promoting a return to a kind of zero-sum thinking, a world where every luxury we indulge in is at the expense of someone else's poverty.

One hundred sixty years ago the population of the United States was less than thirty-one million people. The average life expectancy was forty-three years. There was a telegraph system but no one had a telephone. The average wage was less than 15 cents an hour. Even the very rich had no indoor plumbing, refrigeration, air conditioning, electricity or anesthetics. There were railroads, but less than ten miles of paved roads in all the United States. There were no cell phones, television sets, radios, computers, airplanes or automobiles. As for education, less than one percent of the people graduated from high school, and ninety-nine percent of all doctors had no college education. One out of eight of the U.S. population was enslaved. Most people, except perhaps the 600,000 men who died in the Civil War to abolish slavery, rarely traveled more than a few miles from where they were born. And forests covered about a third of the U.S. and Canada.

Today the U.S. population is ten times as great—over 300 million. Life expectancy in the U.S. (and in most of the industrialized world) is more than seventy-nine years. There are over 250 million automobiles and 2.6 million miles of paved roads in the U.S. Over 85% of the people in the U.S. have graduated from high school and over 25% from college. Nearly everyone has a telephone, a TV set (often more than one), indoor plumbing, refrigeration, air conditioning, electricity and an automobile (often more than one). Drugs cure many diseases that were crippling or fatal to millions of people in former times. Anesthetics make operations possible, painless and usually successful. Most young people today have a cell phone and a computer. Most people in the U.S. and Canada ride regularly in automobiles, trains and airplanes for thousands of miles in their lifetimes. And forests cover about a third of the U.S. and Canada.[102]

---

[102] See: "Forest Resources of the United States:"
<http://www.nationalatlas.gov/articles/biology/a_forest.html>

If resources and wealth were so limited, like a big pie, where did all this new wealth come from? How did three times as many people get hundreds of times wealthier than their poor great-grandparents?

Still other statistics show the resource trend in a different way, that of efficiency, doing more with less, the "light green" way—more wealth and more quality for less work.

Products that only the wealthy could afford in the past are now cheap enough for almost everyone. A Ford Model T automobile in 1920 cost more than 2.25 years worth of factory wages. A Ford Taurus today (quite a bit superior to the Model T) costs just eight month's factory wages. A flickering color television in 1954 cost 562 hours of factory wages. A modern flat-screen TV today costs 23 hours. Air travel of 1000 miles cost 221 hours in 1919. Today it costs 11. Computing power as measured in millions of instructions a second cost 67 hours in 1984. The same computing power today costs 20 minutes of factory wages.[103]

All of these sharp contrasts, to a greater or lesser extent, hold for just about any country in the world, including the two most populous countries, India and China. People all over the world are hundreds of times wealthier, use hundreds of times more natural resources and yes, produce hundreds of times more waste than a much smaller population did a hundred and fifty years ago.

If resources and wealth are both so limited (as many green enthusiasts claim), where did all the resources come from that made this new wealth? If wealth was like a big piece of pie, how come everyone has a bigger piece now (and a much safer and more flavorful one) than his or her great-great-grandparents living in a much simpler world, with a much smaller population, did a hundred and sixty years ago?

The answer to all of these questions is simple. Natural resources may be limited, but wealth is not. Neither wealth nor natural resources are at all like a fixed pie. We do have to use resources to create wealth. But the earth (and the universe!) has far more natural resources than we can even

---

[103] Comparing costs over past years is complicated. Here is a reference that is reasonable and helpful: <http://www.measuringworth.com/uscompare/>

dream of now. The more we use, the more new ones we discover, the more we invent better ways to use the ones we find, and the more wealth we create. Finally, the more wealth we create, the more wealth our children can use to continue the wealth creation process.

Here is still another example from more recent history to illustrate the point. Many experts and many citizens speculated in the mid 20th century that their children would never be able to afford a house and life style equal to their own. In 1958 the renowned economist John Kenneth Galbraith agreed with this prognosis in his popular books *The Affluent Society* and *The New Industrial State*. He claimed that American standards of living had gone about as far as they could go, and that children of his age would never have a lifestyle that equaled his own. It was time, he claimed, to devote more resources and wealth to social goods and public investment.

He was mistaken. As Gregg Easterbrook points out in his new book *Sonic Boom: Globalization at Mach Speed,* "Fifty years later, inflation-adjusted per capita income is three times what it was when Galbraith said incomes had peaked; the average 1,100-square-foot American house of the 1952 has become a 2,400-square-foot house; the average one-car family has become a three-car family; by many other measures, living standards are much higher than when Galbraith said they had peaked."[104]

Yet today prominent scholars like the late Tony Judt, in an article in a 2010 *New York Book Review,* claimed again that, "Something is profoundly wrong about the way we live today." He went on in the article to illustrate this claim: "In contrast to their parents and grandparents, children today in the UK as in the US have very little expectation of improving upon the condition into which they were born."[105]

I won't live another fifty years to collect, but I am willing to wager that Judt will turn out to be as mistaken as Galbraith was fifty years ago.

---

[104] *Sonic Boom: Globalization at Mach Speed* by Gregg Easterbrook, p. 163-164.
[105] "Ill Fares the Land," by Tony Judt in the *New York Review of Books*, Apr. 29, 2010, pp. 17-19.

The point today is we should be proud, not ashamed, that we in the US use 30% of the world's resources because in the process we create more than 30% of the world's wealth! The truth is that the only limit to resources and to wealth is the ultimate natural resource—the creativity of human muscles and minds.

Here is how it works.

As an important natural resource begins to become scarce, it also becomes more expensive. This presents a challenge. Some people take up that challenge looking to make a profit. They begin searching for alternatives. Some people fail. But the failures are personal and society as a whole does not suffer. Some people succeed, make big profits—and their success benefits all.

That is exactly what happened when whale oil began to run out in the middle of the 19th century. People found petroleum in the ground that could do the same job as whale oil and do it more cheaply. More important, humans soon found that petroleum could not only illuminate our lamps and oil our sewing machines—it could power newly invented automobiles and trains and airplanes and bulldozers and tractors and ocean liners. It (along with other fossil fuels like coal and natural gas) could provide the raw material for newly invented materials like plastics and medicines and fertilizers and pesticides and paints and cosmetics. It could replace wood. It could heat homes and offices and schools. It could create electricity and transform agricultural and industrial production. It could help create a world where everyone could get an education. It could be a key link in creating a new world where everyone could potentially be a winner!

You say yes, ok, but we will eventually run out of oil and natural gas and then we will be in a pickle.

First of all, experts have been predicting the world will run out of oil ever since it was first discovered. In 1908 the U.S. Bureau of Mines predicted a total future world supply of oil would be 22.5 billion barrels. (We have used three times that much since 1908 and have at least three times that much in known reserves today.) In 1939 officials predicted the

U.S. oil supplies could last only another thirteen years. In 1979 President Jimmy Carter declared the imminent oil shortage a national crisis of historic dimensions. Like religious cults that have predicted over and over again that the world will end in the near future, that future keeps getting further and further away.

Today new discoveries and new technologies to extract oil and natural gas from the earth have convinced many experts that the U.S. and Canada alone have enough oil and gas under their soil and continental shelf to power the entire world for the next hundred years!

But let's say these optimistic experts are wrong and we do begin to run out of oil. Or, more likely, considerations of possible climate change from burning too much oil (or coal or gas) put a severe restraint on its use. What then?

As oil becomes more expensive and scarce (or laws prohibit its continued use in order to prevent climate change and/or wean us from buying foreign oil), clever people will take up the challenge, find profits in developing new sources of energy, like nuclear power, solar power, natural gas, tidal power, geothermal power, fusion power, hydrogen power, windmill power, large increases in efficiency and who knows what. No one predicted computers, cell phones or satellites sixty years ago. When and if physicists solve the problems of nuclear fusion, that alone could lead to near unlimited energy.

Billions of galaxies are rapidly expanding, propelled by a mysterious form of "dark energy." When and if physicists discover this fourth basic force of the universe in new experiments in Switzerland with the recently completed Large Hadron Collider (LHC) this, too, may lead to energy possibilities no one can predict today.

Whatever, whenever and wherever—these new sources of energy will replace petroleum just as petroleum replaced whale oil.

The same story could be told about other important natural resources. Take wood. True, most of the original forests in the U.S. and Canada have disappeared. When European settlers first arrived on this continent, about half of it was forested. In the 18th and 19th centuries farmers and lumber companies cut down large sections of this natural resource and used the wood to heat homes, to cook food, to fence farms, to make paper, and to build houses, barns, mills and factories.

In the 20th century, however, forests in U.S. and Canada have, for the most part, come back. So much so that today forests cover about one third of the continent and every year they are increasing, not decreasing, in acreage. How does that happen? People plant more trees than they cut down. Nature, too, plants more trees after we cut them down. Trees are a renewable resource. Contrary to what many think, despite the increased demand for wood and paper worldwide in the 21st century, forests in the U.S. and Canada, and in China, India and most other countries, are growing year by year in both quantity and quality. (One exception is tropical rain forests in South America and Southeast Asia. Here the destruction has slowed but not enough yet to reach a steady state where new growth equals harvest, as it has in most other regions.)

Take food. Farms produced enough food for 88 million people in the U.S. in 1908. Using only five percent more farmland, farmers in this country produced more than enough food for 300 million people in the U.S. in 2008 and there was enough left over to help feed many millions of people in India, China, southeast Asia and Latin America.[106] How did they do it?

People invented better ways to farm. They found better ways to select, to breed, and then to genetically modify corn and wheat and soy beans; better ways to keep crops from being eaten by insects and molds. They used tractors instead of horses; etc., etc. A farm family in 1800 could produce just enough food to feed itself and half a person more. By 1940 a farm family could produce enough food to supply 10.7 people more. The average farm family in the U.S. today can feed itself and 128 people more.[107] Unless we follow the advice of green advocates and return to "organic" small farms, the prospect for food abundance worldwide (contrary to doomsters all the way back to Thomas Malthus) is virtually

---

[106] See: <http://www.measuringworth.com/uscompare/>
[107] See: < http://www.agclassroom.org/gan/timeline/farm_tech.htm>

unlimited. And we haven't even considered the possibility of discovering how photosynthesis works. This discovery could lead to factory production of real food and real fiber, and the eventual conversion of much farmland back to a wilderness state!

We gave used immense amounts of iron, copper, aluminum, tin, lead, silver, gold and other metals. Yet today all of these metals are cheaper (that is, in real practical terms, more plentiful) then they were a hundred years ago! How did this happen? People found better ways of extracting metals from their earth-bound ores. People found new sources for ores. People found ways of using metals more efficiently. People found better ways of recycling metals. People found substitutes for many metals.

Another dramatic example of efficiency in the use of resources is computer power. Thomas J. Watson, then Chairman of the Board of IBM, in 1943 was quoted, "I think there is a world market for maybe five computers." One of the first general-purpose computers was ENIAC, completed at the University of Pennsylvania in 1946. It weighed over thirty tons and needed as much electricity as a large apartment building. ENIAC had less processing power than an iPhone does today!

LET'S NOT GO TOO FAR too fast, however. There are at least two exceptions to this good news story about resources—wilderness conservation and species preservation.[108] New forests are not the same as old forests. A species lost cannot be regained. (Although here, new work in genetics may indeed enable us to bring back some extinct species!) Theodore Roosevelt recognized this over a hundred years ago when he pioneered in creating our first national parks and wildlife reserves. Today all over the world, people are carrying forward this work.

Here again, however, the moral is not to denounce wealth, or populations or technology. We need to welcome technology, encourage wealth creation, and improve the free-market economic systems that have brought such technology and wealth to the world. This intelligent use of

---

[108] For a contemporary conservative view that follows the lead of Theodore Roosevelt, see *Hard Green. Saving the Environment from the Environmentalists* by Peter Huber.

technology and free markets to create wealth is the very thing that will make it possible to preserve more wildernesses and prevent more species extinctions. Conversely, the more we turn away from technology and free markets as some green advocates advise, the more farmland we will need to feed the world's growing populations and the less wilderness we will have to preserve species.

A Chinese proverb says: "A peasant must stand for a long time on a hillside with his mouth open before a roast duck flies in." Natural resources are like that. To those who stand pat and wait, resources are few and far between and if we use them up too fast, there will be less for those who come after. But to those who search and work creatively, resources (and wealth) are unlimited.

"The world is so bad off and overpopulated"

I have two children, both boys. From my teaching days I remember a young woman who had just graduated from my high school telling me that she was not sure she wanted to have any children. When I asked "Why not?" she answered, "Oh, the world is so bad off and so overpopulated and polluted already, why add more children and their pollution to the mess."

This view that the world is so overpopulated already that more children would be a burden, not a blessing, gets support from many academics. A justifiably renowned professor of biology at the University of Wisconsin–Madison, Dr. Hugh H. Iltis, is one such person. Dr. Iltis made his reputation by discovering important strains of corn in Mexico that apparently were the origin of modern corn in the U.S. and the world. He often vents his opinions about issues like population and politics. In 1982 he wrote a letter to the local Madison newspaper complaining that the current problems that countries like Poland and Cuba were having with their agriculture were not the fault of socialism, but rather that the countries were overpopulated. Here was my reply.[109]

> Professor Hugh H. Iltis has done some outstanding scientific work in botany. When it comes to public affairs, however,

---

[109] *The Capital Times*, Madison, WI, Jan. 28, 1982.

his pronouncements have more in common with sorcery than with science. For him, as for Paul Ehrlich and a good many other doomsayers, Satan is the population bomb, and heaven, presumably, would be the magical removal from earth of most of its people.

In his most recent diatribe Professor Iltis claims that the current trouble in Poland is plainly due to gross overpopulation. This was also his analysis of Cuba's problems a few months ago. Iltis cites the nearly 50 percent increase in Poland's population over the past 30 years and notes that today Poland is three times as dense with people as our own Wisconsin. Besides that, he says, Poland has "an unfavorable climate" for growing food.

Let's look at the facts. Poland has a density of 299 people per square mile. Wisconsin has 89 people per square mile. What does that prove? Lucky that Iltis does not live and teach in Rhode Island or Connecticut, with population densities of 765 and 521 people per square mile, respectively.

According to his reasoning, these states should have long since gone to long food lines and martial law. Or what about other countries, most of them with soil

and weather conditions no better than
Poland? West Germany has 640 people
per square mile; the United Kingdom 591;
the Netherlands, 886; Japan, 768; South
Korea, 971. Cuba has 227 people per
square mile.

Take the other extreme. Why is it that
the most severe food problems in past
decade have come in extremely sparsely
populated countries? In Chad, for instance, with a density of only 8 people
per square mile; in Mali, with 13; in Mauri-
tania, with 4; and in Niger, with 107.
Drought, yes, but if these countries had
been more "developed" with roads and
communications (all of which improve
greatly with population density) the famines could have been quickly alleviated.

Is it growth then? It is true that Poland's
population has grown by 30 percent in
the past 30 years. The world as a whole
has grown 75 percent in that same time.
What Professor Iltis doesn't tell you is
that world food production has grown
also—by more than 100 percent. In other
words, despite local setbacks, the average
world citizen is over 30% better fed today than 30 years ago.

The truth is, just about every index of
human health and progress you can

measure has shouted to us '"Good News!" over the past century. Life expectancy, infant mortality, food per capita, energy availability and price, mineral resource availability, and price—they have all shown encouraging leaps forward in both the developed and in the underdeveloped world.

These human successes do not in any way imply complacency for the future. But they do encourage hope. And they should make us suspicious of those who continually cry wolf. There are real problems. Solving them is not as simple as Professor Iltis would have us believe.

This exchange was in 1982. A few decades later Jane and I travelled to Poland, and after that, to Cuba. In Poland, now a free-market democracy, food production and population had grown dramatically, as had freedom. Food was plentiful, good and cheap. In Cuba, still rigidly communist, population had also grown (though not as much), but freedom had not. Food there was scarce, not so good and expensive.

Chapter 18

Populations

WITH INTERESTING TWISTS, what we just pointed out about resources is true of populations.

The same biologist who helped coin the I=PAT equation, Paul Ehrlich (his specialty was insects), also wrote a best-selling book in 1968 called *The Population Bomb*. In the first sentence of the book he boldly predicted that, "In the 1970s ... hundreds of millions of people are going to starve to death in spite of any crash programs embarked upon now." India, he claimed, was a basket case. He recommended triage. When there is no hope, we have to simply abandon the effort, steel ourselves to the inevitable and watch people die.

In 1970 Ehrlich doubled down on his predictions and in an article in *Progressive Magazine*[110] predicted that sixty-five million people would die of starvation in the United States by 1990. His math was close. As it turned out, about sixty-five million people in the U.S. were on diets by then.

Just as we haven't run out of oil, metals or wood, so sixty-five million people in America did not die of starvation. The opposite happened. Even though yes, there are still hungry people in the world, many millions fewer are hungry today than when the population of the world was half or a quarter of what it is today. India can feed itself and it is exporting food in the 21st century! The most populous country in the world, China, is the same story.

In the 1970s Ehrlich's view was the popular one among both scientists and citizenry. Ehrlich himself was a frequent guest on Johnny Carson's *Tonight Show*. United Nations commissions in those days echoed the view that overpopulation was a serious problem, perhaps the most serious problem the world faced. The most common recommendation to avoid ecological disaster was then, and is now, to promote "sustainable

---

[110] "Eco-Catastrophe" in *Progressive Magazine*, Apr. 1970.

development." Proponents admit this may require draconian measures to control population and equally draconian ones to enforce conservation.

Howard Odum, one of the founders of modern ecological economics, told an interviewer, me, in 1992 that we needed to cut back the world's population from, "six billion to maybe one billion or thereabouts." He did qualify slightly when he added, "We don't need to do it right away, we have a few generations to do it."[111]

Amartya Sen, the Indian economist who won the Nobel Prize for Economics in 1998, described this view as, "The tendency to see in population growth an explanation for every calamity that afflicts poor people is now fairly well established in some circles, and the message that gets transmitted constantly is the opposite of the old picture postcard: 'Wish you weren't here.'"

The world population has increased from 4.5 billion in 1980 to over 7 billion today. We need to get numbers like that into perspective. A billion is a big number. On the one hand, you could point out that a billion seconds ago it was 1959. A billion minutes ago Jesus was alive. A billion hours ago our ancestors were living in the Stone Age. A billion days ago no one walked on the earth on two feet. Billion is a big number.

On the other hand, you could also point out that today all the people in the world, all six billion of us, could fit—albeit a bit uncomfortably, like at a rock concert or in Times Square on New Year's Eve—into the commercial office space in the United States, which is around 3.5 billion square feet. A recent issue of *National Geographic*[112] pointed out that we expect the world population to top seven billion in 2011. What if you threw a party and invited all seven billion people on earth to attend? A party where everyone needs room to dance would mean each partygoer would need about six square feet. A party like this would take up about 1,500 square miles and could be accommodated in the state of Rhode Island or in the emirate of Dubai. If you wanted to have all seven billion

---

[111] See *Populations on Earth*, a DVD production of Hawkhill Assoc. available on www.Hawkhill.com.
[112] *National Geographic*, January, 2011.

shoulder-to-shoulder you could squeeze them all into the city of Los Angeles. If you wanted them all to live in ranch houses they could fit into the state of Texas. Billion is not such a big number.

MOST SCIENTISTS TODAY WHO study population issues say that, at most, overpopulation is a minor issue as world issues go. Some places, as in Europe and Japan today we need to encourage population growth, not decline. As for developing economies of Asia, Africa and Latin America, the rate of population growth has radically slowed down.[113] As these countries become industrialized and richer, they will almost certainly follow Europe, Japan and North America in having low birth rates and close to or below zero population growth.

In a new book *The Next Hundred Million,* the author Joel Kotkin argues that "United States population is expected to expand dramatically in coming decades" and that is a good thing! Why? Because Europe's and China's populations will be in decline due mostly to their low birth rates. As a result they will be increasingly burdened by a surplus of old people (non-productive consumers) and a shortage of young people (productive workers). The United States, on the other hand, has a birth rate slightly higher than its death rate and, more important, can expect more immigration, especially of productive young people.

In addition, the United States has been from its beginning a magnet for attracting immigrants. Some worry today that some of the new immigrants are bringing poverty and crime, and taking jobs from native citizens. However that might be, there is no question that in the past we have been a nation built by immigrants. Today as well, the good news is that, on the whole, immigrants are contributing more than their share to our national prosperity and well-being. At the unskilled level, like the Irish and the Chinese in former times, they are filling some of the dirty jobs

---

[113] See "Population Estimates Fall as Poor Women Assert Control." *The New York Times,* March 10, 2002, p. 3. India's fertility rate, for example, fell from 2.1 per woman to 1.85.

many Americans don't want in basic industries like agriculture, food processing and manufacturing.

Equally important, at the highly skilled level, immigrants are contributing more and more to our productive professional and creative culture. Hospitals, corporations, government agencies and universities are short of doctors, nurses, engineers, chemists and scientists in all fields. These institutions are becoming more and more dependent on immigrants to fill vacancies, and in many cases to make the discoveries that contribute to our growing entrepreneurial world economy. Immigrants are also providing in many cases the business and government leadership our democracy demands. Google was founded by a Russian immigrant; Intel was co-founded by a Hungarian; Yahoo! by a Taiwanese; the last Governor of California was an immigrant; our former National Security Advisor, Secretary of State and Chairman of the Joint Chiefs of Staff had parents who were immigrants from Jamaica; the President of the United States had a father from Kenya. And so it goes.

Remember, too, the hundred or so European scientists who fled Europe before, during and after World War II and as immigrants led the surge in scientific and technological creativity that made the second half of the 20th century the most prosperous fifty years the country and world has ever seen.

How does it work, population growth and economic development?

When countries are poor, people have more children because children are needed as a work force, and as an insurance policy for old age. Also, most children die before they ever reach working and reproductive age. In England in 1600 half the children died before the age of six. In most agricultural and hunting/gathering villages, infanticide was common when too many children were born.

As industrialization and free-market economics have made countries richer, people have begun having fewer children—and taking better care of them. Most children today do not work in factories or on farms and do live to become adults. For example, in the United States in 1776 the average family had seven children. In 1876 the average family had a bit more than four children. In 2000 the average family had two children.

This same decline in average family numbers is happening all over the world. So long as free-market economics and democratic political systems continue to grow, creative human beings will continue to solve resource challenges to create more wealth, more health, lower birth rates and— believe it or not—more open space, more wild areas!

WAIT! WAIT! THAT'S GOING too far! How could that be? More people, more wild areas?

Well, look at New England today, and compare it to New England 150 years ago. In the 19th century, settlers cleared lumber from most of the hills and mountain valleys and farmed the marginal soils of much of New England. Where they couldn't raise decent crops, they grazed sheep on the denuded hillsides. Populations were lower, yes. But poverty was higher and pollution was more, not less.

Today farms in New England are many fewer (but much more productive), forests are more common and much of the land is open to wildlife and recreational activities for harried urban dwellers from eastern metropolises, where factories and service industries have created the wealthiest coastal region in the world. In New York, Boston, Baltimore, Philadelphia and Washington DC, populations are among the densest in the world, yet access to wilderness recreation is among the best in the world, and pollution is arguably at its lowest level in world history.

You don't agree with this last claim? Well, as the Democrat Al Smith said when he was running for president in 1928, "let's look at the record."

"it's great to be rich"

In the 1970s the late Stephen Schneider (one of the scientific leaders of the environmentalist movement) wrote a book, *The Genesis Strategy: Climate and Global Survival.* In it he predicted that catastrophic cooling was on the way and if we did not take drastic measures, the world would suffer unimaginable catastrophe in the near future. In one passage he suggested we might have to consider using nuclear energy to help melt Arctic glaciers.

A few years later he said that new data had come along to change his prediction. Now it was global warming that was the threat. Whatever the prediction, he did confess that he and his colleagues, "had to offer up scary scenarios, make simplified, dramatic statements, and make little mention of the doubts that we have."[114]

By 1992 he had suppressed any and all doubts and claimed that, "it is journalistically irresponsible to present both sides [of the global warming issue] as though it were a question of balance."[115]

Many followers of Schneider also do not have any doubts, or they suppress them if they do.

---

[114] Jonathan Schell, "Our Fragile Earth," *Discover Magazine*, Oct. 1989. *p.47.*
[115] See Ross Gelbspan, "Racing to an Environmental Precipice," *Boston Globe*, May 31, 1992.

"The debate is over. A threat of unimaginable proportions is likely within our lifetime ... there is no longer any doubt. Global warming is real, and it's scarier than anyone could have imagined."[116]

I was in one of the poorer provinces of China a few years ago, and came on a street festival where performers were no longer chanting Mao slogans about the evils of capitalism, but instead were singing in a chorus line, "It is great to be rich!"

And they were doing just that, getting rich. The half of the world that is still desperately poor wants just as desperately to be rich. And they are strongly moving in that direction. We can help them. But not by air-drying our laundry, leaving our cars home, and carpooling to work. That is kind of like the, "Think of the starving children in China" meme that my mother used to use to get me to eat my beans.

How then? By following the advice of people like Stewart Brand and Bucky Fuller and "doing more with less." By finding ways to keep increasing wealth in environmentally friendly ways.

Today, to increase the energy supply, there are three main choices—coal (along with other fossil fuels), greatly increased efficiency, or a combination of solar and nuclear power. As a former

---

[116] *Wisconsin State Journal,* Guest column by Jeremiah Donahue on the editorial page, Dec. 13, 2006.

director of Greenpeace recently noted, nuclear power[117] is the most practical, the most powerful, and the most environmentally friendly. The fossil fuel natural gas is a close second; especially valuable for the decades it will take to replace fossil fuel energy.

What is the best way to survive and prosper in an ever-changing environment, warmer or cooler? Vague admonitions to "stop war on our world" will not help. My Chinese friends had the better answer, "It is great to be rich."

---

[117] See "Global Warming and Nuclear Power" by Richard A. Meserve, *Science,* Jan. 23, 2004.

Chapter 19

Climate Change

THIRTY YEARS AGO IT IS TRUE that most experts claimed resource depletion and population growth were two extremely serious world problems—in fact the most serious problems the world faced. Today, however, the majority of experts (not necessarily the ones who get the most publicity) agree with the views stated in this book. Natural resources are always limited, but they are unlikely to ever "run out," and in any case they are the least important ingredients in wealth. We are always learning ever better ways to "do more with less," as Bucky Fuller used to advise. Population growth is no longer considered the crisis it once was. In some places it is a negative, and in other places a positive. In both Europe and North America we need to encourage growth of the population, not decline. In no place is it a determining factor in wealth (or poverty) creation.

And finally, the majority of experts on toxic waste issues (again not necessarily the ones who get the most publicity) also agree with the view in this book that toxic pollution is a serious problem in many developing countries, but at most it is a minor problem today in the U.S., Canada, Japan and western Europe.

Bruce Ames, for instance, is arguably the world's most internationally respected expert on toxic waste. He is the inventor of the Ames Test, the standard way to test for carcinogens and mutagens in the environment. He said in an interview that, "All of whatever I have been learning is telling me that pollution [in this country] is pretty much irrelevant to public health. A little problem here and there ... And the whole country seems to be thinking that pollution is very important."[118]

---

[118] See *Disease and Health*, a DVD program from Hawkhill Associates, available on Hawkhill.com. See also an interview in *Reason Magazine*, "Of Mice and Men," by Virginia Postrol, Nov. 1994: <http://reason.com/archives/1994/ 11/01/of-mice-and-men>

There are still many places on earth with serious pollution problems, of course, but environmentalists can take credit for having spearheaded movements in 20th-century North America and Western Europe that have made the air, water and earth cleaner and more healthful than they probably have ever been in human history. For the most part, current scare stories about this or that chemical in the air, water or soil are just that, scare stories. There comes a point when the cost to get rid of the last part per billion (or trillion!) of some potentially harmful chemical is far greater than any conceivable benefits.

THE MAJORITY OF EXPERTS today, however, *do* claim that there is one important exception. Potentially poisonous gases and particulates in the air are on the decrease and pose few health problems, but carbon dioxide in the air is on the increase. Because of this increase, possible climate change is considered a serious worldwide problem.

Here, too, as with resource and population issues of the past, doomsayers have received the most publicity and seem to be the most active and believable. If you read the newspapers and magazines and listen to television news shows, you might be pardoned for thinking it is the view of all reputable scientists.

Strangely though, despite the media publicity, recent polls in the U.S., Canada and Europe show that most ordinary people put possible climate change very low in their estimate of problems we face in the 21st century. When asked to rate the twenty most serious national problems, for instance, climate change (or global warming) almost always comes out last.[119] And when push comes to shove, most legislators put jobs and economic growth far above possible climate change.

---

[119] See Gallup Poll, March 2010, on: <http://www.gallup.com/poll/126716/environmental-issues-year-low-concern.aspx> See also the ranking done by the *Copenhagen Consensus Conference of 2008*. "The World's Biggest Problems" *Reason Magazine*, May 30, 2008. Go to: <http://reason.com/archives/2008/05/30/the-top-ten-solutions-to-the-w>

When it comes to possible climate change and what to do about it, the views in this book are admittedly in the minority. However, this minority includes a substantial number of world-class climatologists, meteorologists, economists and Nobel Prize winners in science.

First of all and worthy of note, the "scientists" often referred to in the media, the "overwhelming majority" that is, who believe climate change is the world's most important problem, are for the most part scientists whose specialty is not climate research. As Richard Lindzen, himself a world-class climatologist at Massachusetts Institute of Technology, points out "… the American Society of Agronomy, the American Society of Plant Biologists and the Natural Science Collections Alliance … have no expertise whatever in climate." Unfortunately they are only too typical of the "overwhelming" scientific opinion that news media refer to on this subject.

Note, too, that climatology itself is not a very large field of science specialization. Until the last quarter of the 20th century, it was a scientific backwater, considered too boring and unpromising for high-potential science students to specialize in. As late as the mid-1970s you would have had difficulty identifying a hundred scientists in the entire world whose research specialty was climate change. Even today, substantially fewer than a thousand scientists worldwide specialize in studying climate change. (Meteorologists, of course, due to the demands of television news, are a much larger group. And perhaps worthy of note, meteorologists today are more uncertain and not climate change activists.[120])

Climate change contrarians like Richard Lindzen, Freeman Dyson, Fred Singer, Roy Spencer and Bjorn Lømborg say that ordinary people may have a point.

---

[120] See the study by George Mason University, "A National Survey Of Television Meteorologists About Climate Change: Preliminary Findings," March 20, 2010. <http://www.climatechangecommunication.org/images/files/TV_Meteorologists_/ Survey_Findings_%28March_2010%29.pdf>

These contrarian climatologists and scientists point out that: (1) even though the climate may change—and probably will—it is not the "unimaginable calamity requiring large-scale, preventive measures to protect human civilization as we know it," and (2) when and if climate change does accelerate in the 21st century, humans will not only cope with it, they will probably end up richer, not poorer. Just as the decline in whale oil led to the discovery of petroleum, just as the explosion of population in the 19th century led the wealth of the 20th century, so the possible warming of the earth may lead to extraordinary progress in efficiency, new energy sources, new ways of controlling nature, new progress in agriculture world-wide, and dramatic progress in healthcare.

In my early days creating and promoting educational media products, I produced and sold a kit for teacher workshops called "Finding Ways to Be Human." One of the suggestions I put on what we called an *Idea Bank* card read: "All of the people of the world could gather in a square 20 miles on a side and be about as crowded as at a rock concert. Suppose they are here and you have ten minutes to teach them something. What will you teach them? Plan your lesson."

A similar task was given to eight of the world's most prominent economists, including four Nobel Prize winners. They met in Denmark a few years ago at the *Copenhagen Consensus*.[121] The economists were challenged to put together an imaginary budget of fifty billion dollars in ways that would be of most benefit to the world's people. They were presented with a list of ten global problems and asked to rank them in order and specify how much of the fifty billion each should receive. To the chagrin of climate change activists, climate change (global warming) came out last again. It would get the least money in other words. In their considered opinion, more than half the money should go to AIDS research and prevention. The number two priority would be a program to provide micronutrients such as iron, iodine and Vitamin A to the billions of people who need these nutrients and now suffer from stunted growth,

---

[121] See the web site of the *Copenhagen Consensus Center*.
<http://www.copenhagenconsensus.com / CCC%20Home%20Page.aspx>

lower IQ or blindness because they are not getting them. These and seven other programs, like malaria protection, clean water supplies, river blindness, etc. would all be, in their opinion, of greater potential benefit to more people in the world than wealth sacrificed now to prevent possible global climate change in the future.

Let's be more specific about the science and the speculations.

ALL INFORMED SCIENTISTS agree that carbon dioxide has been increasing in the atmosphere over the last century. And all agree that the increase has come from humans burning fossil fuels in much larger quantities since the industrial revolution began a century and a half ago. They also agree that there is an atmospheric phenomenon called the "greenhouse effect." Gases in the atmosphere like carbon dioxide, methane, and water vapor (the most important greenhouse gas by far) reflect infrared heat rays back to earth and make our planet a warmer place than it would be without these reflectors. Fortunately. If it weren't for these greenhouse gases, earth would be too cold for life of any kind.

Also noteworthy is that if it were not for carbon dioxide in the air, life as we know it could not exist at all, because plants could not grow. The raw materials for photosynthesis are water and carbon dioxide. So it is not true that carbon dioxide is a harmful pollutant gas. Just the opposite.

Clouds and water vapor are far more important causes of temperature variations on earth than is carbon dioxide, but their influence is mixed and not well understood. On the one hand, clouds cool the earth by reflecting solar rays back to space instead of letting them warm the earth. On the other hand, clouds warm the earth by reflecting infrared rays back to earth as the greenhouse gases do. As you can see, it is complicated and even expert climatologists disagree about many of the details. They do agree, however, that global warming today is real. The world has warmed in the last century, though only about one degree centigrade. Also the bulk of that warming came in the first half of the century when presumably there was less industrial emission of carbon dioxide.

Some climate scientists also point out that man-made carbon dioxide increases in the atmosphere do not necessarily mean that the increase in carbon dioxide has caused the warming, nor that the climate will get still warmer in the 21st century.

They point out that: (1) carbon dioxide is a very minor gas in the atmosphere (less than 0.04%) and of much less importance to the greenhouse effect than water vapor or cloud cover, for instance.

(2) Climate change has occurred throughout earth's history. Many times over the last few thousand years the earth has warmed and cooled. In medieval times Greenland was green, with a thriving agriculture and cattle culture. A few hundred years later there was a "little Ice Age" and people were ice skating on the Thames River in London. These warm and cold periods in the northern hemisphere may or may not have been true for the earth as a whole. The evidence is inconclusive. Some climatologists point out that evidence from ice core research has found that in past climate changes over many thousands of years, the carbon dioxide percentage in the atmosphere has increased *after* the temperature increased, not before. In other words, it has been presumably been an effect, not a cause, of climate change.

(3) Climate is affected by a very large number of variables making long-term predictions very unreliable even with the aid of modern computers.

(4) Detailed predictions about possible rain pattern shifts, sea level changes, disease vectors, destructive storms, etc. due to changing climates are even more unreliable. (A case in point: in the 1950s firms had a contract to build dams in central Africa, and they consulted with climatology experts as to how and when they could expect the largest floods to occur. Climatologists of the day consulted their climate statistics and predicted floods every fifty years on average. They built the dams and found that they had to cope with "fifty-year" floods for each of the following three years.[122] Sadly, another case in point is the magnitude 9.0

---

[122] For corroboration of this story and that "the middle of the 20th century the study of climate was a scientific backwater," see the footnote on: <http://www.aip.org/history /exhibits/climate/climogy.htm#N_28_>

earthquake that is devastating northern Japan as this is being written. You would have to go back over a thousand years to find an earthquake of this magnitude.

Richard Lindzen, the MIT climatology contrarian who was a member of the UN Intergovernmental Panel on Climate Change (IPCC), points out that recent pronouncements of climate change scientists do not add confidence to their predictions of unimaginable catastrophe from climate change. "They then throw in a very peculiar statement (referring to warming)," writes Lindzen, "almost in passing: 'Uncertainties in the future rate of this rise, stemming largely from the 'feedback' effect on water vapour and clouds, are topics of current research.' Who would guess, from this statement, that the feedback effects are the crucial question?"[123]

In other words, they are assuming, without any evidence, that the feedbacks will all be in the direction of more warming. If the atmosphere were to react homeostatically (as our own bodies and most other living things do), the feedbacks from water vapour and clouds will be in the direction of cooling.

All that said, this minority of contrarian climate scientists and economists admit that, yes, some of the doomsday scenarios might happen in coming decades. Sea levels may rise. Rains may change their pattern. Diseases may come to regions immune in the past. Polar bears may be threatened by habitat loss.

They also point out, however, that some regions may benefit from a warmer climate. Farms in Canada, Russia, Scandinavia and northern U.S. will have longer growing seasons, as will farms in South Africa, Chile and Argentina. The Arctic regions (and the far south) may be in for a boom in real estate, manufacturing, tourism and urban development.[124] Opening up of shipping lanes in the Arctic will be of great benefit to many industries, shippers and consumers.

---

[123] See "Climate Science In Denial" by Richard S. Lindzen, in *Wall Street Journal*, Apr. 22, 2010, p. A23.
[124] See "Unfreezing Arctic Assets" by Laurence C. Smith in *Wall Street Journal*, Sep. 18, 2010. p. W2.

More carbon dioxide in the air will act as a stimulant to plant growth worldwide. Since far more people in the world die from cold than die from heat, there will be a net gain of people if the climate worldwide gets warmer. And if rain patterns do change, desert-like conditions in much of Africa, in China and in the American south and southwest may benefit from more rain, even as Midwest and European farms may suffer from more drought.

Benefits or dangers, what should we do about it now? How much of present wealth should we spend to prevent possible future changes in the world climate? And here many contrarian scientists as well as many mainstream economists, say, "Go slow."

In this century they point out there are now, and there will be in the future, many challenges, not just one. The earth's two largest countries, China and India, are both rapidly industrializing, and the people there are growing richer, better fed, with better health and lower birth rates year by year. Just a few decades ago, both countries were being written off as desperately poor, gravely overpopulated, and incurably polluted. Today there has been immense progress on all of these fronts.

If China or India were to drastically cut back on their energy supply by severely restricting the burning of fossil fuels, they realize they would condemn themselves to a heart-breaking relapse into poverty, violent political problems, soaring unemployment, and rampant pollution. They are unlikely to do this voluntarily.

Contrarians also point out that the world has other challenges as well, many that are far more immediate and severe than climate change. Radical Islamic terrorism, for instance. Or disease epidemics like malaria, AIDS, tuberculosis and chronic diarrhea that maim and kill millions of people every year. Poverty, malnutrition, and desperate shortages of drinking water and basic sanitation in many parts of the developing world. If we are to spend vast sums of wealth to help the world's environment, which includes its present population, we would be wise to concentrate on what we know is here today, rather than spending our wealth to protect against speculative dangers fifty or a hundred years from now.

Still, yes, with all of these caveats, contrarians admit that climate change is real. So can we and should we do something now to protect ourselves from the negatives of possible global climate change in the future, while still maintaining, and indeed increasing, our industrial growth and our world-wide progress?

Many scientists, economists and politicians agree with former vice president Al Gore, that we need to take drastic and expensive steps now to cutback fossil fuel use as soon as possible, even if it slows economic growth and wealth creation.

Paul Krugman, Nobel prize-winning economist and *New York Times* columnist agrees, but claims it need not slow economic growth. At least not by very much. He suggests that effective economic policies like substantial carbon taxes, or cap and trade schemes, could significantly slow global warming while only slightly slowing worldwide economic growth. He claims that these new taxes would lead to important incentives for private companies to find ways to operate using less carbon-based fuels, and would only end up costing between one and three percent of the gross world product over the next century. [125]

Contrarians are skeptical of projections like these. Using the same computer data that the doomsayers use, they claim that reducing future climate warming by even a single degree centigrade would require trillions of dollars of wealth today and would severely stunt, if not reverse economic growth in both the industrialized and developing worlds.

Even if unlikely, people do take out insurance against accidents, against fire, against possible threats to their health, wealth and safety. Shouldn't the world take out an insurance policy against global climate change?

"Yes, but ... ," say contrarians.

Contrarians do agree that we should by all means increase our research into new energy systems and new ways of using energy (and all other natural resources) more efficiently. The best way to do this, however, may not be public subsidies that only too often fail to pick winners.

---

[125] See "Green Economics: How We Can Afford Climate Change" by Paul Krugman. *New York Times Magazine*, Apr. 11, 2010, pp. 34-41, 46-49.

We should be wary of relying on rhetoric and propaganda to convince people to lead a greener lifestyle. Many people today give lip service to green lifestyles, and some find recycling and composting satisfying. Very few, however, actually cut back significantly on travel, shopping, home building, landscaping, automobile ownership and mileage, entertainment or any other energy-using carbon-dependent activities.

Back in 1974 then-president Gerald Ford tried to combat inflation with an initiative called Whip Inflation Now (WIN). He had WIN buttons printed by the millions and in nationally televised speeches begged citizens to help in ways similar to green propaganda today.

> Here is what we must do, what each and every one of you can do: To help increase food and lower prices, grow more and waste less; to help save scarce fuel in the energy crisis, drive less, heat less. Every housewife knows almost exactly how much she spent for food last week. If you cannot spare a penny from your food budget—and I know there are many— surely you can cut the food that you waste by 5 percent.[126]

Similar efforts were made by Jimmy Carter to control inflation, as well as to live a more frugal and green lifestyle. Both campaigns were futile.

Instead of rhetoric, it would be better to put our faith in the old-fashioned profit motive that solved so many problems like this in the past. The government did help, but it was to a large extent "robber baron" risk-takers like John D. Rockefeller, J.P. Morgan, Andrew Carnegie and Cornelius Vanderbilt who led us to our present state of national and worldwide wealth. It will more likely be entrepreneurs like Steve Jobs or Bill Gates, or the next scientific breakthrough from people like the physicists at the new Large Hadron Collider (LHC) in Switzerland, or the next marketing or financial genius like Warren Buffett who will discover, pioneer and finance new and presently unknown technologies and

---

[126] See President Gerald R, Ford Address to a Joint Session on the Economy, Oct. 8, 1974.

industries that will make us (and the world) more prosperous, more free in our "pursuit of happiness."

One prominent large corporation today, Google Inc., is already planning an investment of billions of dollars to construct a gigantic power line in the Atlantic Ocean from New Jersey to Georgia. It would take the power from thousands of windmill turbines at sea, and funnel it ashore to provide energy for the eastern seaboard cities. It may or it may not work as planned. Google may or may not make a profit.

No one knows now which new energy system or which new pollution controls will be the most effective. Given time, the free market will sort them out. Some, probably most, approaches will fail. But some will succeed and that success will benefit us all.

We may find, for instance, that genetically engineering new kinds of plants that would be more efficient in removing carbon dioxide and other greenhouse gases from the atmosphere will be successful. We may find that new ways of capturing carbon dioxide from power plant smoke stacks and sequestering it under ground or under the ocean will work well. Or we may want to build hundreds of new nuclear power plants as an alternative way to create electricity, as well as hydrogen for use as a vehicle fuel—a way that will not create any carbon dioxide at all. Or ... who knows? No one could have predicted computer power a hundred or even fifty years ago. We may find technologies to replace fossil fuels that no one can dream of today.

Or we may find that earth is homeostatic and that the increasing quantities of carbon dioxide in the atmosphere will cause the atmosphere to automatically find ways to reduce this concentration.[127] Just as our bodies keep our internal environment remarkably constant so long as we are alive, so, too, the earth seems to have kept the atmosphere remarkably

---

[127] See: Jocelyn Kaiser, "Possibly Vast Greenhouse Gas Sponge Ignites Controversy," *Science*, Oct. 16, 1998. P. 386-387. They do not identify this as homeostatic, but they do give evidence that there are unknown levels of natural "sinks" in North America and Europe that seem to be "sponging up" vast quantities of carbon dioxide.

constant for quite a few million years past with no help or hindrance from human beings.

Still another possibility is new drilling techniques that will, according to many experts, make plentiful natural gas from shale a huge near-term energy source in this country, Canada and Europe. According to energy expert Amy Myers Jaffe, the Wallace S. Wilson Fellow for Energy Studies at the Baker Institute for Public Policy at Rice University, "Shale gas is going to rock the world … [its use] promises to shake up the energy markets and geopolitics. And that's just for starters."[128]

She claims, "By some estimates, there's 1,000 trillion cubic feet recoverable in North America alone—enough to supply the nation's natural-gas needs for the next 45 years." This enormous supply of energy-rich gas could be used for powering vehicles as well as producing electricity. It does produce carbon dioxide, but far less per energy unit than coal or oil. Using this plentiful carbon-based fuel would reduce possibilities for climate change, would drastically reduce our dependence on imported oil, and would give us a substantial breathing space before some new renewable energy source proves itself. Admittedly there are some environmental problems that come from the new drilling techniques but experts are confident they can be solved.

Another possibility: there are just four basic forces in the universe. Gravity, discovered by Isaac Newton 300 years ago, led to the mechanical engineering age of the first Industrial Revolution. Electromagnetism, discovered by scientists like Edison, Maxwell and Faraday, led to the new world of electricity and electronics. Nuclear strong and weak forces, pioneered by Albert Einstein, led to nuclear power. One other basic force of nature is still unknown. The just-completed and now-working Large Hadron Collider (LHC) in Switzerland is designed to discover this force. If physicists do find it, this may yield results in basic science that will lead to new energy sources we have never thought of before.

---

[128] See Amy Myers Jaffe, "How Shale Gas Is Going to Rock the World" *The Wall Street Journal*, May 10, 2010, p. R1.

CONTRARIANS ARE NOT ABSOLUTISTS. Short of direct subsidies, rich countries of Europe, Japan and North America may be able to encourage development of new carbon-free and carbon-sequestering technologies by providing more powerful incentives to the private sector. Putting modest taxes on fossil-fuel use in the form of carbon taxes, increased gasoline taxes, or indirectly by cap-and-trade schemes are examples. Modest, but not crippling, say contrarians.

It's a matter of degree. Contrarians use an analogy here. Just as we could dramatically reduce traffic fatalities by passing laws to reduce maximum speeds to five miles an hour, so we could reduce the chances of future global warming by severely restricting fossil fuel use today. But would that be wise? In other words, there is always cost vs. benefits, no matter how you slice it. Yes, we may find climate change brings serious problems, just as traveling seventy miles an hour leads to serious accidents. Do we want to give up the benefits of vehicle travel to save lives lost in accidents? Do we want to cripple economic growth for the, as yet unknown, possible benefits of reducing climate change?

Radical environmentalists urge us to live a more "green" lifestyle, to have a lower "carbon footprint." In practice, this means driving a smaller car, living in a smaller house, using fewer resources, eating foods grown closer to home, eating more organic food, planting what we used to call "victory gardens" during World War II, cutting back on gadgets and frivolous consumer goods, recycling instead of buying new, sharing more and buying less, biking more and driving less, cutting energy use, and in general making do with less and adjusting to a simpler, lower standard of living. When we have a serious recession in the economy, as we having at this writing in 2011, a "green" lifestyle as described above is uncomfortably close to what we are getting.

We are also getting unemployment, crumbling pension funds, international crises, sinking standards of living in countries where poverty and repression were just beginning to ease, union busting, home and business bankruptcies, bigger deficits, more debt for our grandchildren to pay, less money for schools and for the arts and sciences, more poverty, less health care and fewer rich people. Except possibly for the last, I don't imagine even the greenest of green supporters would approve of these unintended consequences. Be careful what you ask for, you might get it.

Instead of cutting back, as green proponents want us to do, we should be doing more with less, as Bucky Fuller suggested forty years ago, and some "light green" advocates do today. With the emphasis on "doing more." Instead of suppressing powerful new technologies like nuclear power or genetic engineering[129], we should be encouraging them to lead the way to a world where one hundred percent of the people have a good life in a healthy environment.

In the end, as with resources and population, and, as a matter of fact, with Islamic terror, the most promising morals seem to be: technology is a friend, not an enemy; wealth is good, not bad; in this inevitably changing and often chaotic world, free-market economic systems are not perfect, but they have brought a world of material progress and vigorous health to the western world in the last two centuries. It would be foolish and irresponsible in the extreme to abandon (or weaken) them now, just as they are doing the same for the developing worlds of Asia, Africa and Latin America. We don't need "sustainability," we need vigorous growth. If some want a green lifestyle, fine. If some want a luxurious lifestyle, fine. Or anything in between, fine. So long as it is not obviously criminal, everyone in the world should have the freedom to choose any lifestyle they want.

Instead of the doomsayer's equation that makes population, wealth, and technology bad things, we should be paying attention instead to a more promising equation—P=ATCE. (P) Progress (and that includes environmental progress) equals (A) Affluence, multiplied by (T)

---

[129] For nuclear power today see Richard C. Lester, head of the department of nuclear science and engineering at MIT, "Why Fukushima Won't Kill Nuclear Power," *The Wall Street Journal*, April 6, 2011. For genetic engineering see Normal E. Borlaug, 1970 Nobel Peace Prize Laureate, "Continuing the Green Revolution" <http://www.cartercenter.org/news/documents/ op_ed_borlaug_wsj07grnrev2.html>

Technology, multiplied by (C) Creativity, and most important of all by (E) an environment of Freedom.

Unfortunately, often in this world of woe, this prosperous equation is not automatic. The world of politics, of economics, and of culture is full of variables and is immensely difficult-to-understand, much less to predict. A hundred years ago prosperous folks in England and in North America were confident western progress was obvious and enduring. Free-market democracy was on the march and nothing could stop its coming triumphs.

World War I came as a traumatic shock, to be followed closely by the false hopes raised by Lenin and the supposed utopia of command-economy communism. Recovering from the disasters of World War I, there followed the seemingly prosperous days of western democracies in the 1920s. Then came the worldwide depression, the rise of Hitler, and World War II.

What of the 21st century? Will globalization and free-market liberal democracy bring prosperity and peace to the world? Or will the ancient memes of religious and cultural hatreds, false utopian dreams, and fears of resource scarcity continue to handicap our efforts. Will new fears of climate change, population pressures, or excessive debt for expensive social programs in the U.S. and other western democracies so hijack our hopes that we will be condemned instead to a century of gloom and doom?

The politically center-right and usually reliable magazine *The Economist* was hopeful in a late 2009 issue:

"Recognizing the political shortcomings of globalization should redouble Western liberals' determination to defend it: to close the gap in the right way. That involves a myriad of things, from promoting human rights to designing better jobs policies. But it also requires defending the enormous benefits that capitalism has brought to world since 1989 more forcefully than the West's leaders have done thus far. And above all perhaps, taking nothing for granted."[130]

IN THE END I THINK AGAIN that the Chinese sage was wise: "A peasant must stand for a long time on a hillside with his mouth open before a roast duck flies in." To those who search and work creatively, resources (and wealth) are unlimited. We need not fear more people to share the earth's bounty, we need to have confidence that a secular liberal western society can and will prevail over medieval theocracies of Islamic or any other variety of Religious voices. Climate change itself, if it comes, is to be welcomed, not feared. And finally, in so far as freedom and science prevail in the 21st century, we—that is, all the people on this small planet—can and will be winners.

---

[130] "The Berlin Wall: So much gained, so much to lose," *The Economist*, November 5, 2009.

PART FIVE

THE FUTURE OF FREE-MARKET LIBERAL DEMOCRACY

The Whole Earth Catalog

In 1968 one of the students in my chemistry class brought me a copy of the first edition of *The Whole Earth Catalog*. I loved it. In those days this catalog was the latest word in environmental wisdom and know-how. The cover featured the new NASA photo of the whole earth as first seen from space. In those heady days of the late 1960s, we also loved a folk song that came out the same year.

> Those were the days, my friend
> We thought they'd never end
> We'd sing and dance forever and a day
> We'd live the life we choose
> We'd fight and never lose
> For we were young and sure to have our way.

It was the years of the hippie, and even those of us who never joined a commune, never wore beads or shod ourselves in sandals, did share some of the mischief, silliness and fun. Inside *The Whole Earth Catalog* were articles, quotes and ads (with addresses and prices) for thousands of do-it-yourself recipes and gadgets (Swiss Army knives and geodesic domes were some of my favorites) that would lighten the human load on the earth, and give "access to tools" that would help make life better and more earth-friendly!

The man behind the catalog was a quirky genius named Stewart Brand. He peppered the pages with quotes from people like Buckminster Fuller, Henry David Thoreau, Lewis Mumford, E. F. Schumacher *(Small is Beautiful)* and himself. It was, in its way, an early print version of the World Wide Web and Google.

"We are as gods" Brand claimed in the first *Whole Earth Catalog*, "and we might as well get good at it."

Unlike some later environmentalists, Brand was pro-technology. In fact, people like Steve Jobs, founder of Apple, were early supporters. Jobs and other fans later went on to found the personal computer industry. Brand himself had another warning that seems appropriate today, "A blanket rejection of technology is trapping people in an alternate lifestyle of shabby creativity."

Brand distanced himself from the New Left, which was also rising in fame and power in the late 60s and early 70s. He wrote later, "At a time when the New Left was calling for grass-roots political power *Whole Earth* eschewed politics and pushed grassroots direct power—tools and skills. At a time when New Age hippies were deploring the intellectual world of arid abstractions, *Whole Earth* pushed science, intellectual endeavor, and new technology as well as old. As a result, when the most empowering tool of the

century came along—personal computers
(resisted by the New Left and despised by the
New Age)—*Whole Earth* was in the thick of the
development from the beginning."

In those days I was also a big fan of a man
featured often in the Catalog, Buckminster Fuller.
I was fortunate enough to meet Bucky in Chicago
in the early 70s, and get invited to his summer
home on an island off the coast of Maine. With
my two sons, we spent a week with him and his
wife, along with a few other Fuller family friends.
The home and island had no electricity, so we
brought along a small generator to power a slide
projector for an evening entertainment. The
featured presentation was my recently completed first audiovisual production, *Spaceship Earth*.[131]
Bucky, of course, recognized that it was based on
his vision and ideas. He was very appreciative and
I was, of course, ecstatic. It was a memorable way
to launch my new mid-life career as an educational media producer.

After reading and praising my just-published book
of poetry, *A Little While Aware*, Bucky gave me a
copy of a poem that I think he wrote that same
week. It has the best definition of "environment"
I have yet seen. (I learned later that he may have
borrowed the idea from Einstein.)

---

[131] See *Spaceship Earth* on <www.hawkhill.com>

Environment to each must be
All that is, that isn't me.
Universe in turn will be
All that isn't me *and me.*

I still think often of another Bucky quote: "I live
on Earth at present, and I don't know what I am.
I know that I am not a category. I am not a
thing—a noun. I seem to be a verb, an evolutionary process—an integral function of the universe."

Fuller also invented something he called the
"World Game."[132] His idea had always been to
"do more with less," and the goal of the World
Game was to, "Make the world work for 100% of
humanity in the shortest possible time through
spontaneous cooperation without ecological
damage or disadvantage to anyone." Too bad he
is not with us anymore. We could use his
wisdom on getting this done right.

Stewart Brand is still with us, and still writing and
working to help us learn how to be good gods.
Today he has not lost his enthusiasm for the
environment, or for technology. Recently he
came out strongly for reviving nuclear power and
for using more genetic engineering, both
technologies being, in his opinion, essential tools
for helping to slow global warming and making
the world work for 100% of humanity.

---

[132] See: http://www.osearth.com/. Last accessed on 02/21/11.

Brand today is advocating a science-based
"whole-earth discipline" he calls "ecopragmatism."
He rejects the attitudes of many leaders and
rank-and-file fellow followers in the environmentalist movement that he helped to create and
inspire. Their opposition to "factory" foods,
genetic engineering and nuclear power, Brand
says, is anti-science, anti-intellectual and counter-
productive, especially to what Brand considers
the most serious environmental challenge of our
lifetime, climate change. He goes even further
and says to environmentalists today, "you're
harmful."

I got my philosophy degree working under the
late Sydney Hook, professor at New York
University and well-known international leader in
democracy studies and activities. Hook was a
follower of John Dewey, the eminent proponent
of pragmatism. In one of Dewey's seminal works,
Reconstruction in Philosophy, he wrote lines that I
think would please Steward Brand as much as
they please me.

> Conceptions of possibility, progress, free
> movement and infinitely diversified op-
> portunity have been suggested by mod-
> ern science. But until they have displaced
> from imagination the heritage of the im-
> mutable and the once-for-all ordered and
> systematized, the ideas of mechanism and
> matter will lie like a dead weight upon the
> emotions, paralyzing religions and dis-

torting art. When the liberation of capaci-
ty no longer seems a menace to organization and established institutions ... art will
not be a luxury, a stranger to the daily
occupations of making a living. Making a
living economically speaking will be at one
with making a life that is worth living. And
when the emotional force, the mystic
force one might say, of communication,
of the miracle of shared life and shared
experience is spontaneously felt, the
hardness and crudeness of contemporary
life will be bathed in the light that never
was on land or sea. [133]

---

[133] John Dewey, *Reconstruction in Philosophy*, Vol. 10 of the *Collected Works of John Dewey, The Middle Works* (Carbondale: Southern Illinois University Press, 1982, pp. 200-201).

Chapter 20

The Future of Free-Market Liberal Democracy

LET'S GO THE BASIC QUESTION of this book—the future of free-market liberal democracy. (*Liberal* in the classic Enlightenment sense of freedom from governmental and clerical domination. See pages 44-46.)

In 1902 Lenin wrote his short book *What Is to Be Done?* In it he cautioned that "to belittle socialist ideology *in any way*, to deviate from it in the slightest degree means strengthening bourgeois ideology." He went on to urge his followers to form small, intellectually led, tightly disciplined revolutionary cells that would lead the world to a socialist utopia.

Lenin, it turned out, was misled by ideas (memes) that turned out to be tragically dysfunctional. It was not only his misguided faith in socialism that led to such tragic consequences, but also his fanatic conviction that he and only he had the true faith. It is this kind of either/or, absolutist, fundamentalist, agricultural-age, utopian-religious, single-way of thinking that is severely handicapping our ability to solve world problems today in economics, politics, and environment.

Lenin wrote his book to provide a recipe for destroying free-market liberal bourgeois democracy. I am writing this book to provide rough hints for nudging, enhancing, protecting and making free-market liberal bourgeois democracies more common and more successful on earth.

The world knows how hellish Lenin's socialist utopia turned out to be. The death of communism in 1991 was the death of a secular religion. Communism for the better part of a century inspired millions of people in all countries of the world, before it destroyed them (along with millions more who did not share their secular religion). The world thought that when the Soviet Union entered the dustbin of history we had driven a stake through the heart of the evil vampire. Now in the 21st century we are finding that it is not quite dead. To change the metaphor, we are getting some nasty cases of shingles because we once had chicken pox.

How about 9/11? What are the lessons there? And finally, what can we learn from the long and often tortured history of economics, of science and technology, and of religion? Big questions, I know. And they deserve big answers, not easy recipes. Whatever the answers, it pays to remember as Judge Learned Hand put it, "The spirit of liberty is the spirit that is not too sure that it is right."

To my way of thinking, the answers to these questions break down into three categories: economics, science/technology, and religion. The synergetic mix is all-important, but let's take them one at a time before we consider the synergy. Economics first.

ZERO-SUM VS. WIN-WIN ECONOMICS

IN MY VALEDICTORIAN SPEECH when I graduated from high school in 1944, I urged my classmates and our parents to "Return to Religion." I think now that was not a brilliant idea in 1944. It is an even worse idea today. Instead of returning to religion, we should instead consider returning to somewhere close to where we were in the late 18th century. That insight, it seems to me, is the kernel of wisdom, often encased in a chaff of fluff, that best defines what is called the Tea Party today.

We obviously do not want to literally return to those days, nor to any other days of the past. Most certainly we do not want to return to anyplace in the late 18th century world but the northeastern coast of North America. It was there—in Philadelphia, Boston and New York—that truly revolutionary things were happening. Not things that would point to, or lead to a utopia, but ones that *have led* to genuine progressive increases in human freedom, security and prosperity. Things that have not led to perfection, but have led to a substantial decrease in poverty, disease and violence.[134] Things that made, and still make, our country the exceptional

---

[134] See *The Better Angels of our Nature: Why Violence Has Declined.* Stephen Pinker.

country it is. And things (memes), we seem to have neglected or severely mutated in the late 20th and early 21st centuries. Sometimes for the better, but sometimes for the worse.

A favorite book of libertarians is Friedrich Hayek's *The Road to Serfdom*. It was written between 1940 and 1943, during the most devastating worldwide war ever. This chapter, *The Future of Free-Market Liberal Democracy,* is a personal view of what I think Hayek might write today with the advantage of seventy years of hindsight. (I realize that Hayek had a wider, more philosophic approach than my more mundane efforts. Nevertheless, I think there is enough in common to presume a relationship.)

For instance: One of the most important and revolutionary ideas to come out of the last two centuries was a new view of wealth.

For at least ten thousand years past, wealth was measured in land, gold and slaves, serfs or peasants. The richest families, the richest villages, the richest cities, the richest countries, the richest kingdoms and empires, were the ones that controlled the most land, had the biggest hordes of gold, and the most slave (or serf or peasant) workers. It was a zero-sum system.

The total wealth (GDP) of any tribe, group, or society was like a large pie and dividing it up was an often-deadly game. If I win, you lose. If you win, I lose. If I get a big piece, you will have to be content with a small one. The inevitable result was that if a village, a city, or an entire country or civilization wanted to become wealthier, it had two choices: theft or war.

The road to serfdom was well worn, not only in the ten-thousand-year-long agricultural age, but also in the many millennia of hunting/gathering tribes on this small planet.

When the agricultural revolution took hold about ten thousand years ago, it was a huge leap forward in worldwide wealth and populations. But then for the next ten thousand years, there was little gain. The world's GWP (Gross World Product), in other words, barely nudged up or down. Empires rose and fell. Tribes became better off or worse off. Individual family dynasties rose and fell. But the total population and the median wealth of the world's citizens changed barely at all. You can't make more land, more gold, or get more slaves no matter how smart, how powerful or how persuasive you are. The best you can do is to hang on to what you have, or pilfer a bit from your neighbor. Rich folks were usually good at hanging on to what they had, and even better at pilfering from their neighbors (including their own slaves, serfs or peasants). Hence comes our envy, fascination and resentment of rich people today.

It was around the time of the American Revolution that this view began to change.

The Scottish moral philosopher of the Enlightenment, Adam Smith, led the way intellectually with his classic book *The Wealth of Nations*. It was published the same year our Declaration of Independence was signed, 1776. In his book he sketched details of how to *create* wealth, *new* wealth. It was a way that Great Britain and the American colonies took to heart and put to work. It was, you might say, the first firm step on the road to a modern Free-Market Liberal Democracy. Smith's new idea stressed three principles: private property, division of labor and free trade. He added a fourth condition that was necessary for the other three to be effective, a strong government. The government, Smith advised, should take all steps necessary to keep the peace, to enforce contracts, to protect the commonwealth from foreign threats, to protect private property and to promote free trade. If villages, cities or nations would adopt these principles, the result would be powerful incentives to create new wealth, which would massively expand the societies' Gross Domestic Product (GDP). For the first time in human history, the wealth pie could increase in size. And increase it did. Dramatically.

In America especially, foundations were laid for a new win-win economics on a continental scale. In a free trade, Smith pointed out, both sides win. Wealth will not depend on how much land or gold, or how many slaves you have. Wealth will come from the sweat, creativity and invention of the ultimate unlimited resource, the human hand and mind. This meant that theft or violence would no longer be necessary to get rich. Theft and violence might linger on, as they have, but they would no longer be necessary.

Agricultural-age kingdoms at that time, in Europe and elsewhere, had objections to these principles. Memes thousands of years old told their elite leaders (as well as their servile followers), that land, gold and slaves were the only secure ways to live. Trade was fine (for the ruling class) to get luxuries, weapons, and sometimes food too, that the kingdom could not provide for itself; private property was fine, so long as the ownership was confined to hereditary lords and anointed clergy; and division of labor was fine, so long as it was understood that it was the slaves (or serfs or peasants) who did the scut work and the nobles who protected, governed, and got the bulk of the benefits. As the folk song goes, "It's the same the whole world over/'tis the poor what gets the blame/While the rich has all the pleasure/Now ain't that a bloomin' shame."

Thomas Jefferson, on the other hand, wrote that, "the mass of mankind has not been born with saddles on their backs, nor a favored few, booted and spurred, ready to legitimately ride them." In 1787 the founding fathers rejected some of these authoritarian agricultural-age zero-sum ideas and voted for new liberal republican ones. Instead of kings, nobles and clergy riding on the backs of serfs, slaves and peasants, it was to be, "We the people of the United States, in order to form a more perfect union, establish justice, insure domestic tranquility, provide for the common defense, promote the general welfare, and secure the blessings of liberty to ourselves and our posterity, do ordain and establish this Constitution of the United States of America."

Freedom was to be the key. In our new system there would be citizens, not subjects.

And they sketched out the mechanics of how this could happen. In a well-defined separation of labor (following precedents set centuries before in the early Roman Republic), republican government would work best by dividing it into three separate independent branches—executive, legislative and judicial. In the Fifth Amendment to this new Constitution of the United States, ideas of Adam Smith were made explicit. "No person shall ... be deprived of life, liberty, or property, without due process of law; nor shall private property be taken for public use, without just compensation." In enumerating the limits to the powers of Congress, they even added a free trade provision, "No Tax or Duty shall be laid on Articles exported from any State."

Thomas Jefferson went further in the Adam Smith direction, "Agriculture, manufacture, commerce, and navigation, the four pillars of our prosperity, are the most thriving when left most free to individual enterprise." And he also added "a wise and frugal government, which shall restrain men from injuring one another, shall leave them otherwise free to regulate their own pursuits of industry and improvement, and shall not take from the mouth of labor the bread it has earned. This is the sum of good government."

This commitment to hands-off government, leaving citizens free to "regulate their own pursuits," has paid rich dividends through the 200-plus years of our national existence. Instead of fighting about ways to more fairly "divide up the pie," as zero-sum feudal theory would dictate, our pioneer ancestors proposed to massively increase the size of the pie. That way everyone could have a bigger piece.

That did not and does not mean there are no disputes about the distribution of the newly created wealth.

Even a determined win-win capitalist society has zero-sum transactions as well. In the 19th and 20th centuries, for instance, there were bitter fights about how fairly to distribute the bigger pie created by the new system. And although no one today doubts that the pie is bigger, there are still bitter disputes about how to divide the riches.

When a business makes a profit from its win-win transactions, that profit must be distributed. People with a strong claim to the profits include management, workers, owners and the government. Dividing up the profit is a zero-sum game. If management gets a bigger share, the workers get a smaller share. And vice versa. And then there are the owners, who advanced the capital needed to produce the income and the profits. The wild card is the government.

The government is essential. It also has the most power in any transaction. Like rulers of old, the government has a monopoly on force and the potentially unlimited power of taxation. In a modern liberal democracy, the government also has a major constraint. It must appeal to a majority of voters to win the next election. One of the best ways to please the majority is to offer more services. As George Bernard Shaw once quipped, "A government that takes from Peter to pay Paul can always depend on the support of Paul." Here's where it can get sticky, especially when it comes to government employees.

More and better services mean more and better employees to deliver those services. Governments don't make a profit as such, so, unlike private companies, there is no surplus to share. There is the power to tax, and the power to borrow. Governments also cannot go bankrupt (short of a complete collapse and ensuing revolution), and they have almost unlimited borrowing power.

When a government employee union demands higher pay and more benefits for its members, the easiest course for elected officials is to give in and offer higher pay and more benefits. The result, often, is that a bigger and bigger share of the government's taxation and borrowing funds (which in the end come from the net wealth of the entire society) go to government employees and become unavailable for profit-making enterprises. Nor are they available for infrastructure projects or education programs that might in the long run help grow the economy. The short-run effect of generous government employee benefits, though, is to please the government workers, who also vote.

In modern times this has resulted in serious imbalances. Firefighters, cops, teachers, municipal bus drivers, prison guards, secretaries, lawyers, engineers, diplomats, government administrators of all kinds can often retire in their fifties (or earlier), and be supported by generous pensions and health care services for the rest of their lives. Since the life span has increased dramatically by the 21st century, this means many billions of dollars are needed for their support when they are no longer able to offer useful services (i.e. participate in win-win transactions).

This is happening not just in America, but it is happening all over the liberal democratic world. It is even more of a problem in Europe, where social welfare systems and government bureaucrats are more entrenched and well rewarded than in America, and where the population is also more heavily skewed to the elderly. Recently this imbalance brought on a crisis in France when the government tried to raise the minimum retirement age from 60 to 62. General strikes, burning effigies and violent protest marches of government employees, as well as young and old supporters, opposed the change. Recent protests of government workers in Great Britain, Spain, Greece and France turned violent. Protests in Wisconsin, Ohio and other states of the U.S. have led to serious social unrest.

One of the many damaging effects of excessive government benefits is the restraint it puts on government investments that might indeed be win-win transactions in the long run. In the 19th and 20th centuries the government was able to invest millions of dollars in the canals, railroads, roads and airports that proved critical in our wealth-creating prosperity. President Truman invested billions of dollars in the Marshall Plan that saved Europe. President Eisenhower was able to invest today's equivalent of trillions of dollars on an Interstate Highway System that has had enormous payback for the U.S. economy since the 1950s. After World War II, the U.S. government was able to invest what would today be billions of dollars in a GI Bill of Rights that provided college educations to millions of young men and women (including me) who might never have seen the inside of a college classroom without this aid.

After the Civil Rights reforms of the 1960s, the government was able to invest billions of dollars in education, enforcement and affirmative action programs that have empowered over half the U.S. population (African-Americans and women) to achieve and contribute to our national wealth.

All of these investments by the government were win-win transactions in the long run. The government *and* the economy benefited. And so, in the short run, did the workers who built the canals, railroads, Interstate Highway Systems and airports; who contributed to the Marshall Plan that saved Europe; who taught in the colleges and administered the Civil Rights reforms.

Today there are still plenty of opportunities for long-range infrastructure investments, transportation projects, and programs to improve health and education. However, governments, federal, state and local, are often under severe fiscal restraints due in large part to their excessive pension fund and health care obligations (made worse by good things like the stabilizing of population growth, early retirement and increasing life spans).

A new tunnel under the Hudson River from New Jersey to Manhattan, for example, would probably be a win-win project. It would help both New Jersey and New York expand industry and commerce in the long run, as well as provide many construction jobs in the short run. However, the recently elected New Jersey governor has stopped construction on this billion-dollar project because his state is near bankruptcy due to its excessive public salary, health care and pension benefit packages. These New Jersey benefit packages for state employees, for instance, are forty-two percent more expensive than those offered by the average Fortune 500 Company.[135] And these benefits are rising by sixteen percent a year. California, New York and many other states face similar problems. States are required by law to balance their budgets each year. The Federal Government has no such constraint.

The Federal government not only has the problem of federal government employee benefits, it is also responsible for expensive entitlement programs for the entire country—Social Security, Medicare, Medicaid, Food Stamps and the new Health-care programs for all citizens. Popular and desirable as these entitlement programs are, they are for the most part not win-win transactions and do not add to the national wealth pie.

---

[135] See column by David Brooks "The Paralysis of the State" in *The New York Times*, Oct. 12, 2010. Last accessed on 04/26/11. <http://query.nytimes.com/gst/fullpage.html?res=9E04E5D6163EF931A25753C1A9669D8B63&ref=davidbrooks>

In still another non-economic demand, environmentalists are pushing for new investments in green technology that, in many if not most cases, will end up doing less with more. That is, they will create products, like a new high-speed train infrastructure or new biofuel, windmill or solar installations, which will cost more than they will return. Many will turn out to be zero-sum, or even lose-lose transactions. One result is that our national debt is skyrocketing. Good ideas on how to control it are in short supply.

This is not a new problem. But in modern times it seems more serious than it was a hundred or two hundred years ago.

DESPITE THE PROBLEMS, the economic history of this country since 1787 gives strong evidence to support the overall wisdom of win-win free-market capitalist principles. The population of the United States according to the first census in 1790 was 3 million people, 2.4 million free and 600,000 enslaved. The vast majority of the free people were poor farmers. Today the population of the United States is over 300 million, all free, the vast majority middle class urban dwellers, just about all of whom have living standards better than the richest of our founding fathers.

Without question this gain in population, in resources and in wealth was due to free-market capitalism operating in an environment of liberal democracy. That is so, even though as many scholars have pointed out, the United States in the 19th and 20th centuries has often modified or ignored some of Adam Smith's principles.

The government, for instance, has not always followed Jefferson's advice to allow business people to be "free to regulate their own pursuits of industry and improvement." It has often restricted free trade in order to protect and subsidize domestic industries and agriculture. It has often undertaken massive programs to create new jobs and new industries on its own initiative, bypassing "free enterprise." Despite these compromises, on the whole we have been a nation following free-market principles— respect for private property, diversity of talent and reward, and free trade. But in a pragmatic way. Never as a dogma written in stone.

One of the best examples of the triumph of free-market win-win capitalist principles is the success of the Marshall Plan after the Second World War. (See page 20-27.)

More recent international examples of the power of win-win free-market capitalism are the two most populous countries in the world, India and China. Using free-market capitalist ideas, both India and China have gone from being desperately poor to challenging western nations for jobs and economic growth.

India has been a liberal democracy from its origins after the Second World War, but it was hampered for many decades by socialist-leaning, state-dominated command-economy policies. Once it opened up to allow more free-market private enterprise in the late 20th century, it has made huge gains in wealth and well-being for its still growing population. (Brazil in South America has gone through a similar history.)

China was desperately poor and brutally suppressed under Mao's communist regime. Deng Xiaoping changed the economy to a free-market capitalist one. In a remarkably short time, China has become the most productive exporter, and one of the wealthiest bankers in the post-communist world. As yet China has not embraced liberal democratic memes, but some predict that will follow sooner rather than later. It happened before in formerly authoritarian states like South Korea, Taiwan, Singapore, Brazil, Spain and Chile. For that matter, in formerly totalitarian states like Germany and Japan!

THE SAME COMMITMENT to free-market win-win economics may work some day with Islamic societies. It may be a long while before free-market liberal democratic memes can overcome dogmatic Islamic ones. On the other hand, it might come faster than many guess today. Muslim countries like Indonesia, Turkey, India (Hindu majority, but sizable Muslim minority), Morocco and a few others, are already on their way. Even Iraq, Pakistan, Egypt, Lebanon, Libya and Afghanistan are lurching hesitantly toward free-market liberal democracy. Recent unrest and revolt in many Arab countries in the Middle East and North Africa are also telltale signs of movement in Western directions. Western societies succeeded in transforming Christian memes for the better once free markets showed a better way to amass wealth. My bet is that it may take longer, but in the end Muslim-dominated countries, too, will take the leap.

CRITICS

I RECOGNIZE THAT THE LEFT-LIBERAL intellectual community, and the new green sustainable community, do not accept much of what I claim about capitalism and win-win economics. There has been recently, among some left-liberal leaders and environmental intellectuals, a strong movement away from free trade, free markets and capitalism. The idea that the United States is "exceptional" is also unpopular among this elite.

It is true that the new system of "we the people" was not perfect in 1787. And certainly it is far from perfect today. "We the people" in 1787 did not include enslaved people from Africa. Nor did it include Native Americans. In many ways it did not include the half of the population that is female. In part at least, it was constructed to preserve elite wealth (a zero-sum hangover at the very beginning), and to prevent what the founding fathers feared would be the chaos of a direct democracy (they took pains to make clear it was to be a representative republic, not a democracy). It is also true that other reactionary ideas from the past were not addressed, nor did they disappear overnight. Many still linger in weakened forms today.

Memes, for instance, that said women should be confined to childbearing and domestic duties. Memes that justified male dominance; memes that encouraged aggressive violence to preserve male honor; memes that justified aggressive action to enforce female submission, gender prejudice, homosexual isolation and persecution. Memes that excused violence against other ethnic groups—like our wars against the Native American inhabitants of the continent; our violent oppression of enslaved Africans; our atrocious treatment of freed African-Americans, immigrant Irish-Americans, Swedish-Americans, Norwegian-Americans, Japanese-American, Latino-Americans, etc. Memes that looked on religions other than Christianity as inferior, if not blasphemous.

Far-right individuals and groups who sponsor racist, ethnic and sexist violence are trying to resurrect some of these negative memes today.

It was not utopia, in other words. And it still isn't.

Severe left-liberal critics today, like the popular Harvard scholar Noam Chomsky (as well as a significant host of leftist academic scholars who should know better), go further. They routinely denounce our country as a "rogue state," "fascist," "imperialist," "racist," a "terrorist" nation that, above all others, has adopted "rape and pillage" as a routine foreign policy. They base some of this on historical fact. In this they sometimes have the facts right, but are guilty of gross historical malpractice in applying today's moral standards to the past.

Every society in the world in the late 18th century shared most of these reactionary and destructive memes. Slavery was the norm everywhere on all continents, including Native America.[136] Gender prejudice, violence between ethnic groups, imperialistic wars, racism and male dominance had been the norm for ten thousand years everywhere in the world. Imperialism, getting more wealth by making war against your neighbor, was the way it had been done, and the only way it was done, for hundreds of thousands of years in every society, including primitive tribal ones.[137] Most, if not all, of these reactionary memes were closely allied, if not directly caused, by the very nature of a zero-sum economic system.

The genius of our founding fathers was to take the first giant steps to make things better, to move away from zero-sum ideas and implement, instead, win-win ones. The fact that they did not solve all the problems at once is not surprising, nor does it justify such ridiculously unfair labeling.

---

[136] See *1493: Uncovering the New World Columbus Created*. Charles C. Mann.

[137] For corroboration on this point see Part 1 (pp. 1-146) of Azar Gat's well-documented book *War in Human Civilization*.

Chomsky and like-minded critics go further, and claim that the United States not only always was but still is, "fascist," "imperialistic" and "racist."

Compared to what?

It was the United States that took the lead in abolishing slavery in the western world at the cost of 600,000 American lives in the Civil War. It was the United States that spent billions of dollars, and devoted millions of acres of land, to repay and restore Native American rights and wealth. It was this country, far more than any other country on earth, that has been and still is struggling—successfully for the most part—to accommodate, enrich and expand a multi-racial, multi-ethnic, gender-blind, tolerant and progressive democratic society.

Chomsky claims to be an anarchist, not a communist. It is time he and his fellow travellers did some comparison-shopping before condemning their own country so viciously and unfairly.

Historically, for instance, how much did the Iroquois nations do, yesterday or today, to recompense the Algonquians (and other tribes) that their ancestors tortured, murdered, and forced out of the Northeast North America? How much did the tribes in southern North America do to recompense the tribal warriors they had enslaved for centuries?[138] It was the same story with most Native American tribes. Wars between these tribes, like those between all agricultural, as well as all hunter/gatherer groups, were the norm for thousands of years before the United States was imagined.[139] Again, it was always and everywhere a zero-sum game. Steal or be stolen from. Kill or be killed.

And how about internationally? How much have the West African nations done to punish, or even acknowledge, the crimes of their ancestral tribal brothers who were the ones who kidnapped and sold their

---

[138] See pages 93-99 in *1493: Uncovering the New World Columbus Created*. Charles C. Mann.

[139] See *Dinner with a Cannibal* by anthropologist Carole A. Travis-Henikoff for details on life with hunter/gathering tribes. For a shorter article on same subject see Ann Gibbons, "Archaeologists Rediscover Cannibals," *Science*, vol. 277, Aug. 1, 1997, pp. 635-637.

neighbors to Arab, English, Indian and Chinese slave-traders? (They also murdered far more fellow Africans than the slave-traders or slave-holders did.) Why not condemn Cuba because it imported more slaves than the entire North American continent? Or Brazil, a country that had far more slaves than the United States and did not emancipate them until the 1880s. Or the Arab states whose ancestors made slaves of more Africans than all the Europeans and North America colonies combined (and some of them still today practice slavery!). Slave or be enslaved. Steal or be stolen from. Kill or be killed. It's the zero-sum way.

Finally, what country has done more to assimilate and integrate large numbers of racial and ethnic groups within its economy and society in the 19th, 20th and 21st centuries? What country has devoted more energy, money and lives to opposing reactionary and imperialist regimes in this imperfect world? I am talking not only about Nazi Germany, Fascist Italy, Totalitarian Soviet Union and militaristic Japan, but also Maoist China, Communist North Korea, Cuba, Nicaragua, Vietnam, as well as today's reactionary regimes in Iraq, Iran, Afghanistan, Palestine and Somalia. In fact, what country has done more to protect Muslim people from terror in their own Muslim-majority countries like Indonesia, Iraq, Libya and Afghanistan, and from other ethnic and religious aggressors, as in Kosovo, Palestine and India? The defense rests.

I doubt whether the prosecution will let up. Why not?

This is a good question that is not considered often enough. Why are so many obviously intelligent, well-intentioned and well-informed intellectuals in western democracies so bitterly opposed to the United States and its policies, indeed to Western society itself? There have always, fortunately, been critics in western societies, but today some of the critics seem more impassioned, more illogical, and more destructive than before.

Some critics of western societies in the past were liberal progressives who left a legacy of genuine progress in this country and in the world. Giants of the past come to mind like Martin Luther King, Nelson Mandela, Abraham Lincoln, Thomas Jefferson, along with thousands of unsung union leaders, abolitionists, suffragettes, freedom riders, etc.

These progressives loved their country, and worked and fought to make it freer, better, more just and more prosperous.

I give credit to many progressives today who work and fight to lessen prejudice, increase health-care access, cut back violence and bring more equality and justice in education, employment and income. I wish sometimes that they were a bit more generous in acknowledging the progress we have made in the past, but as to the future, go for it. We are not perfect. We are not utopia and never will be. We want and need to continue to progress in all areas.

That does not, however, explain or excuse the excessive, vulgar, damaging, and untrue words of so many harsh, bitter and unfair critics like Noam Chomsky, Howard Zinn, Jeremiah Wright, Lynne Stewart, Barbara Kingsolver, Bernardine Dohrn, Bill Ayers, Eric Foner, Alexander Cockburn, Todd Gitlin, Ramsey Clark, Helen Caldicott, Wim Wenders, Susan Sontag, Norman Mailer, Herbert Marcuse, Michael Moore, Sarah Sarandon, Barbara Lee and thousands of other academic, literary, and political celebrities who can be counted on to regularly denounce this country, no matter what the issue, and no matter how ridiculous the charge or how paltry the evidence.

I think one key to understanding these destructive critics can be found in the career and writings of the leftist critic Gerda Lerner. Lerner was a Jewish refugee from Germany who came to the United States immediately before World War II to escape Hitler. She later made a name for herself in women's history studies. She was a dedicated and devout communist in Germany and in the U.S., until she broke with the party after Khrushchev's speech denouncing Stalin in 1956. She apparently had doubts in 1939 when Stalin and Hitler signed their non-aggression pact, but she put aside the doubts and continued to be a reliable and strong supporter of the Soviet Union until her defection a decade and a half later. Writing an autobiography many years later, she expressed some regret for her support of Stalin, but wrote, "Like all true believers, I believed as I did because I needed to believe: in a utopian vision of the future, in the possibility of human perfectibility ... And I still need that belief, even if the particular vision I had embraced has turned to ashes."

This is speculation, but it seems to me that the extreme anger and anti-American sentiments of so many modern critics (especially in academia and many mainstream media outlets) come from a toxic marriage of two memes: (1) an idealistic true-believer demand for utopian perfection (as described by Gerda Lerner) and (2) an arrogant revengeful conviction that the world has conspired against them. The first meme has its origin in traditional religious sources. The second was sometimes justified. At least it was in the case of Gerda Lerner reacting to the horrors of Nazi Germany, and even perhaps of politically aware Americans and Europeans reacting to the hardships of the great 1930s depression.

For many younger radicals in this country, however, the second kind of anger seems to me to have grown out of a common adolescent fantasy greatly exacerbated in the Vietnam War days. Students and intellectuals, previously protected, catered to and admired, were suddenly threatened with serious harm in defense of a cause they did not understand or believe in. As a result they became fiercely and lastingly anti-American.

This revengeful conviction that the world (especially the United States) is conspiring against them is not likely to diminish until the current crop of Vietnam dissidents retires or dies. Unfortunately for America, because of draft deferment policies in the Vietnam days, many able and idealistic radical students went on to become professors and media stars. Today, as professors, they dominate the faculties of most universities in this country. As media stars they dominate Hollywood, the major networks, and the new Internet blogs. Unfortunately this also means that many of their students and followers may carry some of these destructive memes into the mid-21st century.

I have concentrated my ammunition here on critics from the far-left. There are, of course, serious challenges from the right as well. Here I am talking about militia groups, abortion clinic bombers and crazies like Timothy McVeigh who killed 116 people when he set off a bomb in front of the Federal Building in Oklahoma City in 1995. These critics from the far right, however, have not made many, if any, significant inroads in the dominant media and academic world and I doubt that many, if any, of their partisans are likely to read this book.

It is probably not a good idea, however, to dismiss them so cavalierly. Hitler and his Nazi thugs were also on the fringes of the literate liberal social-democratic society of Germany in the 1920s. They were only able to make a dent and finally to take absolute command when the economic situation became grim. The moral of the story here is not to let our economic situation deteriorate. We will always have thugs with us, but we need never let them command.

Let's now move on to the second of our liberal democratic categories, science and technology, especially as it relates to environment.

SCIENCE, TECHNOLOGY AND ENVIRONMENT

SO FAR AS SCIENCE AND TECHNOLOGY goes, the American Revolution was from the start friendly to all the sciences, basic and applied. Benjamin Franklin was a prominent politician, businessman, inventor and ladies man. He was also one of the most important and acclaimed scientists of the 18th century. Thomas Jefferson, too, was famous for his work in science as well as in politics. And on the new continent of North America, pioneer farmers and craftsmen were encouraged to innovate and be scientific and economic entrepreneurs. And they were. New England soon became a leader in textile manufacturing, iron-making, shoe manufacture, hydraulic energy, lumbering and farm technology.

Since those revolutionary days, America has continued to be a world leader in science and technology. Today it is surely no accident that, according to *Washington Post* columnist Charles Krauthammer:

The U.S. leads the world by an immense margin in just about every measure of intellectual and technological achievement: Ph.D.s, patents, peer-reviewed articles, Nobel Prizes. But in the end, it's the culture, stupid. The economy follows culture, and American culture today, as ever, is uniquely suited for growth, innovation and advancement.

The most obvious bedrock of success is entrepreneurial spirit. The U.S. has the most risk-taking, most laissez-faire, least regulated economy in the advanced Western world. America is heartily disdained by its coddled and controlled European cousins for its cowboy capitalism. But it is precisely American's tolerance for creative destruction—industries failing, others rising, workers changing jobs and cities and skills with an alacrity and insouciance that Europeans find astonishing—that keeps its economy churning and advancing.[140]

A serious challenge to this leadership, and indeed to world progress today, comes from Western culture haters, critics of globalization and the more radical communicants of the new quasi-religion, Radical Environmentalism. Karl Marx claimed his new secular religion was based on science. Radical environmentalists today also claim their secular religion is based on science.

Environmental doomsayers today resemble earlier leftist fellow travelers in their demand for immediate action to radically change free-market liberal democracy in order to save the earth and avoid a worldwide Armageddon. (Actually leftist critics and environmental radicals are often one and the same. Both readily adjust their arguments and evidence to fit their goal of command-economy utopian *progress*.)

Critics like Paul Ehrlich, John Holdren (currently science advisor to the president of the United States), Jeremy Rifkin, Helen Caldicott, Bill

---

[140] "Don't Believe the Hype. We're Still No. 1," by Charles Krauthammer, *Time Magazine*, Feb. 5, 2006, p.41. Also available on *Time's* website: <http://www.time.com/time/magazine/article/0,9171,1156589,00.html>

McKibben, James Hansen, Howard Odum, Edward Abbey, Jared Diamond, Al Gore and Stephen Schneider claim that resource depletion, population growth and climate change will bring catastrophic collapse to present industrial societies unless we dramatically change our ways.

In practice, this means that we must work to drastically reduce our population, adopt a "green lifestyle," dramatically reduce our use of energy and material resources. To do this the presumption again is that we need to change gears and move beyond free-markets and free-trade capitalism to a kind of benign command-economy socialism. Proponents do not like to use the word socialism, preferring to dodge the issue by denouncing "labels" like socialism and capitalism as out-dated reactionary terms and politics.

Some of these critics think we have already passed the point of no return, and there is no way now to prevent a catastrophic collapse. The best we can do as individuals and small groups is to try to survive the collapse by retreating with our like-minded friends and neighbors into organic gardens and self-help communities.

I have analyzed and critiqued this challenge in the previous three chapters. Suffice here to note once again how seriously this dogma conflicts with the tenets of win-win free-market capitalism, how closely it resembles agricultural-age zero-sum ideas, how closely it resembles utopian socialist fantasies, and, in fact, how closely it resembles some of the Radical Islamic challenges. Both Osama bin Laden and Al Gore think our western lifestyles are decadent, unjust and certain to bring catastrophe to the world. They differ on their prescriptions to save the world.

The Radical Islamists want suicide bombers to bring our civilization down. Most Radical Environmentalists do not approve of violence, though there are exceptions. *Earth First* supporters spike trees so that lumbermen are hurt; bomb SUVs; and look to "take out a McDonald's or Starbucks"[141] or two. And then there was the Unabomber, Ted

---

[141] See "Aftermath of Terror," *The Wall Street Journal*, Sept. 12, 2001, p. A4.

Kaczynski,[142] who murdered three scientists and injured twenty-two more with mail bombs designed to call attention to his crusade to bring down industrial societies and send us back to hunter/gathering days.

In so far as Radical Environmentalism is a new secular religion, and I think it is, let's conclude with a look at religions—all religions—and their relevance to the future of free-market liberal democracy. This is the most confusing and most controversial of all issues today.

RELIGION

THE AMERICAN REVOLUTION at the end of the 18th century did not originate win-win economics, but it did give it a strong foothold on the world stage. It provided a shining example of its power to the rest of the world, and in doing so dealt a serious blow to zero-sum economic ways of life.

It also pioneered a new way of looking at religion. And that new look is one we should seriously consider once more in trying to pave the road to a new century of progress in free-market liberal democracy.

The new U.S. Constitution in 1787 significantly advanced a process that began in the Enlightenment and that many, including myself, believe will eventually result in the decline and near death of most traditional supernatural dogmatic religions. If we are really lucky, in the decline and near death of secular dogmatic religions as well. This death will probably not happen in my lifetime or that of most readers. On the other hand, the decline has already developed more momentum than many expected just a few decades ago.

Note I say "dogmatic religions," supernatural and secular. I am not talking about morality, or about faith in God or divine providence, or spiritual quests into the mysteries of the unknown. I am also not talking

---

[142] See interesting comments by liberal writers on the Unabomber: Daniel J. Kevles in *The New Yorker*, Aug. 14, 1995, pp. 3-4; and Joe Klein in *Newsweek*, Apr. 22, 1996, p. 38.

about serious secular attempts to understand and control the body politic so long as they remain open to doubt and change.

The fortunes of fundamentalist dogmas, religious and secular, have waxed and waned over the years. They are on the mildly waxing side in America today, and on the waning side in Europe. Unfortunately they seem to be explosively waxing today in some parts (not all) of the Islamic world.

IN THE FIRST AMENDMENT to the Constitution it was specified that there must be "no law respecting an establishment of religion, or prohibiting the free exercise thereof." Thomas Jefferson added later that there should be a "wall separating religion and state." To my knowledge, nowhere else in the world had this ever been so formally stated or tried. And today in many places in the world—the remaining communist countries, Israel and many Islamic countries (not all)—there is still a tenacious union of religion and state.

While the American experiment in republican government separated religion and state, it did not abandon or denigrate all religious-derived values, and, if anything, it took a firm stand in favor of a belief in divine providence and spiritual quests.

Moral lessons (memes) from Judeo-Christianity, in fact from whatever source, have always been welcomed in America, so long as they contribute to the "general welfare." Examples of Judeo-Christian derived virtues are admonitions to forgive your enemies, honor your parents, give alms to the poor, refrain from backbiting and slander, pay your debts, obey legitimate authority, be compassionate to the sick, the poor and the downtrodden, respect your elders, be generous in your love and, in sum, be honest, fair, brave and honorable in all dealings with your neighbors.

Some other "moral" lessons (memes) of past Judeo-Christian religious practice, however, were not welcomed. In fact they were sent to the ash-heap of history. For example: banning or burning heretics; using torture and other unusual punishments for suspects and for criminals; using the civil authorities to punish heretics, to ban blasphemy, to censor speech or print; using taxes to financially support religious schools or churches; using religious dogma to suppress scientific inquiry; using the state to demand adherence to religious holidays or rituals; demanding religious affiliation to run for public office. All these and more had been standard practice in many, if not most, societies in Europe and elsewhere in the world of the 18th century and before. (Some of them are still present in many European countries, even though rarely enforced.)

In addition to the welcomed moral lessons, our founding fathers, and probably the majority of our pioneer ancestors, had strong convictions about God and a deep faith in divine providence. Jefferson in the Declaration of Independence wrote, "that all men are created equal, that they are endowed *by their Creator* with certain unalienable rights, that among these are Life, Liberty and the pursuit of Happiness."

"Four score and seven years" later, Lincoln said, "this nation, *under God*, shall have a new birth of freedom …"

Lincoln had a deep (tinged with tragic) faith in a divine providence whose will was beyond our earthly wisdom, but somehow guided us in our quest for a just and prosperous society "conceived in liberty, and dedicated to the proposition that all men are created equal."

John Winthrop (no friend of democracy) in 1630 said of the Massachusetts Bay Colony that it was to be a Biblical "city upon a hill." John F. Kennedy rekindled this view of America as "exceptional" in a 1961 address.

> But I have been guided by the standard John Winthrop set before his shipmates three hundred and thirty-one years ago, as they, too, faced the task of building a new government on a perilous frontier.
>
> "We must always consider," he said, "that we shall be as a city upon a hill—the eyes of all people are upon us."
>
> Today the eyes of all people are truly upon us—and our governments, in every branch, at every level, national, state and local, must be as a city upon a hill—constructed and inhabited

by men aware of their great trust and their great responsibilities.[143]

And Ronald Reagan in his farewell address to the nation captured still once again this exceptional spirit.

> I've spoken of the shining city all my political life, but I don't know if I ever quite communicated what I saw when I said it. But in my mind it was a tall proud city built on rocks stronger than oceans, wind-swept, God-blessed, and teeming with people of all kinds living in harmony and peace, a city with free ports that hummed with commerce and creativity, and if there had to be city walls, the walls had doors and the doors were open to anyone with the will and the heart to get here. That's how I saw it, and see it still.[144]

In other words, faith in God, faith in the inexplicable, in the ever-so-deep sources of life and love, and respect for the "mysterious that is the source of all true art and science," as Albert Einstein put it, have been and still are a source of vital strength in American life and religion. Some think this kind of deep faith in divine providence played a significant role in the pioneer's settling of the west and in our "manifest destiny" to make the North American continent a model for human progress. Some think it also played a role in our triumphs in World War II, and in the Cold War against atheistic communism.

Faith in God and in divine providence does not, however, necessarily mean faith in any particular religious dogma, whether that dogma comes from religious or secular sources. Once religion, supernatural or secular, is linked with a particular theologically based dogma, it has often led to tragedy.

---

[143] JFK's last formal address before assuming presidency. Boston, MA. Jan. 9, 1961.
[144] Ronald Reagan's Farewell address to the nation. Jan. 11, 1989.

Faith in a dogmatic fundamentalist reading of the Christian Bible, for instance, led to the Salem Witch Trials in 17th-century Massachusetts. It played a part in the South's faith in the righteousness of slavery. Today it plays a role with many fundamentalist churchgoers in this country in their demands for sexual purity, bans on abortion, male superiority, rejection of homosexuality, and bans on birth control.

Faith in a dogmatic fundamentalist reading of the Koran led to the 9/11 destruction of the World Trade Center. Faith in the superiority and triumph of the Aryan peoples led to World War II and to the Holocaust. Faith in a dogmatic reading of Marx and Engels led to communist massacres, slave-labor camps and famines in which over 100 million people paid with their lives.

Communism was a secular religion. So was Nazism. And so today is Radical Environmentalism. Instead of God, all of these secular religions have a worldly substitute. In the case of Communism it is the ultimate triumph of a Socialist Utopia. In the case of Nazism it was the triumph of the Aryan People. In the case of Radical Environmentalists it is the triumph of Mother Earth. All of these religions had and have good intentions.

Communists thought they had the final answer to history's riddles. They were, and still are, convinced they are doing the bidding of science and history, and that their good intentions and their dedicated work will bring health and happiness to the world's people. Eventually.

Devout and dogmatic Christians and Muslims in the past and present are convinced that their beliefs and their efforts to promote their faiths will bring health, happiness, and in addition eternal salvation to anyone who believes and follows their example. Eventually.

True-blue believers in Radical Environmentalism are convinced their views and efforts are backed up by solid ecological science and will save the earth. Eventually.

True believers in Buddhism, Hinduism, Ecological Economics, and countless other Multicultural and New-Age religions also think they have

The Answers that will save humankind and make the world a better place. Eventually.

Perhaps we need more humorists to bring a bit of sanity to the world. Like the cartoonist, Sidney Harris, who has a bearded scientist looking at arcane equations on his blackboard while a pretty woman behind him is saying, "I am your guardian Angel, Stanley, and I hate to tell you this but I am afraid you have been barking up the wrong tree for 40 years."

WE HAVE A WONDERFUL human gift—consciousness. Like most gifts, it comes with unexpected and sometimes unpleasant consequences. As the cliché goes, a good deed rarely goes unpunished. One of the gifts that consciousness has brought to the human race is religion. Other animals don't have religions. There is some evidence that all of our human religions, supernatural and secular alike, are the offspring of that pre-conscious time in human history when people first heard voices in their heads to guide them through troubled times. Today those voices are beginning to grow fainter. Everywhere.

I suggest that it is the time to learn more humility, and to look to free ourselves, as Abraham Lincoln once advised, "from dogmas of the quiet past" which are "inadequate to the stormy present ... As our case is new, so we must think anew, and act anew. We must disenthrall ourselves, and then we shall save our country."

We do not need to free ourselves from some of the healthy and good moral and practical lessons (memes) that religions of the past and of the present have given and are still giving us. Nor do we want to free ourselves from quests to explore the mysteries of what believers call divine providence, or the mysteries that Einstein thought were the true sources of all art and science.

It is time though, high time, to disenthrall ourselves from the *dogmas* of the not-so-quiet past and the definitely stormy present, if we are to save our country and our world.

Some of the moral and practical lessons from both supernatural and secular religious dogmas are not only desirable; they are necessary for human progress. Indeed they are necessary for the future of free-market liberal democracy.

The trick is, which ones? Which moral lessons are good, which are not so good, and which are downright evil? And how do we decide?

FOR STARTERS, WE SHOULD reject any and all claims to infallibility. I mean by that not only the traditional Catholic Church's position on the Pope's being infallible, but also Lenin's claim that "to belittle the socialist ideology in any way, to turn aside from it in the slightest degree means to strengthen bourgeois ideology." Or Hitler's dogma that the Jews were responsible for all of Germany's troubles. Or Osama bin Laden's Muslim creed that condemns Western lifestyles as the work of Satan and fit only to be destroyed. Or the Radical Environmentalist dogma that condemns excessive consumption, and demands that we adapt a green lifestyle, no matter if it sacrifices the world economy.

Consider what the world might have been like in the 20th century if we had been able to free ourselves, even a little, from infallible dogmas of supernatural and secular ideologies.

The world might not have suffered through the communist trauma, which was due in large part to devotion to a powerful secular religion— Marxism-Leninism—that promoters considered scientifically infallible. We would not have had a Holocaust, which was due to a mindless anti-Semitic dogma in Europe yoked to a Germanic Nazi religion. We would not have suffered a 9/11 attack on New York and Washington, which was due to a Radical Islamic dogma. Israel and Palestine would not be at each other's throats were it not for infallible Jewish and Islamic dogmas grafted on to human beings ethnically and genetically so much alike. India and Pakistan would not be such enemies if each could soften (or abandon) some of their respective Hindu and Islamic dogmatic beliefs. Thousands would not have died in Kosovo if it had not been for dogmatic Christian/Muslim differences. Afghanistan would never have come under Taliban rule. Iraq and Iran would not have lost millions of young men in their 1980s war were it not for bitter Shiite/Sunni dogmas. Northern

Ireland would have been spared countless deaths and indignities were it not for dogmas of Catholic Christianity in conflict with dogmas of Protestant Christianity.

In a different but equally tragic case, millions of Africans and Asians might not have died from malaria, if the United States government had not been pressured into banning a useful chemical, DDT, due to irrational devotion to a radical environmentalist dogma. Africans in Zambia would not have been threatened with starvation if western environmentalists had not convinced their president that genetically engineered corn was poisonous. We would not have to worry as much about increased carbon dioxide in the air if environmentalist dogma had not virtually destroyed the growing nuclear power industry in the 1970s. (I remember the days when engineers were predicting that with the growth of nuclear power, electricity would be so cheap we would not need to meter it and—just as important—coal-fired plants would be historic antiques.)

I KNOW. I KNOW. IF WISHES WERE HORSES, beggars would ride. How can we rid ourselves of these destructive dogmas? One clue would be to admit that most dogmas have a positive side along with their more obvious negatives.

I have already mentioned some of the positive sides to Judeo-Christian dogmas. Not only the healthy and necessary moral memes, but the evidence from history that our Western civilization itself, including our free-market liberal democratic values, arose out of a Judeo-Christian history in Europe.

William McGurn, editorial writer for the *Wall Street Journal*, pointed out in a recent lecture[145] that it was an "odd assortment of Christians and agnostics" in England and "Christians [who] were joined in the Republican Party by ... men who might be described as Chamber of

---

[145] "The Not So Dismal Science: Humanitarians v. Economists" by William McGurn. In *Imprimus*, a publication of Hilldale College, Vol. 40. Number 3. March, 2011. Last accessed 4.14.11. <http://www.hillsdale.edu/images/userImages/ mvanderwei/Page_6907/Imprimis_Mar11.pdf>

Commerce types" who opposed and eventually succeeded in abolishing slavery in the Western world. In England that group included William Wilberforce, John Stuart Mill, Charles Darwin, and Thomas Huxley. Some humanitarian and literary figures of the day, including Charles Dickens, John Ruskin and Alfred Tennyson, in fact, sometimes opposed them. In America, Abraham Lincoln led a liberating combination of evangelical Christians and agnostic liberal business types to bring an end to slavery in the United States.[146]

Secular religions like Communism, Fascism and Radical Environmentalism also have lessons valuable for future human progress—so long as the lessons do not calcify into destructive dogmas.

Communism, for instance, teaches that equality and fairness are desirable virtues. They are. In context, and in balance with freedom and common sense. Exploited workers are a fact, and we do need to find better ways to protect people from the abuses that come with unfettered capitalism. Effective industrial trade unions are one answer. Western liberal democracies have already taken other important steps to bring about more equality and fairness. National health care systems, safety welfare nets, unemployment insurance, social security and environmental legislation are all examples. And all are common in modern western liberal free-market democracies today.

One danger is that in implementing these social welfare programs, we so handicap the basic engine of wealth creation—win-win free-market capitalism—that we end up with less wealth to distribute. A smaller pie means all must have a smaller piece, rich and poor alike. For the rich this may not be so tragic, for the poor it could be catastrophic.

If we go too far in the Fascist direction, we also lose freedom and so damage efficiency with command-economy social planning that the economy will shrink instead of expand. Hitler can never be forgiven for claiming the Jews were the cause of Germany's problems. But he, and other fascists, were right in claiming that people are not all equal in talents

---

[146] For details on this history of religions and its importance today, see Chapters 10 and 11 of this book.

or productivity. One of the three critical components of Adam Smith's capitalist advice is division of labor. This implies diversity of talents and inequality of results.

Hitler's criminal record has made it ever since politically suicidal to point to obvious facts—that people differ significantly in all human characteristics. He was wrong that the so-called "Aryan" race was "superior," and in claiming that Jews, Africans and other non-Aryans were "inferior." He and other racists are wrong today in suggesting that any group is "inferior" or "superior." But he and many other people today are right to claim that people differ in any and every trait you can name.

It is simply a fact that for all living creatures—plant, animal and human—there are bell curves for all measurable characteristics.

In human beings that means that there are bell curves for height, weight, athletic ability, strength, intelligence, speed, musical ability, sensual acuity, susceptibility to diseases, introversion, extroversion, longevity, social skills. You name it, there is a bell curve.[147]

It is not politically correct to say this. Probably no politician today could be elected if he or she calls undue attention to the bell curves. But that does not mean they are not there; nor that almost everyone knows they are there; nor that the bell curves do not play a strong part in the political, social and economic life of all countries in the world.

Bell curves do not have to reinforce prejudices however. Most people are smart and wise enough to distinguish between individuals and groups. Recognition of the bell curve reality can offer hope for reconciliation and progress. While Jews and Orientals may be, on the average and on the median, superior when it comes to academic and scientific achievement, they may also be, on the average and on the median, inferior when it comes to other important human activities and achievements. While African-Americans may be, on the average and on the median, superior when it comes to many sports, they may not be so when it comes to other important activities and achievements. So? Let it be.

---

[147] See the controversial but also solidly documented book, *The Bell Curve: Intelligence and Class Structure in American Life* by Richard J. Herrnstein and Charles Murray.

Many other traits—speed, strength, social skills, street smarts, musical ability, sports skills, empathy, verbal fluency, sense of humor, empathy[148] and ability to convince others, elocution, selling skills—are often far more important and far more prized by most people than academic or scientific achievements. Certainly far more important than scores on any test.

Most important of all, "average" and "median" have no meaning and no relation to *individuals* in any given social, ethnic or racial group.

Knowledge and acceptance of these bell curves and their irrelevance for individuals is especially important in the early 21st century when people from all countries, regions and ethnic groups are mingling, merging, interacting, marrying and often clashing with one another. Jews with Slavs in Russia, Chinese with Philippines in Southeast Asia, Tutsis with Hutus in Uganda, Muslims with Europeans in Europe, African-Americans with Latin-Americans and Whites in the U.S., whites with native Africans in Zimbabwe and South Africa, Mexican immigrants with Anglo-Saxon citizens in the U.S., Latinos with blacks and Puerto Ricans, Japanese with Koreans, and hundreds if not hundreds of thousands of other racial and ethnic groups in societies around the world, with hundreds if not hundreds of thousands of competing racial and ethnic groups in societies around the world.

What should be done about the bell curve differences?

My solution sounds simplistic and callous. Nothing. A wag once said all comparisons are odious. And so they are. Let's have a moratorium on group comparisons. Border collies on the average are more intelligent than cocker spaniels. Greyhounds on the average are faster than golden retrievers. People love all four with equal passion. Jersey cattle on the average give more butter fat than Holsteins. Holsteins on the average are more productive of raw milk. Everyone has his or her favorite variety of tomatoes. Writing great books is valuable. So is cleaning the house,

---

[148] See "Social Class, Contextualism, and Empathic Accuracy" by Michael W. Kraus, Stephane Cote and Dacher Keltner. *Psychological Science*, Oct. 25, 2010, <http://www.rotman.utoronto.ca/facbios/file/Kraus%20Côté%20Keltner%20PS%20in%20press.pdf>

collecting the garbage, playing in the Super Bowl, giving speeches, writing songs, playing the guitar and mining the iron ore. Provide the maximum of opportunity, live with a variety of outcomes, and respect all good people as unique individuals for what they do and what they can't do.

Of course doing nothing is more an intellectual solution than a practical one. When there are bitter ethnic or racial conflicts, intellectual solutions are feeble. Here is where the humanistic influences of religion can help: forgive your enemies and be kind to your neighbors is not just good religion, it is good politics, good economics and good morality. It worked well after the Second World War in our relations with defeated Germany and Japan. It worked well as championed by Nelson Mandela in South Africa, where he not only led the forces that overcame the apartheid system, but then established and fostered a policy of forgiveness. It worked well in Germany when the Berlin Wall came down and East and West were united again. It worked well when the Irish Catholics and Protestants found a way to make peace in Northern Ireland after so many centuries of bitter conflict.

Another result of free markets causes problems today. Free markets reward achievements in any and all human activities, but they reward some achievements more than others. How much income and how much reward free markets give individuals is a democratic choice and a democratic decision. Let the chips fall where they may. Let the people decide. Everyone wins. Some win more than others, it is true. But if you try too hard to get equal outcomes, you end up with equal misery.

The dancer Martha Graham put into words an ideal we should strive for, individually and as a society, "There is a vitality, a life force, an energy, a quickening that is translated through you into action, and because there is only one of you in all of time, this expression is unique. And if you block it, it will never exist through any other medium and it will be lost. The world will not have it."

SO IF WE ADMIT THAT DOGMATIC solutions are no solutions at all, how else can we know what directions are good and what directions not so good unless we have some principles to go by? Once we reject infallible dogmas, are there any principles we can use to judge how best to defend and advance the fortunes of free-market liberal democracy?

Just stating these questions, we have clues to answering them. Programs that advance free markets will probably be good. Programs that advance liberal ideals (liberal meaning freedom, in the classical sense of 18th-century Enlightenment philosophers) will probably be good. And finally, programs that advance human welfare will probably be good. Programs that synergistically advance all three have the greatest chances to be good.

I said "probably" in all these cases. In the short run and in the long run politicians and citizens will have to make up their own collective minds about any particular program. And there will inevitably be mistakes. We may have to all be like Supreme Court justices and judge a given program by whether it contributes to "a more perfect Union, establishes Justice, insures domestic tranquility, provides for the common defence, promotes the general welfare, and secures the Blessings of Liberty to ourselves and our posterity."

I realize, as Tony Blair comments in *A Journey*, "Most people, most of the time, don't give politics a first thought all day long. Or if they do, it is with a sigh or a harrumph or a raising of the eyebrows, before they go back to worrying about the kids, the parents, the mortgages, the boss, their friends, their weight, their health, sex and rock 'n roll."[149]

But most people, most of the time, do know when and where the shoe pinches. In a well functioning free-market liberal democracy, that means there is a certain homeostatic equilibrium that usually brings the ship of state back to a more or less even keel. Not always. We did have to go through a terrible civil war to get rid of slavery. But with that important exception, the United States has managed to make more or less steady progress in advancing life, liberty and the pursuit of happiness for over two centuries. Not many countries can say as much.

---

[149] *A Journey: My Political Life* by Tony Blair, p. 70.

And so we come back to the road to future progress. This will not be exactly the same road our founding fathers traveled. But the general direction is there. Limited government to tame the beast, reduce the debt, and encourage individual responsibility. More science and technology to improve efficiency—to do more with less—and to increase intelligence— more reason and fewer *voices*. And finally a return to the best parts of humanistic religion—reduce crime and violence, forgive your enemies, calm ethnic differences, and increase the health and well-being of all.

No political party will be able to accomplish all of this. There is no free lunch and there is no magic wand. Everything is compared to what. The Democratic Party today is too beholden to the unions, the trial lawyers and the radical environmentalists. The Republican Party today has become too beholden to large corporations and bankers. The new Tea Party is beholden to two groups. One is libertarians, whose hallmark is freedom. In *Give Us Liberty: A Tea Party Manifesto*, the authors, Dick Armey and Matt Kibbe write, "We just want to be free. Free to lead our lives as we please, so long as we do not infringe on the same freedom of others."

But Jonathan Haidt, a social psychologist at the University of Virginia, points to another side, "the passion of the tea party movement is, in fact, a moral passion. It can be summarized in one word: not liberty, but karma."

> The notion of karma comes with lots of new-age baggage, but it is an old and very conservative idea. It is the Sanskit word for "deed" or "action," and the law of karma says that for every action there is an equal and morally commensurate reaction. Kindness, honesty and hard work will (eventually) bring good fortune; cruelty, deceit and laziness will (eventually) bring suffering. No divine intervention is required; it's just a law of the universe, like gravity. ...

In the tea partiers' scheme of things, the federal government got into the business of protecting the American people— from market fluctuations as well as from their own bad decisions—under Franklin D. Roosevelt. During the Great Depression, most Americans recognized that capitalism required safety nets here and there. But Lyndon Johnson's effort to build the Great Society, and particularly welfare programs that reduced the incentives for work and marriage among the poor, went much further. ...

Now jump ahead to today's ongoing financial and economic crisis. Again, those guilty of corruption and irresponsibility have escaped the consequences of their wrongdoing, rescued first by President Bush and then by President Obama. Bailouts and bonuses sent unimaginable sums of the taxpayers' money to the very people who brought calamity upon the rest of us. Where is punishment for the wicked?

As the tea partiers see it, the positive side of karma has been weakened, too. The Protestant work ethic (karma's Christian cousin) holds that hard work is a duty and will bring commensurate rewards. Yet here, too, liberals have long been uncomfortable with karma, because even when you create equal opportunity, differences in talent and effort result in unequal outcomes. These inequalities must then be reduced by progressive taxation, affirmative action and other heavy-handed government intervention. ...[150]

---

[150] "What the Tea Partiers Really Want" by Jonathan Haidt, *The Wall Street Journal*, Oct. 16, 2010. <http://online.wsj.com/article/SB10001424052748703673604575550243700895762.html>

Voices

SADLY MANY, IF NOT MOST, of the conflicts and horrors of this sad world today are brought on by people hearing authoritarian "voices" from their teachers, parents and media stars, as well as their political leaders, whether clerical or secular, that tell them in one way or another that their religion is the only true religion, their views are the only morally right views, and if only everyone would follow them, the world would be a better place.

The only honest answer is, of course, that there is no answer, at least not one with a capital A. Utopia chasing, like true believing, is not only counter-productive, it can be evil. If we can learn nothing more from the collapse of communism and the challenge of Radical Islam, it should be a lesson of humility. We should be very wary of people who claim to have *The Answer* and listen instead to more modest folks like the late physicist Richard Feynman who urged us to pursue ...

> A satisfactory philosophy of ignorance, and the progress made possible by such a philosophy, progress which is the fruit of freedom of thought.
>
> I feel a responsibility to proclaim the value of this freedom and to teach that doubt is not to be feared, but that it is to be welcomed as the possibility of a new potential for human beings. If you know that you are not sure, you have a chance to improve the situation. I want to demand this freedom for future generations.[151]

Considering the passionate hold that religions, clerical and secular, still have on so many billions of human beings, can we realistically expect to

---

[151] Richard P. Feynman, *The Meaning of It All: Thoughts of a Citizen-Scientist,* Reading, MA: Perseus Books, 1998.

get freedom from any and all true-believing infallible faiths and yet retain the progressive memes that come with all religions?

From Christianity (and most other supernatural faiths): forgiveness of enemies, tolerance, kindness to strangers, concern for the poor and downtrodden, explorations into the "mysterious that is the source of all true art and science," plain civility in everyday life, love. Why not?

From Communism: fairness, equality and justice. Why not?

From Fascism: acceptance of inequalities in human society and a commitment to order. Why not?

From Radical Environmentalism: passion for clean air, water and soil and preserving earth's ecosystems. Why not?

Can we realistically expect to ever escape the intolerant "voices" of dogmatic "experts" and demagogues that plague all of these religions, secular and supernatural? Why not?

IN 1787 OUR FOUNDING FATHERS showed us the way, though we may have slipped backwards in this country in recent years. In some ways Europe may be showing us the road to freedom from some of these religious absolutes in the 21st century. Perhaps the depths of Europe's hideous descents into secular religious barbarisms in the 20th century have taught them important lessons and now they can be the leaders.

The growing strength of the idea that says wealth is not zero-sum, but potentially win-win, will be helpful. One surprising finding recently highlights the importance of wealth in opening people's minds and shaking their faith in utopias and gurus. As millions of people worldwide move into the much-derided but also much-imitated middle class, their consciousness goes through changes, most of them desirable. Contrary to some literary myths, middle class people worldwide are more diverse and more tolerant than poor people. And the wealthier they become, the more varied and open-minded they become. It turns out that not only did the proletariat of Marx and Lenin not become more alienated, exploited and impoverished. They became more bourgeois.

Middle class people on the whole are more open-minded, take more care in raising their children, take more interest in political and social issues, and are more influenced by abstract values than by traditional ones. On the whole, too, they are less likely to be caught up in mindless irrational mass movements, though I realize this has in the past been more honored in the breach than in the reality.

Middle class people are also becoming smarter (see page 216). A psychology researcher in New Zealand, James Flynn, found that on the average people's IQs are increasing at a rate of 3 points a year. In effect this means that teenagers today who score an average 100 on intelligence tests, if they were to take the IQ tests of 1911 would score at the 130 gifted level.[152]

Stephen Pinker in his book *The Better Angels of our Nature: Why Violence Has Decreased* claims that the decrease in violence in recent decades has two major causes. One is the increase in trade (moving away from zero-sum transactions), the other is the increase in intelligence (the Flynn Effect).

Unfortunately, the rapid expansion of social welfare programs in Europe as well as in the United States over the last few decades has had a powerful negative side.[153] As more and more citizens in Europe and in America have become more dependent on government subsidies, the freedom and self-reliance necessary for free-market progress has suffered. Recent riots in European countries, as well as noisy protests in this country in reaction to cutbacks in government subsidies, demonstrate how difficult will be the return to a healthy free market.

The impressive popularity of "green" lifestyles presents another and different challenge to free-market liberal democracy. Fortunately, most people who intellectually subscribe to many of the tenets of radical environmentalism do not choose to live that way. When push comes to

---

[152] Review in NY Times by Peter Singer, Oct. 6, 2011. <http://www.nytimes.com/2011/10/09/books/review/the-better-angels-of-our-nature-by-steven-pinker-book-review.html?_r=1&scp=2&sq=book%20review%20pinker&st=cse>
[153] "The Coming White Underclass" by Charles Murray, *Wall Street Journal*, Oct. 29, 1993. See also his influential book, *Losing Ground: American Social Policy, 1950-1980.*

shove, most people choose comfort and freedom over austerity and denial, despite the preaching and scolding of gurus like Paul Ehrlich, Bill McKibben, Michael Moore and Al Gore (most of whom are themselves not famous for austerity and denial). The same observation applies to most members of Congress, the Judiciary, and the Executive Branch.

AS TO ESCAPING THE TYRANNY of traditional religious dogmas, my own Catholic background offers hints. I made a difficult but in the end clean break with the church and no longer consider myself a practicing Catholic. Many millions of other Catholics, in my own family and in the world, have migrated to a kind of quasi-Catholic point of view in their beliefs and in their actions. Probably due to the increasing wealth and prosperity (increasing intelligence too?) of Catholic families in this country and in Europe, this has been a big change in my lifetime.

Good, even devout, Catholics today still go to Church. They still pray. They still believe in a life after death. But they no longer religiously follow the dogmas of their faith, or the commands of the Pope. Not to the letter, nor even to the spirit. Catholic birth rates, for example, have plummeted in all European countries, especially so in the most Catholic countries of all, Italy and Ireland. This has happened despite the Pope's often-repeated condemnation of artificial birth control and abortion. Young Catholic couples in Europe and in America pay little heed to the Pope's and the bishop's condemnation of pre-marital sex. And of course we know now how fragile the clergy's commitment is to the church's puritanical embrace of chastity.

These same movements are also apparent in many Protestant families and to a perhaps lesser degree in middle-class and wealthy Muslim families. No doubt we will probably not see the end of the tenacious hold that faith and supernatural beliefs have on many people in any of our lifetimes. Even though reason tells us that prayer is stunningly unreliable, and that life after death is a comforting myth, most people want to believe in the power of prayer and in an afterlife. Neither of these beliefs causes much damage to society, at least not in their present-day form. (In

Christian Medieval days they did bring much damage, and in their Islamic form today they are only too often tragically destructive.) Many people still do want to believe in the infallible wisdom of many religious and secular gurus of politics, science and popular media. These beliefs today do cause damage.

Examples of major countries that presently seem to operate successfully in a kind of quasi-religious noosphere are the Scandinavian countries, Sweden and Denmark. A book, *Society Without God* by Phil Zuckerman, a sociologist at Pitzer College in Claremont, California, provides evidence that such a society is not only possible, but is desirable. "Many religious folks in this country imagine that a world that abandons the Bible and strong religious beliefs would be rampant with immorality, full of evil and teeming with depravity," writes Zuckerman. After fourteen months studying and interviewing people in Sweden and Denmark he found that their society was on the contrary, and on the whole "a markedly irreligious society that was above all, moral, stable, humane and deeply good."

People there do retain membership in Christian churches and do not consider themselves atheists. Instead they simply seem to have lost interest in the dogmatic supernatural aspects of their religion. Zuckerman found that when he asked educated Swedes and Danes basic questions about God, Jesus, death, and the afterlife, the most common response was, "I really have never thought about that." Less than four percent of Swedes attend church in an average week.

Yet a few hundred years ago both Sweden and Denmark were deeply religious monarchies that fought many bitter wars with each other as well as with Russia, France and other European powers. These wars, like most wars of the agricultural ages, had zero-sum economic causes, but they also were passionately supported by dogmatic religious convictions. Note also that some of their most prominent intellectuals and Nobel Prize winners in the late 19th and early 20th century—Henrik Ibsen, August Strindberg and Søren Kierkegaard—were deeply involved in religious questions.

They were a long way from, "I really have never thought about that." Times change.

I know you could argue that German middle-class educated people did get caught up in the mass movements of the Nazi era, and even made up the core support for hideous national crimes. The middle classes of the early 20th century, however, are not the middle classes of the early 21st century. They are smarter for one thing. They are also wealthier. And today all over Europe, including Germany, authoritarian supernatural and secular religions seem to be in decline.

We can hope it is an irreversible decline. While people still label themselves Catholic, Communist, Protestant, Royalist, Green, or Socialist, they rarely attend church, rarely participate in mass religious or political rallies, and in general are more interested in their own personal "life, liberty and pursuit of happiness." (See a few paragraphs above, however, for how this self-interest pursuit can cause problems when governments try to rein in expensive social-welfare benefits.) On the whole the "voices" seem to be fading, and perhaps soon they may not be heard at all. These irreligious, but moral Europeans are, as a matter of fact, moving closer to the views of our founding fathers, Washington, Jefferson, Adams, Franklin, Paine and Madison.

Unfortunately there is an important exception in Europe and that is the growing population of Muslim immigrants whose numbers and devotion to authoritarian voices seems to be strong. Here the progressive push for multi-cultural values may have backfired. Germany, France, Holland, Denmark, Sweden and other countries of Europe are struggling to assimilate and integrate Muslim immigrants into western cultures. So far they do not seem to have made much progress.

On the other hand, recent progress in Iraq offers hope that Muslim cultures are changing right in the heart of the Middle Eastern caldron of extremism. A recent article in *The New York Times*, "Baghdad's Shiite Heart Beats Freely as War Ebbs," offers hope. In the predominately Shiite Sadr City section of Baghdad, a "neighborhood known for its black-clad militiaman and strict Islamic codes, this was the scene on a recent evening: young men with angular haircuts shooting pool at curbside tables; coffeehouses bursting with hookah smokers and American movies; a raucous wedding party banging drums in celebration; photo studios displaying pictures of women with bared shoulders" A young man hanging out with three friends said, "No one is harassing us to think one way. Religion is available, and I worship God, but people who are praying and going to the mosque are also playing billiards and going to the coffee shops." [154]

SO FAR AS SOCIAL AND POLITICAL progress is concerned, the United States was the world leader back in 1787 as it still is today. Our founding fathers—Franklin, Jefferson, Adams, Washington, Hamilton, Paine, Madison, Monroe and the rest—were a small elite group who made a big difference. While it is not accurate to say they freed us from religion, they made a good start in freeing us from clerical authority and infallible dogma.

It worked. The steps, that is, toward a separation of church and state, and the steps toward rational science and away from the dogmas of both supernatural and secular religion. It worked so well that two hundred and some years later over half the world is following our lead.

I realize that today there is backsliding, as there was in periodic waves throughout the past two centuries. Religious revivals and fundamentalist preachers yesterday and today often made and make the claim that America is founded on dogmatic Christian religious principles. As I have tried to make clear in this book, it is true only in a very limited way. It is true that western free-market liberal democracies have medieval Christian ancestors. It is also true that much of our social welfare progress and humanitarian moral spirit has a Judeo-Christian base. But it is also true that it took a Renaissance, a Reformation, and Enlightenment—and a political revolution in America—to update that Christian ancestry, to change it radically to serve the modern world.

---

[154] John Leland, *The New York Times*, Oct. 30, 2010, p. A1.

SO ONCE AGAIN, and for the last time—what is to be done today?

Continue to lead in the direction of freedom. Reject the voices of infallible dogma and unreasoned faith, both religious and secular variety. Promote, nurture and continue to improve free-market liberal democracy and free-inquiry science. Encourage and facilitate legal immigration. Make the United States the heartland of vigorous international free trade and entrepreneurial expansion movements. Encourage private enterprises, small and large. Fine tune social welfare programs to avoid, as much as possible, ones that encourage self-destructive dependence on the government. Promote programs that lead to good karma, healthy moral values and vigorous economic growth. Make sure that our environment is healthy but make equally sure the costs do not massively outweigh the benefits.

Instead of following voices of authority and dependence, we should preach and live a life of joyful freedom or, as I once put it in a youthful poem:

> Add our increment of honest meaning
> to the not-quite-finished universe.

As Friedrich Hayek pointed out in his book *The Road to Serfdom*, the goals of both socialism and fascism are one thing, the means to reach those goals are often another story. Hayek claimed that command-economy planning is common to both socialism and fascism. Unfortunately and ultimately command-economy planning, whether in a socialist or a fascist state, often leads to ends not desired by socialists, fascists, or anyone else. He thought, and I think, the confusion between noble ends and fallible means is unfortunate. If we use the means first dramatically and exceptionally brought into play by our founding fathers in 1787—free-market liberal democratic ones—in the long run we are more likely to achieve ends we all can agree are desirable and good.

Ironically when freedom is the means we may better approach the ends that the good socialist, Maxim Gorky, wrote about so movingly in *Mother: The Great Revolutionary Novel.*

> There will come a time, I know, when people will take delight in one another, when each will be like a star to the other, and when each will listen to his fellow as to music. The free men will walk upon the earth, men great in their freedom. They will walk with open hearts, and the heart of each will be pure of envy and greed, and therefore all mankind will be without malice, and there will be nothing to divorce the heart from reason. Then life will be one great service to man! His figure will be raised to lofty heights—for to free men all heights are attainable. Then we shall live in truth and freedom and in beauty, and those will be accounted the best who will the more widely embrace the world with their hearts, and whose love of it will be the profoundest; those will be the best who will be the freest; for in them is the greatest beauty. Then will life be great, and the people will be great who live that life.

At this moment of human history one country, and only one country, the United States of America, can still lead the way. If we mind our p's and q's, as Lincoln said a hundred and sixty years ago, we will continue to be "the last best hope of earth."

BIBLIOGRAPHY

Allende, Isabel. *Paula: A Memoir.* New York: HarperCollins, 1995.

Ames, Bruce. *"Dietary Carcinogens and Anti-Carcinogens,"* Science, p. 1256, 23 September, 1983.

Andrews, Antony. *The Greeks.* New York: W.W. Norton, 1978.

Applebaum, Anne. *Gulag: A History.* New York: Anchor Books, 2004.

Arendt, Hannah. *The Origins of Totalitarianism.* New York: World Publishing Co., 1951.

Armey, Dick and Matt Kibbe. *Give Us Liberty: A Tea Party Manifesto.* New York: William Morrow, 2010.

Armstrong, Karen. *Islam: A Short History.* New York: Modern Library, 2002.

Ash, Timothy Garton. *Free World: America, Europe, and the Surprising Future of the West.* New York: Random House, 2004.

Atkins, Peter. *Galileo's Finger: The Ten Great Ideas of Science.* New York: Oxford Univ. Press, 2004.

Bailey, Ronald. *Eco-Scam: The False Prophets of Ecological Apocalypse.* New York: St. Martin's Press, 1993.

Bailyn, Bernard. *The Ideological Origins of the American Revolution.* New York: Random House, 2004.

Bainton, Roland H. & Jaroslav Pelikan. *The Reformation of the Sixteenth Century.* Boston: Beacon Press, 1985.

Bauer, Susan Wise. *The History of the Medieval World: From the Conversion of Constantine to the First Crusade.* New York: W. W. Norton, 2010.

Beaud, Michel. *A History of Capitalism, 1500-2000.* New York: Monthly Review Press, 2001.

Berger, Suzanne and the MIT Industrial Performance Center. *How We Compete: What Companies Around the World Are Doing to Make It in Today's Global Economy.* New York: Doubleday, 2006.

Bettmann, Otto L. *The Good Old Days—They Were Terrible!* New York: Random House, 1974.

Blair, Tony. *A Journey: My Political Life.* New York: Alfred A. Knopf, 2010.

Blankley, Tony. *The West's Last Chance: Will We Win the Clash of Civilizations?* Washington, DC: Regnery Publishing, 2005.

Bloom, Alan and Saul Bellows. *The Closing of the American Mind.* New York: Simon and Shuster, 1988.

Boas, Marie. *The Scientific Revolution, 1450-1630.* New York: Harpers, 1962.

Boot, Max. *War Made New: Technology, Warfare, and the Course of History 1500 to Today.* New York: Gotham Books, 2006.

Bush, George W. *Decisions Points.* New York: Crown, 2010.

Butterfield, Herbert. *The Origins of Modern Science.* New York: Macmillan, 1957.

Brand, Stewart. *Whole Earth Catalog.* San Francisco: Portola Institute, 1968.

—- *Whole Earth Discipline: An Ecopragmatist Manifesto.* New York: Viking, 2009.

Brands, H. W. *American Colossus: The Triumph of Capitalism, 1865-1900.* New York: Doubleday, 2010.

The First American: The Life and Times of Benjamin Franklin. New York: Anchor, 2002.

Brooks Michael. *13 Things That Don't Make Sense.* New York: Vintage Books, 2008.

Bronowski, J. *The Ascent of Man.* Boston: Little Brown & Company, 1973.

Brown, Archie. *The Rise and Fall of Communism.* New York: Ecco, 2009.

Bruchey, Stuart. *The Wealth of the Nation: An Economic History of the United States.* New York: Harper and Row, 1998.

Buruma and Avishai Margalit. *Occidentalism: The West in the Eyes of Its Enemies.* New York: The Penguin Press, 2004.

Cahill, Thomas. *Mysteries of the Middle Ages: And the Beginning of the Modern World.* New York: Anchor, 2008.

—— *How the Irish Saved Civilization.* New York: Anchor, 1996.

Capponi, Niccolo. *Victory of the West: The Great Christian-Muslim Clash at the Battle of Lepanto.* New York: Da Capo Press, 2008.

Carson, Rachel. *Silent Spring.* New York: Mariner Books Reprint, 2002.

Çhang, Jung. *Wild Swans: Three Daughters of China.* New York: Simon and Shuster, 1991.

—— with John Halliday, *The Unknown Story of Mao.* New York: Alfred Knopf, 2005.

Cheney, Edward Potts. *European Background of American History 1300-1600.* New York: Collier Books, 1984.

Chernow, Ron. *Alexander Hamilton.* New York: Penguin Books, 2005.

Chomsky, Noam. *Failed States: The Abuse of Power and the Assault on Democracy.* New York: Henry Holt Metropolitan Books, 2006.

—with Lois Meyer and Benjamin Maldonado. *New World of Indigenous Resistance.* San Francisco: City Lights Publishers, 2010.

Chua, Amy. *World on Fire: How Exporting Free Market Democracy Breeds Ethnic Hatred and Global Instability.* New York: Doubleday, 2003.

Cipolla, Carlo M. *Faith, Reason and Plague in Seventeenth-Century Tuscany.* New York: W. W. Norton, 1981.

Codrescu, Andrei. *Ay, Cuba!* New York: St. Martin's Press, 1999.

Cohen, Daniel. *Globalization and Its Enemies.* Cambridge, MA: MIT Press, 2006.

Cohen, Stephen. *Rethinking the Soviet Experience: Politics and History since 1917*. New York: Oxford Univ. Press, 1986.

Commanger, Henry Steele. *Jefferson, Nationalism and the Enlightenment*. New York: George Braziller, Inc., 1975.

Constable, Pamela and Arturo Vobrizuela. *A Nation of Enemies: Chile under Pinochet*. New York: W. W. Norton, 1993.

Conquest, Robert. *The Great Terror: A Reassessment*. New York: Oxford Univ. Press, 2007.

—- *The Harvest of Sorrow: Soviet Collectivization and the Terror-Famine*. New York: Oxford Univ. Press, 1987.

Cotterell, Arthur and David Morgan. *China's Civilization*. New York: Holt, Rinehart and Winston, 1961.

Crankshaw, Edward. *Khrushchev: A Career*. New York: Viking Press, 1966.

Crowley, Roger. *1453: The Holy War for Constantinople and the Clash of Islam and the West*. New York: Hyperion, 2005.

Dalrymple, Theodore. *Life at the Bottom: The Worldview That Makes the Underclass*. New York: Ivan R. Dee, 2003.

Daniels, Robert Vincent. *Red October*. New York: Beacon Press, 1997.

Darwin, Charles. *On The Origin of Species By Means of Natural Selection*. Abridged and introduced by Richard E. Leakey. New York: Hill and Wang, 1979.

Dawkins, Richard. *The Selfish Gene*. New York: Oxford University Press, 1976.

—- *The God Delusion*. New York: Mariner Books, 2008.

Dennett, Daniel C. *Breaking the Spell: Religion as a Natural Phenomenon*. New York: Viking, 2006.

—-*Freedom Evolves*. New York: Penguin Books, 2005.

Dewey, John. *Reconstruction in Philosophy*. New York: Beacon Press, 1971.

Diamond, Jared. *Guns, Germs, and Steel: The Fates of Human Societies*. New York: W.W. Norton, 1999.

—- *Collapse: How Societies Choose to Fail or Succeed*. New York: Penguin, 2005.

Dickstein, Morris. *Dancing in the Dark: A Cultural History of the Great Depression*. New York: W. W. Norton, 2010.

Donkin, Richard. *Blood Sweat and Tears: The Evolution of Work*. New York: Texere, 2001.

Drexler, K. Eric and Chris Peterson with Gayle Pergamit. *Unbounding the Future: The Nanotechnology Revolution*. New York: William Morrow, 1991.

D'Souza, Dinesh. *What's So Great about America?* Washington, DC: Regnery Publishing, 2002.

Dukes, Paul. *A History of Russia: Medieval, Modern, Contemporary, 1882-1996.*. Durham, NC: Duke University Press, 1997.

Dubois, Rene. *The Wooing of Earth*. New York: Charles Scribner, 1980.

Dyson, Freeman J. *The Sun, The Genome and the Internet*. New York: Oxford University Press, 1990.

—*Disturbing the Universe*. New York: Basic Books, 1981.

Easterbrook, Gregg. *Sonic Boom: Globalization at Mach Speed*. New York: Random House, 2009.

Ehrlich, Paul R. *Human Natures. Genes, Culture and the Human Prospect*. Washington, DC: Island Press, 2000.

—- and Anne H. Ehrlich. *The Dominant Animal: Human Evolution and the Environment*. New York: Island Press, 2009.

—- *Population Bomb*. New York: Ballantine Books, 1968.

Eisley, Loren. *Darwin's Century: Evolution and the Men Who Discovered It*. New York: Barnes & Noble, 2009.

Ellis, Joseph J. *Founding Brothers: The Revolutionary Generation*. New York: Alfred A. Knopf, 2002.

Erdoes, Richard. *AD 1000: Living on the Brink of Apocalypse*. New York: Harper and Row, 1988.

Evans, Richard J. *The Coming of the Third Reich*. New York: The Penguin Press, 2004.

Ferling, John. *A Leap in the Dark: The Struggle to Create the American Republic*. New York: Oxford Univ. Press, 2003.

Ferris, Timothy. *The Science of Liberty: Democracy, Reason, and the Laws of Nature*. New York: Harper, 2010.

Ferguson, Niall. *The Ascent of Money: A Financial History of the World*. New York: Penguin Press, 2008.

Feynman, Richard. *What Do You Care What Other People Think? Further Adventures of a Curious Character*. New York: W. W. Norton, 2001.

—*Surely You're Joking, Mr. Feynman! (Adventures of a Curious Character)*. New York: W. W. Norton, 1997.

—*The Meaning of It All: Thoughts of a Citizen-Scientist,* Reading, MA: Perseus Books, 1998.

Findley, Carter Vaughn. *The Turks in World History*. New York: Oxford Univ. Press, 2005.

Fischer, Louis. *The Life of Lenin*. New York: Weidenfeld & Nicolson History, 2001.

Fonseca, Isabel. *Bury Me Standing: The Gypsies and Their Journey*. New York: Vintage, 1996.

Friedman, Milton. *Capitalism and Freedom*. Chicago: University of Chicago Press, 1982.

—and Rose Friedman. *Free to Choose*. New York: Harcourt, Brace and Jovanovich, 1980.

Friedman, Thomas J. *The Lexus and the Olive Tree*. New York: Random House, 2000.

Friendly, Fred W. and Martha J. H. Elliot. *The Constitution: That Delicate Balance*. New York: Random House, 1984.

Fromm, Erich. *Marx's Concept of Man*. New York: Continuum, 2004.

Fulcher, James. *Capitalism: A Very Short Introduction*. New York: Oxford Univ. Press, 2004.

Fuller, R. Buckminster. *Operating Manual for Spaceship Earth*. New York: Lars Muller Publishers, Reprint, 2008.

—*Utopia or Oblivion: The Prospects for Humanity*. New York: Lars Muller Publishers, 2008.

Fukuyama, Francis. *The End of History and the Last Man*. New York: HarperCollins, 1992.

Fulsom, Burton, Jr. *New Deal of Raw Deal? How FDR's Economic Legacy Has Damaged America*. New York: Simon and Shuster, 2008.

Gaddis, John Lewis. *The Cold War: A New History*. New York: Penguin Books, 2006.

Galbraith, John Kenneth. *The Affluent Society*. Boston: Houghton Mifflin, 1958.

—*The New Industrial State*. Princeton, NJ: Princeton University Press, 2007. First published in 1967.

Gat, Azar. *War in Human Civilization*. New York: Oxford Univ. Press, 2006.

Gilder, George. *Wealth and Poverty*. New York: Basic Books, 1981.

Ginsberg, Alan. *Howl and Other Poems*. San Francisco: City Lights, 2001.

Global 2000 Report to the President, Vols. I, II, and III. Washington, DC: U.S. Government Printing Office, 1980.

Gold, Herbert. *Best Nightmare on Earth: A Life in Haiti.* New York: Prentice Hall, 1991.

Goldhagen, Daniel Jonah. *Hitler's Willing Executioners: Ordinary Germans and the Holocaust.* New York: Random House, 1997.

Goldstein, Thomas. *Dawn of Modern Science: From The Ancient Greeks To The Renaissance.* New York: Da Capo Press, 1995.

Gordon, John Steele. *Empire of Wealth: The Epic History of American Economic Power.* New York: Harper Perennial, 2005.

Gore, Al. *Earth in the Balance: Ecology and the Human Spirit.* New York: Rodale Books, 2006.

Gorky, Maxim. *Mother: The Great Revolutionary Novel.* New York: D. Appleton and Company, 1921.

Gutierrez, Pedro Juan. *Dirty Havana Trilogy.* New York: Farrar, Straus & Giroux, 1998.

Hamburger, Philip. *Separation of Church and State.* Cambridge, MA: Harvard Univ. Press, 2002.

Hamilton, Alexander and John Jay and James Madison. *The Federalist Papers.* New York: Penguin Classics, 1987.

Handlin, Oscar and Lillian Handlin. *Liberty and Equality 1920-1994 (Liberty in America, 1600 to the Present).* New York: HarperCollins, 1994.

Hansen, James. *Storms of My Grandchildren: The Truth About the Coming Climate Catastrophe and Our Last Chance to Save Humanity.* New York: Bloomsbury USA, 2009.

Harcourt, Bernard E. *The Illusion of Free Markets.* Cambridge. MA: Harvard University Press, 2010.

Harris, Sidney. *Einstein Simplified, Revised Edition: Cartoons on Science.* New Brunswick, NJ: Rutgers University Press, 2004.

—*Can't You Guys Read: Cartoons on Academia.* New Brunswick, NJ: Rutgers University Press, 1991.

Harrison, Lawrence E. & Samuel P. Huntington. Sidney. *Culture Matters: How Values Shape Human Progress*. New York: Free Press, 2001.

Hayek, F. A. *The Road to Serfdom*. Chicago: Univ. of Chicago Press, 1956.

Heather, Peter. *The Fall of the Roman Empire*. New York: Oxford University Press, 2006.

—- *The Goths*. Oxford: Blackwell Publishers, 1996.

Heller, Mikhail and Aleksandr M. Nekrich. *Utopia in Power: The History of the Soviet Union 1917 to the Present*. New York: Summit Books, 1982.

Herrnstein, Richard J. and Charles Murray. *Bell Curve: Intelligence and Class Structure in American Life*. New York: Free Press, 1996.

Himmelfarb, Gertrude. *The Roads to Modernity: the British, French, and American Enlightenments*. New York: Alfred A. Knopf, 2004

Hoffman, Abbie. *Woodstock Nation*. New York: Random House, 1969.

Hoffman, Eva. *Exit Into History: A Journey Through the New Eastern Europe*. New York: Thomas Dunne Books, 2002.

Hook, Sidney. *Revolution, Reform and Social Justice in the Theory and Practice of Marxism*. Oxford: Basil Blackwell, 1976.

—- *Sidney Hook on Pragmatism, Democracy and Freedom: The Essential Essays*. New York: Prometheus Books, 2003.

—- *Out of Step: An Unquiet Life in the 20th Century*. New York: HarperCollins, 1987.

Hopkins, Keith. *A World Full of Gods: The Strange Triumph of Christianity*. New York: Plume, 1999.

Horowitz, David. *Unholy Alliance: Radical Islam and the American Left*. Washington DC: Regnery Publishing, 2004.

Huber, Peter. *Hard Green: Saving the Environment from the Environmentalists*. New York: Basic Books, 1999.

Hughes, Bettany. *The Hemlock Cup: Socrates, Athens and the Search for the Good Life*. New York: Knopf, 2011.

Ishay, Micheline. *The History of Human Rights: From Ancient Times to the Globalization Era*. Berkeley, CA: Univ. of California Press, 2004.

Jardine, Lisa. *Ingenious Pursuits: Building the Scientific Revolution*. New York: Nan A. Talese, Doubleday, 1999.

Jay, Peter. *The Wealth of Man*. New York: Public Affairs Press, 2000.

Jaynes, Julian. *The Origin of Consciousness in the Breakdown of the Bicameral Mind*. New York: Houghton Mifflin Company, 1976.

—- *Reflections on the Dawn of Consciousness: Julian Jaynes's Bicameral Mind Theory Revisited*. Edited by Marcel Kuijsten. Henderson, NV: Julian Jaynes Society, 2006.

Jefferson, Thomas. *Thomas Jefferson: Writings: Autobiography: Notes on the State of Virginia; Public and Private Papers, Addresses, Letters*. New York: Library of America, 1984.

Judt, Tony. *Ill Fares the Land*. New York: Penguin Press, 2010.

Kahn, Herman. *The Coming Boom: Economic, Social, And Political*. New York: Horizon Book Promotions, 1982.

Kidd, Thomas S. *God of Liberty: A Religious History of the American Revolution*. New York: Basic Books, 2010.

Kirchner, Walther. *Western Civilization from 1500*. New York: HarperResourse, 1975.

Kirsch, Jonathan. *God Against the Gods: The History of the War Between Monotheism and Polytheism*. New York: Penguin Books, 2004.

Kotkin, Joel. *The Next Hundred Million: America in 2050*. New York: Penguin Press, 2010.

Kramer, Hilton. *The Twilight of the Intellectuals: Culture and Politics in the Era of the Cold War*. New York: Ivan R. Dee, 1999.

Kramer, Mark and Stephane Courtois, Jean-Louis Panne, Andrzei Paczkowski, Karel Bartosek and Jean-Louis Margolin. *The Block Book of Communism: Crimes, Terror, and Repression*. Cambridge, MA: Harvard Univ. Press, 1999.

Krugman, Paul. *The Conscience of a Liberal*. New York: W.W. Norton, 2009.

—- *Essentials of Economics* with Robin Wells, and Martha Olnev. New York: Worth Publishers, 2007.

Landes, David S. *The Wealth and Poverty of Nations. Why Some Are So Rich and Some So Poor*. New York: W.W. Norton, 1998.

Leakey, Richard E & Roger Lewin. *Origins Reconsidered: In Search of What Makes Us Human*. New York: Anchor, 1993.

Lenin, V. I. *What Is To Be Done? Burning Questions of Our Movement*. New York: International Publishers, 1902.

—- *The State and Revolution*. New York: Martino Fine Books (reprint 2009), originally 1917.

Lerner, Gerda. *Living with History/Making Social Change*. Univ. North Carolina Press, 2009.

Levy, David. M. *How the Dismal Science Got Its Name: Classical Economics and the Ur-Text of Racial Politics*. Ann Arbor, MI: University of Michigan Press, 2002.

Lewis, Bernard. *What Went Wrong: Western Impact and Middle Eastern Response*. New York: Oxford Univ. Press, 2002.

—- *Islam in History: Ideas, People, and Events in the Middle East*. New York: World Publishing Co., 1993.

Lewis-Williams, David and David Pearce. *Inside the Neolithic Mind: Consciousness, Cosmos and the Realm of the Gods*. New York: Thomas & Hudson, 2009.

Lipset, Seymour Martin and Gary Marks. *It Didn't Happen Here: Why Socialism Failed in the United States*. New York: W. W. Norton, 2001.

Lomborg, Bjørn. *The Skeptical Environmentalist: Measuring the Real State of the World*. New York: Cambridge Univ. Press, 2001.

—- *Cool It: The Skeptical Environmentalist's Guide to Global Warming*. New York: Vintage Reprint, 2008.

—- *How To Spend $50 Billions To Make the World a Better Place*. Cambridge, UK: Cambridge Univ. Press, 2006.

Lovelock, James. *The Ages of Gaia*. New York: Holt, Rinehart & Winston, 1963.

Lovins, Amory. *Soft Energy Paths*. New York: Harper & Row, 1979.

Lynn, Richard, *The Global Bell Curve: Race, IQ, and Inequality Worldwide*. Augusta, GA: Washington Summit Publishers, 2008.

Malthus, Thomas R. *Essays on Population*. Includes essays by Julian Huxley and Frederick Osborn. New York: New American Library, 1960.

Mango, Cyril, Edited by. *The Oxford History of Byzantium*. New York: Oxford University Press, 2002.

Mann, Charles C. *1493: Uncovering the New World Columbus Created*. New York: Alfred Knopf, 2011.

—*1491: New Revelations of the Americas Before Columbus*. New York: Alfred Knopf, 2006.

Marx, Karl and Friedrich Engels. *The Communist Manifesto*. New York: CreateSpace reprint, 2010.

—*Capital: An Abridged Edition*. New York: Oxford Univ. Press, 1999.

—*The Portable Karl Marx,* Edited by Eugene Kamenka. New York: Viking Penguin, 1983.

McCullough, David. *Truman*. New York: Simon and Shuster, 1993.

—*John Adams*. New York: Simon and Shuster, 2002.

McKibben, Bill. *The End of Nature*. New York: Random House, 1983.

—— *Eaarth: Making a Life on a Tough New Planet,* New York: Times Books, 2010.

McMahon, Robert J. *The Cold War: A Very Short Introduction.* New York: Oxford University Press, 2003.

McNeill, J. R. and Paul Kennedy. *Something New Under the Sun: An Environmental History of the Twentieth-Century World.* New York: W. W. Norton, 2001.

Mesarovic, Mihajlo and Eduard Prestel. *Mankind at the Turning Point: The Second Report of the Club of Rome.* New York: E. P. Dutton, 1974.

Millard, Candice. *River of Doubt: Theodore Roosevelt's Darkest Journey.* New York: Anchor, 2006.

Mokr, Joel. *The Gifts of Athena: Historical Origins of the Knowledge Economy.* Princeton, NJ: Princeton University Press, 2004.

Montefiore, Simon Sebag. *Young Stalin.* New York: Simon and Schuster, 1982.

Moore, Barrington. *Social Origins of Dictatorship and Democracy: Lord and Peasant in the Making of the Modern World.* Boston: Beacon Press, 1993.

Morgan, Ted. *Reds: McCarthyism in Twentieth-Century America.* New York: Random House, 2003.

Morris, Edmund. *Dutch: A Memoir of Ronald Reagan.* New York: Modern Library, 2000.

Mueller, John E. *Capitalism, Democracy, and Ralph's Pretty Good Grocery.* Princeton, NJ: Princeton University Press, 2001.

Murray, Charles. *Losing Ground: American Social Policy 1950-1980.* New York: Basic Books, 1984.

—and Richard J. Herrnstein. *The Bell Curve: Intelligence and Class Structure in American Life.* New York: Free Press, 1996.

Naimark, Norman M. *Stalin's Genocides.* Princeton, NJ: Princeton University Press, 2010.

Nekrich, Aleksandr. M. and Mikhail Heller. *Utopia in Power: The History of the Soviet Union from 197 to the Present.* New York: Simon and Shuster, 1986.

Nelson, Robert H. *The New Holy Wars: Economic Religion vs. Environmental Religion in Contemporary America.* University Park, PA: Pennsylvania State University Press, 2009.

Novak, Michael. *The Spirit of Democratic Capitalism.* New York: Random House, 2007.

Carson, Rachel. *Silent Spring.* New York: Mariner Books Reprint, 2002.

O'Toole, Randal. *Gridlock: Why We're Stuck in Traffic and What to Do About It.* Washington DC: Cato Institute, 2010.

Odum, Eugene P. *Ecology.* New York: Oxford Univ. Press, 1963.

O'Rourke, P. J. *On The Wealth of Nations: Books That Changed the World.* New York: Grove Press, 2007.

——- *Give War a Chance: Eyewitness Accounts of Mankind's Struggle Against Tyranny, Injustice, and Alcohol-Free Beer.* New York: Grove Press, 2003.

Overy, Richard. *The Dictators: Hitler's Germany, Stalin's Russia.* New York: W. W. Norton, 2004.

Paine, Thomas. *Rights of Man.* New York: Penguin Classics, 1984.

Pearson, Richard. *Driven to Extinction: The Impact of Climate Change on Biodiversity.* New York: Sterling Publishing, 2011.

Perlmutter, Amos. *Modern Authoritarianism.* New Haven: Yale University Press, 1981.

Phillips, William. *A Partisan View: Five Decades in the Politics of Literature.* New York: Transaction Publishers, 2004.

Pinker, Stephen. *The Better Angels of Our Nature: Why Violence Has Declined.* New York: Viking Adult, 2011.

Pipes, Richard. *Property and Freedom*. New York: Vintage Books, 2000.

——*The Russian Revolution*. New York: Vintage Books, 1991.

——*Communism: A History*. New York: Modern Library, 2003.

Porter, Roy. *English Society in the Eighteenth Century.* New York: Penguin Classics, 1990.

Quran, The. Edited by Muhammad Zafruita Khan. New York: Interlink Publishing Co., 1991.

Radosh, Ronald. *Commies: A Journey Through the Old Left, the New Left and the Leftover Left*. San Francisco: Encounter Books, 2001.

Reagan, Ronald. *The Reagan Diaries*. New York: HarperCollins, 2007.

Reither, Joseph. *World History: A Brief Introduction*. New York: McGraw-Hill Companies, 1973.

Revel, Jean-Francois. *Last Exit to Utopia: The Survival of Socialism in a Post-Soviet Era*. New York: Encounter Books, 2000.

Ridley, Matt. *Genome: The Autobiography of a Species in 23 Chapters (P.S.)* New York: Harper Perennial, 2006.

Rifkin, Jeremy. *Algeny: A New Word—A New World*. New York: Penguin, 1984.

——*The Empathic Civilization: The Race to Global Consciousness in a World in Crisis*. New York: Tarcher, 2009.

Rosenblatt, Roger. *Consuming Desires: Consumption, Culture and the Pursuit of Happiness*. New York: Island Press, 2006.

Roy, Olivier. *Holy Ignorance: When Religion and Culture Part Ways*. New York: Columbia University Press, 2010.

Ruberstein, Richard E. *Aristotle's Children: How Christians, Muslims, and Jews Rediscovered Ancient Wisdom and Illuminated the Dark Ages*. New York: Harcourt, 2003.

Rummel, R. J. "War isn't this century's biggest killer." *Wall Street Journal*, July 7, 1986.

Rumsfeld, Donald. *Known and Unknown: A Memoir*. New York: Penguin Sentinel, 2011.

Russo, Enzo and David Cove. *Genetic Engineering: Dreams and Nightmares*. New York: W. H. Freeman, 1995.

Samson, Paul and David Pitt, Edited by. *The Biosphere and Noosphere Reader: Global Environment, Society and Change*. New York: Routledge, 1999.

Samuel, Raphael. *Theatres of Memory*. New York: Verso, 1996.

Schell, Orville. *Mandate of Heaven: The Legacy of Tiananmen Square and the Next Generation of China's Leaders*. New York: Simon and Schuster, 1994.

Schneider, Stephen. *Global Warming: Are We Entering the Greenhouse Century*. San Francisco: Sierra Club Books, 1989.

—-*The Genesis strategy: Climate and Global Survival*. New York: Dell, 1977.

Sheehan, Neil. *A Fiery Peace in a Cold War: Bernard Schriever and the Ultimate Weapon*. New York: Random House, 2009.

Shostakovich, Dmitri. *Testimony: The Memoirs of Dmitri Shostakovich*. New York: Harper and Row, 25th Anniversary Edition, 2004.

Silver, Lee M. *Remaking Eden: Cloning and Beyond in a Brave New World*. New York: Avon Books, 1993.

Simon, Julian. *Populations Matters*. New Brunswick, NJ: Transaction Press, 1990.

—*The Ultimate Resource*. Princeton, NJ: Princeton University Press, 1981.

—and Herman Kahn, eds. *The Resourceful Earth: A Response to Global 2000*. New York: Basil Blackwell, 1994.

Smail, Daniel Lord. *On Deep History and the Brain*. Berkeley, CA: University of California Press, 2007.

Smith, Adam. Edited by Edwin Cannan. *The Wealth of Nations*. New York: Modern Library, 2000.

Snyder, Timothy. *Bloodlands: Europe Between Hitler and Stalin*. New York: Basic Books, 2010.

Sobel, Dava. *Galileo's Daughter*. New York: Walker and Company, 1992.

Sobel, Robert. *Coolidge: An American Enigma*. New York: Regnery, 2000.

Solomon, Lawrence. *The Deniers: The World Renowned Scientists Who Stood Up Against Global Warming Hysteria*. New York: Richard Vigilante Books, 2008.

Salomoni, Antonella. *Lenin and the Russian Revolution*. New York: Interlink Publishers, 2004.

Solzhenitsyn, Aleksandr I. *The Gulag Archipelago*. New York: Harper Classics, 2007.

Sowell, Thomas. *A Conflict of Visions: Ideological Origins of Political Struggles*. New York: William Morrow, 1987.

—-*Basic Economics 3rd Ed: A Common Sense Guide to the Economy*. New York: Basic Books, 2007.

—*Economic Facts and Fallacies*. New York, NY: Basic Books, 2011.

Spencer, Roy W. *Climate Confusion: How Global Warming Hysteria Leads to Bad Science, Pandering Politicians and Misguided Policies That Hurt the Poor*. New York: Encounter Books, 2010.

Spofford, Peter. *The Merchant in Medieval Europe*. New York: Thames & Hudson, 2004.

Stark, Rodney. *The Victory of Reason: How Christianity Led to Freedom, Capitalism, and Western Success*. New York: Random House, 2005.

Stone, Norman. *The Atlantic and Its Enemies: A History of the Cold War*. New York: Basic Books, 2010.

Stonebarger, Bill. *A Little While Aware*. Madison, WI: Wisconsin House, 1971.

Tagliaferro, Linda. *Genetic Engineering: Progress of Peril?* New York: Lerner Publications, 1997.

Tannahill, Reay. *Sex in History.* New York: Abacus, 1989.

Toai, Doan Van and David Chanoff. *The Vietnamese Gulag: A Revolution Betrayed.* New York: Simon and Shuster, 1986.

Thoreau, Henry David. *Walden.* Many editions available.
Thurow, Lester C. *The Zero-Sum Society: Distribution and the Possibilities for Economic Change.* New York: Basic Books, 2001.

Tocqueville, Alexis de. *Democracy in America.* New York: Echo Library, 2007.

Toland, John. *Adolph Hitler: The Definitive Biography.* New York: Anchor Books, 1991.

—*The Rise and Fall of the Japanese Empire: 1936-1945.* New York: Modern Library, 2003.

Toye, Richard. *Churchill's Empire: The World that Made Him and the World He Made.* New York: Henry Holt and Company, 2010.

Travis-Henikoff, Carole A. *Dinner with a Cannibal: The Complete History of Mankind's Oldest Taboo.* Santa Monica: Santa Monica Press, 2008.

Trotsky, Leon. *My Life: An Attempt at an Autobiography.* New York: Dover Reissue, 2007.

Tuchman, Barbara W. *A Distant Mirror: The Calamitous 14th Century.* New York: Ballantine Books, 1987.

—*March of Folly: From Tory to Vietnam.* Alfred A. Knopf, 1985.

Turner, Henry Ashby, Jr. *German Big Business and the Rise of Hitler.* New York: Oxford University Press, 2003.

Vajk, J. Peter. *Doomsday Has Been Cancelled.* New York: Peace Press, 1978.

Valladares, Armando. *Against All Hope: A Memoir of Life in Castro's Gulag.* New York: Alfred A. Knopf, 1986.

Wahab, Shaista and Barry Youngerman. *A Brief History of Afghanistan*. New York: Facts on File, 2007.

Walter, Carl E. and Fraser J. T. Howie. *Red Capitalism*. New York: Wiley, 2011.

Ward, Barbara. *Spaceship Earth*. New York: Columbia University Press, 1968.

Warsh, David. *Knowledge and the Wealth of Nations: A Story of Economic Discovery*. New York: W. W. Norton, 2007.

Wattenberg, Ben J. *The Good News Is the Bad News Is Wrong*. New York: Simon and Schuster, 1984.

Weatherford, Jack W. *Genghis Khan: and the Making of the Modern World*. New York: Crown Publishers, 2004.

Wildavsky, Aaron. *Searching for Safety*. New Brunswick: Transaction Books, 1988.

Wilentz, Sean. *The Rise of American Democracy: Jefferson to Lincoln*. New York: W. W. Norton, 2005.

Willett, John. *Art and Politics in The Weimar Period: The New Society 1917-1933*. New York: Da Capo Press, 1996.

Wilson, Edward O. *In Search of Nature*. Washington, DC: Island Press, 2002.

—*Sociobiology: The New Synthesis*. Cambridge, MA: Harvard University Press, 2000.

Wolf, Martin. *Why Globalization Works*. New Haven, CT: Yale University Press, 2005.

—*Fixing Global Finance*. Baltimore, MD: Johns Hopkins University Press, 2010.

Woodworth, Steven E. *Manifest Destinies: America's Westward Expansion and the Road to the Civil War*. New York: Alfred A Knopf, 2010.

Wooster, D. *Nature's Economy*. San Francisco: Sierra Club Books, 1996.

Wright, Robert. *NonZero: The Logic of Human Destiny*. New York: Random House, 2009.

—*The Moral Animal: Why We Are, the Way We Are: The New Science of Evolutionary Psychology*. New York: Vintage Edition, 1995.

Zakaria, Fareed. *The Future of Freedom*. New York: W. W. Norton, 2003.

Zeldin, Theodore. An Intimate History of Humanity. New York: HarperCollins, 1994.

Zinoviev, Aleksandr. Translated by G. Clough. *Yawning Heights*. New York: Bodley Head Ltd., 1979.

Zinn, Howard. *A People's History of the United States: 1492 to Present*. New York: Harper and Row, 1980.

Zubok. Vladislav M. *A Failed Empire: The Soviet Union in the Cold War from Stalin to Gorbachev*. Chapel Hill, NC: Univ. of North Carolina Press, 2007.

Zukerman, Phil. *Society without God: What the Least Religious Nations Can Tell Us About Contentment*. New York: NYU Press, 2010.

INDEX